The Heart of Buddhism

Nanzan Studies in Religion and Culture

JAMES W. HEISIG, GENERAL EDITOR

Hans Waldenfels, *Absolute Nothingness* (1980)
Keiji Nishitani, *Religion and Nothingness* (1982)
Frederick Franck (ed.), *The Buddha Eye* (1982)

THE HEART OF BUDDHISM

In Search of the Timeless Spirit of Primitive Buddhism

Takeuchi Yoshinori

Edited and Translated by
JAMES W. HEISIG

CROSSROAD · NEW YORK

1991

The Crossroad Publishing Company
370 Lexington Avenue, New York, NY 10017

Printed in the United States of America

Library of Congress Cataloging in Publication Data

Takeuchi, Yoshinori, 1913–
The heart of Buddhism.

(Nanzan studies in religion and culture)
Includes bibliographical references and index.
1. Buddhism—Doctrines—Addresses, essays, lectures.
I. Heisig, James W., 1944– . II. Title.
III. Series.
BQ4165.T34 1983 294.3'42 82-23453
ISBN 0-8245-0577-8 ; ISBN 0-8245-1070-4 (pbk)

Contents

Foreword

Notulae on the Buddhist-Christian Encounter

Many today see Islam as the great challenge to Christianity. From a politico-economic and also from a religious-missionary point of view, Islam does indeed fit this description—from North Africa, via the Middle East, all the way to Malaysia. However, from a philosophical and theological viewpoint, it may rather be Buddhism that poses the greatest challenge: it forms the strongest counter-position to Christian faith and, with its profound and encompassing philosophy and its meditational praxis, has exerted a special attraction on many alert minds in the West since the nineteenth century.

We can meet this challenge only by trying to understand the Buddhist reality and claim. For this understanding, it is not enough to know the ever-impressive history of the Indian prince Gautama, who went out from a life of luxury and sensual pleasure into homelessness and solitariness in order to find the imperishable in this evanescent and pain-filled life and to become the *Buddha,* the "Enlightened One." Nor is it sufficient to be conversant with the imposing history of Buddhism, as it spread out from India: first in the form of the "Smaller Vehicle" (*Hīnayāna,* but preferably called *Theravāda,* "Doctrine of the Elders," by its own adherents) to Sri Lanka, Burma, and Thailand; and then, in the first centuries A.D., in the form of the "Greater Vehicle" (*Mahāyāna*) to China, Korea, and Japan. If we really want to meet the challenge of Buddhism, we must endeavor to understand its innermost intention, its "heart."

It is precisely this that Professor Takeuchi Yoshinori, one of the leading figures of the famous Kyoto School of Japanese philosophy, in the tradition of Nishida Kitarō, Tanabe Hajime, Watsuji Tetsurō, and Nishitani Keiji, aims at: to guide us into the core, the heart, of Buddhism. To this endeavor Takeuchi brings exceptional qualifications. As a university professor and a Buddhist priest, he not only knows Buddhist philosophy but knows and practices Buddhist religion. He is a believing philosopher of religion who highly regards Western philosophy (especially Heidegger's) and theology (especially Bultmann's) and nevertheless remains fully rooted in the religion and philosophy of the Orient, that is, the "northern" Mahāyāna Buddhism of Japan.

This Japanese scholar endeavors to correct some misunderstandings that are still rampant in the West, for example, concerning the silence of the Buddha about metaphysical doctrines (Isn't Jesus' message also remarkably unphilosophical?) or, again, concerning the alleged "nihilism" or "pessimism" in Buddhism (Doesn't Christianity also show a sense of the vanity of things and an existential pessimism directed toward salvation?). But he does far more than this. Mainly he tries to guide the Western reader to a critical and self-critical understanding of two tenets that are as central to Buddhism as they are hard to grasp.

Part I: Centering deals with the doctrine of *contemplation,* in its different stages, as the spiritual way to a conversion of one's knowing through enlightenment and of one's acting through mercy. Part II: Freeing considers the doctrine of *dependent origination* (in the West often misunderstood as causal nexus), which denotes the mutual dependency of all phenomena of the universe past, present, and future, and thus the relational nature of all things and ideas, and which seeks to clarify the unsubstantiality in origin and decline, and the liability to suffering, of all beings.

In all of this, Takeuchi Yoshinori, who may be more familiar with historico-critical exegesis of the Bible than any other Buddhist philosopher, constantly returns in his analyses to the original meaning of the Buddhist concepts in Indian Buddhism, as found in the classical Pali and Sanskrit texts. At the same time, however, he invariably adduces Western philosophers and theologians for comparison. In this way, oriented toward both a historical-philological and a philosophical-systematic approach, he succeeds in conceiving of the eternal in the temporal and in bringing to life the fundamental doctrines of contemplation and dependent origination, which often enough appear fossilized in Buddhist scholasticism. He also succeeds, through the frequent use of comparisons drawn from daily life, in making them freshly intelligible to the contemporary person and conducive to insight and conversion in view of a religious-existential realization.

What is it, in our times, that brings Buddhist and Christian thought together? Mainly the impact of the question how an old religion can survive in a new age. In secularized Japan this is at least as urgent a question as in the West. Here, at least as to the point of departure, we find strong common elements between the Buddhist philosopher of religion and the Christian theologian. They are: a common concern—the concern for the future of religion and of man in a world thoroughly structured by technology; a common hope—the conviction that the old religion will survive in a renewed form for the benefit of humankind; and a common method—a harking back to the origins (Ur-Buddhism and Ur-Christianity, the persons of Buddha and Christ), in order to provide inspiration for the way of contemporary man. And, finally, that Buddhism is a matter of religion (and not only of philosophy, as is often mistakenly thought in the West) becomes abundantly clear in Takeuchi's book.

At this point, the question naturally arises to what extent a rapprochement is possible, in the realm of content and doctrine, between two religions as different as Christianity and Buddhism. I am not of the opinion, held by many Christians as well as Buddhists, that a rapprochement is only possible on the level of praxis or religious experience, and that on the theoretical-doctrinal level the contradictions are irreducible. For it is precisely when a common quest for a deeper understanding of the real common ground of both religions is intended, rather than mere conceptual delineation and apologetic demarcation, that one should not forget that religious experience, Christian as well as Buddhist, is already *interpreted* experience—interpreted differently according to the particular religious paradigm, the system of beliefs, the theoretical-practical context wherein the believer is situated. Here it would be an illusion to imagine true mutual understanding to be possible in religious experience without a clarification of the fundamental doctrinal structures and contents, both philosophical and theological. How far mutual understanding can go, especially in the two central doctrines treated by Takeuchi is hard to foresee—for we are, after all, only at the beginning stage of the Buddhist-Christian dialogue—and to try to take a position on this point would, in any event, exceed the scope of a foreword.

Which kind of Buddhism is presented in this book? In the West today, Buddhism has become known mainly in its Zen, or experiential, variety. Takeuchi, however, is the most significant philosophical representative of a second orientation within Japanese Buddhism, the Pure Land School (which in Japan has an even greater number of adherents). Herein he differs from most other philosophers of the Kyoto School, which on the whole is rather Zen-oriented. In order to understand Takeuchi's investigations, the Western reader should at least know the following. *Jōdo Shinshū* ("True Pure Land" sect, sometimes called "Shin Buddhism") is the form of Amidism or Pure Land Buddhism that originated with Shinran Shōnin, a contemporary of Thomas Aquinas in the thirteenth century.

Shinran had been introduced to faith in Amida by his master, Hōnen Shōnin. It is to this Shinran that Takeuchi constantly refers.

Here we must say a word about Shinran's special understanding of man, which is very important for Takeuchi and which in many respects sounds familiar to Christian ears: A human being is a weak and imperfect ego, subject to *karma* and unable by its own power to liberate itself and overcome its sufferings. This image is very different from the well-known Buddhist teaching on self-liberation, or salvation by one's own power (*jiriki*).

How then is one to be saved? According to the Shinshū doctrine, the only possibility lies in faith in the Vow or Promise (*hongan*—in Christian language one is tempted to translate as *evangelium*) of Amida, the Buddha who, in limitless love and almost like another Christ, vowed to save all sentient beings. The decisive point here is that Buddha's Vow refers indiscriminately to all human beings, provided they trust in the power of the Promise, precisely this "Other Power," (*tariki*) which offers itself to the human being in its weakness. What matters is that one completely forsake all power of one's own and leave all activity to the Other Power. The being that is capable of such selflessness is the Bodhisattva who, out of his love for all, vows not to enter Nirvana as long as not all are saved. In faith in the power of this Vow, a person is sure of salvation—in faith, yes one could truly say: in faith alone, *sola fide*.

What is meant here by faith? Certainly not a belief in the objectively represented person of the Buddha or in definite doctrinal propositions. Faith here denotes a freedom from self-power and total trust of the believing heart in the Other Power of the Vow. Such a faith has nothing to do with human endeavor; it originates solely in the turning of the Buddha's heart toward the human being. For it is Buddha alone who can elicit faith. And how does this faith work itself out in life? With the establishment of faith, a turn-about occurs in the human being, a "conversion of heart," in total spontaneity, "naturally," "in an instant." That is, in this world of suffering the believer can already be assured of liberation. Since he is adopted by Amida, the believer does not fall back any more—he is born in the Pure Land. This new birth is no longer a future happening after death; rather it occurs in the moment of the coming-to-faith, in a tension between "already" and "not yet" reminiscent of that found in the announcement of the Kingdom of God in the New Testament. The Pure Land is realized there where human beings believe, divest themselves of their own power, and recognize that of themselves they are capable of nothing. Where there is no longer any egoism, suffering, anxiety, and where the false ego has been overcome, the Pure Land has already become reality. Enlightenment, Nirvana, salvation, liberation are thus already found in this present world and not just in an other-worldly paradise beyond death—as it is also said in ancient Buddhism.

No long explanations are needed here to make clear that there is a wide field of convergence between this kind of faith-Buddhism and the faith stance not only of the Protestant Christian but also to a great extent of the contemporary Catholic as well, since, according to the New Testament, one is justified not through one's devout efforts and performances, nor through meditation, but on account of one's unconditional trust, one's faith, in the Power of God.

Many a starting point could be found here for a dialogue, in which so eminent a representative of Christian theology as Karl Barth already attempted to engage in his *Church Dogmatics,* and which is carried further, for example, by a book on Shin Buddhism by Christiane Langer-Kaneko of our Institute for Ecumenical Research. Still, the Christian recipient must beware of the danger of interpreting the corresponding Buddhist concepts all too directly from the conceptuality and thought structures of the Christian tradition. Faith in Amida Buddha should not be understood in a simply dualistic way as a faith in an over-against (*ein Gegenüber*). It does not do to understand Amida Buddha as highest personal God, and the Pure Land as a world of the beyond, in an objective way. The total Buddhist context must be carefully considered here: The goal, liberation or salvation, is reached in the perfect supreme enlightenment or in the realization of Nirvana; and this consists in being one with true reality (suchness, *shinnyo*), which in turn is to be understood as emptiness (*kū*).

This aspect of emptiness is of the utmost importance for philosophical reflection. There is intended here a kind of "negative theology," which is also native to Christianity and which shuns positive statements about the Absolute, preferring silence instead. On the other hand, if, rather than on the philosophical elaborations of Amida Buddhism, one focuses on the liturgical celebrations in honor of Amida Buddha—in which one can share also as a Western observer—one must say that this decisive negativity scarcely shows at all. This liturgy, which apparently influenced Takeuchi deeply, is totally directed at the pronunciation-acclamation of the Name of Amida as an expression of faith: "Namu Amida Butsu."

Takeuchi is deeply convinced that, beyond the differences, there exists a profound convergence between faith Buddhism (Pure Land), which expects salvation from an Other Power (*tariki*), and meditation Buddhism (Zen), which relies on the self-efforts of man, the own power (*jiriki*). Moreover, Takeuchi is carried by the hope that also between Buddhism and Christianity an albeit limited common ground is becoming visible, which will have to be elaborated more clearly in the future. To me it seems that the concept of "reasonable trust," which I have tried to develop in a philosophical-theological way in the horizon of contemporary nihilism, forms a good starting point for the discussion also of other disputed tenets. "Reasonable trust," which also finds expression in the Buddhist basic experience of suffering and its overcoming, was seen by me as a presupposition of all-trust in an Absolute—the fundamental trust in reality as presupposition of "trust in God."

I must have already gone beyond the permissible limits of a foreword! In conclusion, I want to thank the theologians of the Nanzan Institute for Religion and Culture who have made available to us in English Takeuchi's extremely important introduction to the heart of Buddhism: the translator and author of the introduction proper, Dr. James Heisig, and the director, Dr. Jan Van Bragt, and the staff of the institute with which Takeuchi has closely collaborated since his retirement from Kyoto University, and which hospitably received me during my visit to Japan in 1982, and which labors in many ways for a better understanding between Buddhism and Christianity. May the number increase of those who cooperate toward the objective which the American theologian and pioneer of the Buddhist-Christian dialogue John Cobb expressed in his recent book *Beyond Dialogue:* namely, to arrive, beyond mere dialogue, at "a mutual transformation of Christianity and Buddhism."

Hans Küng

Institute for Ecumenical Research
Tübingen
January, 1983

Translator's Introduction

The essays brought together in this book span a period of twenty years, and the questions they treat represent the focus of published researches in the philosophy of religion that go back twice that far. A lot can happen to one's thought over so many years, especially in the fevered pace of change and impatience for novelty that academia has contracted from twentieth-century urban life. Add to that the profound shaking that Japan's intellectual world experienced in the aftermath of the war, the author's ongoing contact with scholars in Europe and the United States, and his travels throughout the Buddhist lands of Asia, and we have every reason to expect a teeter-totter of time-bound ideas that, even if duly accounted for as "the development of one's thinking" and highlighted at certain moments by weighty contributions to scholarship, would do little to recommend itself as a true witness to the "timeless spirit" of a religious tradition. In fact, it is quite the opposite with Takeuchi Yoshinori. Throughout his work we find a remarkable single-mindedness of standpoint and critical method that both lends unity to his own ideas and makes them all the more accessible to readers in the grip of the same questions as he. There is a sense in which the steady flow of this undercurrent is the key to the timeliness of Takeuchi's thought, and it is that sense I should like briefly to explore by way of introduction.

Takeuchi has the rare gift of getting right to the heart of the matter at hand, where others less inspired with a sense of purpose get distracted or waylaid into the mere exercise of some expertise or other they picked up in the course of their scholarly training. He is like the master potter who can slap a puddle of clay upon his wheel and within a few turns achieve a "centering" where tool and matter, body and mind can work harmoniously as one. To look only to the final result all shaped and fired and glazed and compare it with the models after which it was fashioned is to miss the most important point, the "freeing" that takes place within the artist in whom skill and idea wrestle together and transform each other.

To entitle this book *The Heart of Buddhism* was therefore a natural choice: it gets to the heart of Buddhist teaching, and it gets there with a distinctively Buddhist heart. Indeed, as I think these pages will demonstrate clearly enough, there is no other way to arrive at what is timeless in a religious tradition than to locate its philosophical reflection in time as part of the religious quest itself. In that sense, this book is every bit as much a work of Buddhist praxis as it is a work of Buddhist theory.

All of this does not of course relieve one of the responsibility of presenting one's data accurately and respecting the methods that scholarship has devised to take care of history. Rather it endows reflection with the added responsibility of belonging fully to a particular time and place in history, as an individual possessed of particular experiences and insights. The "timeless" quality of religion, Takeuchi argues, does not reside in propositions that hold true always and everywhere regardless of who speaks them and who hears them, but in the continued experimentation with its truth in the midst of the things of life, opening religion to new questions and forging from it new responses: " 'The crab digs its hole to the size of its shell.' My sentiments exactly. I prefer digging holes to my own measure over stepping into rented quarters" (p. 67). Religious reflection for Takeuchi is not a cumulative science in which one generation can build on the foundations of its predecessors; it is a conversion that needs to be repeated fundamentally again and again. No one can secure religious truth for another; the whole length of the road spreads out anew before each individual, beginning to end. In one of his books Takeuchi likens his position with regard to the great religious figures of the past to a man standing on a dark street outside of a lighted room and looking for something: "The window and the curtains cut me off from what is inside the room, and I probably have no way of ever really knowing what is in there. But if I am able with the aid of that lamp to see something that I might not otherwise have seen out here on this street, that is enough for me."[1]

The point bears repeating not because Takeuchi himself is ambiguous about it, but because the demands he makes on his readers to follow his often circuitous and spirated Japanese logic, or to keep up with everything he presumes in the way of background knowledge, might well obscure his basic intent. What is more, Takeuchi works on several levels at the same time, which can be disconcerting in the extreme for Western readers who would be more comfortable with a methodology of *divide et impera*. He works over the actual Palı texts of primitive Buddhism, blending textual criticism with commentary and interpretation; occasionally he pauses to race through some aspect of Buddhist history or other; he compares and contrasts the details of Buddhist doctrine with Western philosophy and theology; he weaves in illustrations from everyday life and the contemporary world; he abstracts to the universal dimensions of the phenomenon of religion; and he relates everything, often in covert fashion, to his own faith as "a Pure Land believer of extremely conservative stamp" (p. 132).

The two major pivots around which everything in the book revolves are the doctrines of primitive Buddhism concerning contemplation and dependent origination, which roughly account for its division into two parts. Before we take a closer look at the organization of these themes and the way in which Takeuchi kneads them together in the text, it would be good to trace the background of influences formative of his religious and philosophical interests.

Takeuchi Yoshinori was born in 1913, the eldest of four children, and spent his youth in the northern Japanese city of Sendai. At the time, his father, Takeuchi Yoshio, was teaching Chinese philosophy at Tōhoku University, a field in which he was to distinguish himself as a scholarly authority,[2] all the while maintaining a lively interest in Buddhist studies. Some years later he moved to the town of Yokkaichi, near Nagoya in central Japan, to assume the responsibility for a small temple of the Pure Land Buddhist Takada sect that had been in the family for fifteen generations and that would later pass into the hands of the young Yoshinori.[3]

As a youth, Takeuchi had been interested in the study of mathematics, but his father, knowing the problems his son had with arithmetic, persuaded him to turn to broader cultural studies. But Takeuchi did not give in so easily and continued to study on his own. In high school he read a book on the philosophy of mathematics written by Tanabe Hajime and made up his mind that he would study under the celebrated philosopher when it came time to go to university. In his final year of high school he ploughed through Tanabe's difficult treatise on *Dialectics and Hegelian Philosophy,* which had just been published the year before. At the time, Marxism was much debated, and Takeuchi took what he understood of Tanabe's critique of Marxist dialectics as his own standpoint, thus gaining a certain familiarity with philosophical argumentation even before he had studied it formally.

The following year he did indeed enroll in Kyoto University, specializing in philosophy (which of course meant Western philosophy), and hoping to receive further instruction in the philosophy of mathematics from Tanabe, who had succeeded Nishida Kitarō, Japan's first great philosopher, as the principal figure of what had already come to be known as the "Kyoto School."[4] To his initial disappointment, Takeuchi discovered that Tanabe avoided the treatment of mathematics in his lectures. As a third-year student, however, he had occasion to enroll in a seminar with Tanabe to begin a meticulous study of Hegel's *Phenomenology of Mind.* After graduation in 1936 he remained at Kyoto and for a full ten years continued to study the work with Tanabe—in its original German, since it had not yet been translated into Japanese. Following that, he was directed by Tanabe for three years in the study of Hegel's philosophy of religion and also in ethics, which had become the focal point of the latter's concerns after the war,[5] broadening out to include the works of Fichte, Schelling, and other nineteenth-century German thinkers. During this period of postgraduate work he also studied the philosophy of religion under Nishitani Keiji, who was later to succeed Tanabe as the dean of the Kyoto School. He had first been introduced to Nishitani as a second-year undergraduate and used to frequent his home for philosophical discussions. At the time, Nishitani was doing work in Aristotle, whom Takeuchi was also reading in one of Tanabe's seminars. The following year he enrolled in Nishitani's classes and over the years was introduced to the application of ontological hermeneutics and existential philosophy to Zen, which has become one of the distinguishing traits of Nishitani's work.[6]

As a first-year undergraduate, his interest in primitive Buddhism was awakened through the reading of Watsuji Tetsurō's *The Practical Philosophy of Primitive Buddhism* and Ui Hakuju's *Studies in Buddhist Thought.* Watsuji was the only major figure in the Kyoto School doing studies in primitive Buddhism, and in addition was perhaps the single most important person responsible for introducing existentialism into Japan through his books on Nietzsche and Kierkegaard.[7] Through his lectures, Takeuchi was inspired in both directions, and it is not without a certain irony that his criticisms of Watsuji's neo-Kantian approach to primitive Buddhism that appear in this book focus on its lack of existentiality (pp. 72–73).

Two years after completing his undergraduate studies, Takeuchi was ordained a priest in the Takada sect of Shin Buddhism. In addition to the training in Pali and Sanskrit that he received at the university, he was supervised in the reading of sūtras and other priestly duties by his uncle, Nakazawa Kenmyō, a member of the Ōtani sect of Shin Buddhism, for which purposes he commuted each weekend from Kyoto to the family temple at Yokkaichi. Though not a professional academic, Nakazawa was exceptionally well informed in Shinran's thought and had a keen appreciation of its practical aspects, which left a deep impression on Takeuchi. Nakazawa authored one book during his lifetime, *The Wellsprings of the Pure Land,* and after his death Takeuchi arranged for the publication of another of his manuscripts, *The Shinran of History.* Three years after his ordination, Takeuchi was married.

Almost immediately upon entering graduate studies, Takeuchi was encouraged by Tanabe to turn his attention to Shinran, since there was no want of scholars working on Hegel but few on Shinran. At first he resisted the idea, feeling he had been betrayed by his teacher, but in time he was to see the wisdom of the counsel, even though he continued to study Hegel for many years with Tanabe. As a result of his work on Shinran, in 1941 Takeuchi published a book on *The Philosophy of the Kyōgyōshinshō*[8] while still a graduate student.

In 1946 he began lecturing at Kyoto University, and two years later was named assistant professor in the Department of Religious Studies. In 1959 he became full professor, and in 1963 served as a director of research for religious studies in the graduate division of the Faculty of Letters. At the time he began teaching, interest in "primitive religions" was strong throughout Japan, and especially in Kyoto University, but Takeuchi was more interested in world religion, or what he calls, with Bergson, "open" religions (p. 25). While a lot of work was going on in the study of Sanskrit Buddhism, very little was being done on the Pali texts in the Department of Religious Studies at the University of Kyoto, and literary criticism and comparative studies were almost unknown—a fact that, in spite of the achievements of Watsuji, held true until recently in the Kyoto School. From the start, Takeuchi made use of the research on form criticism being carried on by Christian exegetes to study primitive Buddhism. In this regard, the earlier efforts made by Harnack in his three-volume *History of Dogma* were also influential in opening Takeuchi's eyes to the way in which a religious tradition develops and can become alienated from its origins. All of this helped him to have a second look at the apparently crude and stereotyped texts of primitive Buddhism and to realize how an existential hermeneutic could disclose their true depths. This conviction has remained with Takeuchi throughout his scholarly career. Indeed, one might say that this attempt to fathom the meaning of primitive Buddhism brought together for the first time and crystallized his disparate interests in German philosophy, Shinran, existentialism, and theological exegesis.

Takeuchi visited Germany in the fall of 1960 to attend an International Congress on the History of Religions at Marburg, where he remained for the winter semester as a guest professor, lecturing on Buddhist philosophy. While in Marburg he made the personal acquaintance of Bultmann and met with him frequently. One such meeting is recorded in the final chapter of this book. He also had occasion to strike up a friendship with Friedrich Heiler, to whom he later dedicated a collection of German articles published in 1972 as *Probleme der Versenkung im Ur-Buddhismus.* In 1961 he was invited by Columbia University in the United States as a visiting professor for one academic year. He returned to the United States in 1967 as a visiting professor at Williams College, and has since been to Europe on several occasions to participate in international conferences.

Takeuchi retired from Kyoto University in 1976 as professor emeritus and took up a post that same year at the Aichi Gakuin University, where he continues to teach at present in addition to carrying on his duties as a Buddhist priest. In 1977 he was awarded the Purple Ribbon by the Japanese government in recognition of outstanding academic achievement. Among his current projects is the preparation of two volumes on Buddhist spirituality for an encyclopedia of world spirituality being edited by Ewert Cousins of Fordham University, and collaboration in the English translations of important works of Nishida and Tanabe, all of which has brought him into close contact with the Nanzan Institute for Religion and Culture during the past several years.

The wide range of influences on Takeuchi's thought discussed above are all mirrored in *The Heart of Buddhism,* which stands as a powerful tribute to the particular philosophical ethos that has come to characterize the Kyoto School as a major force in current Japanese thought.[9]

In an address delivered to a gathering of eminent Buddhist and Christian scholars in 1981 in the town of Mödling outside of Vienna, Takeuchi took up the problem of self-power (*jiriki*) and Other-power (*tariki*) in connection with his own standpoint, which he characterizes as a "Buddhist existentialism."[10] Simply put, *tariki* signifies an exclusive trust in the gracious power of the Other, who is Amida Buddha, and is a key notion in Pure Land Buddhism and in the thought of Shinran (1173–1262). *Jiriki* points to the opposite tendency, stressing rather self-deliverance, as we see especially in Zen Buddhism and in the thought of Dōgen (1200–1253), a contemporary of Shinran. Now, for Takeuchi the return to primitive Buddhism offers us a standpoint from which these two radically opposing orientations can be seen as correlative and from which the close kinship between the personalities and convictions of Dōgen and Shinran can be brought to light.

By identifying with the questions that the Buddha asked himself with regard to our common human condition, we discover the impulse both to set out on the same "noble quest" as he and to open ourselves to becoming the object of the Buddha's own compassionate quest to save not only himself but all living things.

Thus, on the one hand, Takeuchi speaks of a *transcendental way* that entails the exercise of one's own efforts to arrive at enlightenment. But this way proceeds by stages and is perpetually "on the way," in danger of corruption or despair. It thus needs to be complemented, on the other hand, by the contrary direction, which he calls the *transdescendental way,* the actual encounter with the power of the Other to deliver us once and for all from the sea of suffering in which we, together with all of reality, founder. It is when these two ways cross, when our own religious quest meets with the noble quest of Amida Buddha, that Takeuchi sees salvation taking place. The attempt to disengage the self from its finiteness meets with the attempt of the Buddha to engage the self in the compassionate deliverance of all things.[11]

In this book, Takeuchi treats this twofold dynamic in terms of the two core doctrines of primitive Buddhism: the teaching on the stages of contemplation and the teaching on the causal chain of dependent origination. These two doctrines cannot simply be identified as teaching *jiriki* and *tariki* respectively but involve both correlatively and hence naturally flow into each other. It was with this understanding that the book has been divided into two parts: Centering (contemplative insight) and Freeing (breaking the chain of causal dependency).

Chapter 1 actually presents the same problem of *jiriki* and *tariki,* albeit in somewhat elliptical form, through a reflection on the silence of the Buddha with regard to metaphysical questions. Takeuchi is forthright in rejecting interpretations that see this silence as equivalent to a repudiation of metaphysics altogether, just as he rejects the idea of a nihilistic fatalism in Buddhism that renders all philosophical thought "useless" for the goal of nirvāṇa. Instead, he argues that it is the unique quality of that goal that requires a complete philosophical metanoia before it can come to touch everyday life. The so-called pragmatic approach to the Buddha's silence gets close to this insight but fails to account for the constructive role that philosophical thinking can play in the holy quest. This leads us to a consideration of the Buddha's silence in terms of contemplation, which is the subject of the lengthy second chapter.

Takeuchi tries to show how the Buddhist idea of a state of contemplative insight (samādhi) was from the start part of a more wide-reaching doctrine of spiritual practice, including preliminary disciplines, meditational methods, and the distinguishing of various stages (dhyāna) of contemplation. Throughout this chapter, he selects from the wealth of material on the subject in primitive Buddhism and the Indian traditions that preceded it to stress the two goals of transformation that appear in contemplation: the transformation of insight through enlightenment and the transformation of action through compassion.

Chapter 4 shifts our focus to the philosophical content of what primitive Buddhism teaches about the structure of the human condition and existence as a whole by means of its doctrine of dependent origination (paticca-samuppāda), the causal chain through which ignorance and suffering come into the world and through whose undoing they can be made to disappear. This two-directional movement of insight into the linkage of the chain and the breaking of the chain—the forward and backward progressions of dependent origination and dependent extinction—show the same relationship between insight and action that we saw in contemplation. The influence of Watsuji's interpretation of the theory of dependent origination as a philosophy of the a prioris of everyday life is strong here, but at the same time Takeuchi stresses the need to go beyond Watsuji to save the doctrine from becoming mere abstract theory *about* freeing, to the neglect of the actual practice of freeing itself. Merely to know the conditions for the possibility of human existence does not suffice; life itself must be opened to transformation through participation in the noble quest of the Buddha. The silence of the Buddha demands as much, and this leads Takeuchi to consider the role that existential philosophy's reflections on the *Lebenswelt* might play to clarify this dimension of the doctrine of dependent origination.

In chapter 5 the point is taken up in an extended argument on the relationship between vijñāna (consciousness) and nāmarūpa (the *Lebenswelt* of name-form) as one of co-dependency, which the noble quest seeks to break. This is a somewhat bold and original interpretation of the doctrine of dependent origination, but one to which Takeuchi is driven by his insistence that the doctrine not be seen as mere empty metaphysical speculation but as a concretely practicable metaphysical metanoia. This in turn draws him back to many of the concerns taken up in chapter 2.

Chapter 6 turns the enigma of the Buddha's silence around by focusing on the actual questions that the Buddha himself faced and showing their metaphysical and existential dimensions. In this way he both confirms the conclusions arrived at in chapter 1 and reiterates them in terms of the relationship between centering and freeing.

Chapters 3 and 7, which fall at the end of the two major divisions, serve as a sort of counterpoint to the movement of the argument as a whole. The intent of each is the same: to show that it is only in trusting in the world beyond, the Pure Land of Amida Buddha, that true transformation can occur in history and consciousness. Here we have the goal of the noble quest in terms of which all philosophy must be constructed, weighed, and evaluated. In these two chapters the timeless truth of the noble quest is set within the concrete symbolic beliefs of a particular tradition, Shin Buddhism, and its principal figure, Shinran.

I cannot pretend that the book makes easy reading, any more than it made easy translating. The deceptive familiarity of the conclusions and the tormented route by which we are led to them requires that the book be read more slowly and meditatively than one might at first be led to believe. In any case, in order to save the reader from what are really unnecessary tangles with jargon, I have appended a brief glossary of Pali and Sanskrit words at the end; and I have taken the liberty of using the more commonly known of the terms, even when this meant referring to a Pali text with a Sanskrit word. The idea was to make the text accessible to as wide a readership as possible, and to require no more than a passing knowledge of Indian philosophical vocabulary in order to follow its main argument.

The material that makes up this book has appeared in various revisions and languages, all of which had to be consulted in the preparation of the translation. The first two chapters were originally delivered as part of the Joachim Wach Lectures to the Theological Faculty of the University of Marburg in 1960–61. Chapter 1 was also the basis for a talk given to the Philosophical Faculty of the University of Hamburg in 1961; a transcript from that talk was translated into Italian and published in *Il Pensiero* (1962) as "Il silenzio del Buddha." After some reworking, it appeared in English in volume 6 of *Philosophical Studies of Japan* (1967) as "The Silence of Buddha." After one more revision, it was published in the 京都大学文学部紀要 (Journal of the Faculty of Letters of Kyoto University) in 1968 (no. 9). Chapter 3 was a lecture first delivered to the International Congress of the History of Religion at the University of Marburg in 1960. These three chapters were then included in a 1972 book of Takeuchi's German lectures, *Probleme der Versenkung im Ur-Buddhismus,* edited by Ernst Benz (Leiden: E. J. Brill, 1972). The bulk of chapter 2 was also published in Japanese in two parts as 原始仏教に於ける禅定の問題 (Problems of Contemplation in Primitive Buddhism) in 宗教研究 (Religious Studies), numbers 152 and 155 (1957–58). Chapters 4, 5, and 6 were published in 1982 under the title 縁起思想 (The Idea of Dependent Origination) in 講座・仏教思想 (Lectures on Buddhist Thought), volume 5, edited by Saigusa Mitsuyoshi (Tokyo, Risōsha). Chapter 7 was taken from the second chapter of 親鸞と現代 (Shinran Today), published in 1974 (Tokyo, Chuōkōronsha), and in English translation as "Shinran and Contemporary Thought" in *The Eastern Buddhist,* volume 12, number 2 (1980).

I would like formally to express my thanks to the various journals and publishers listed above for permission to use their material in the preparation of this translation. Special thanks are also due to Jan Van Bragt, who reviewed my work in its entirety and offered numerous suggestions for improvement.

A few days ago Professor Takeuchi came to our home to discuss some revisions in another manuscript we were working on together. Later he turned to reminiscing on his student days, providing me with much of the material for this introduction. At some point early in our conversation—I really did not notice when—he quietly slipped out of his chair and onto the living room carpet. For the better part of three hours we sat there, he sipping tea and squatting on the floor, I drinking coffee and leaning back in an easy chair. We talked of many things, finally of the role of religion in contemporary history and the need for constructing a spirituality commensurate with the technological modes of thought that have shaped the consciousness of humanity in new ways and alienated it from the agrarian imagery religion could once rely on for communicating its truth. He spoke with equal disappointment of the failure of Christianity and Buddhism to face this task. It struck me then, as it has many times, that what could have become lines of separation—Buddhist versus Christian, East versus West, old versus young—had become rather borderlands that are the domain of everyone and no one, of all disciplines and none. The standpoint from which Takeuchi speaks is neither one of interreligious "dialogue" nor one of "cross-departmental" research. His focus is not on the divisions that we have created and now strain to pull down, but on the concrete, living reality of men and women troubled by religious questions that ultimately care little what names we call them by and only cry out to be recognized in order that the hope they conceal may be released and channeled to the benefit of all living things. If this book can help others to encounter something of that same timeless spirit in the heart of Buddhism, the labors that went into its publication will more than have received their reward.

James W. Heisig

Nanzan Institute for Religion and Culture
Nagoya, Japan
August, 1982

·I·

CENTERING

·1·

The Silence of the Buddha

For Buddhism the philosophy of religion consists in philosophical reflection on the heart of Buddhism. It is in the very nature of Buddhism as a religion to be permanently bound up with such philosophical reflection. This is not to say, however, that the two are the same. In Buddhism religion always needs philosophy (or, more accurately, metaphysics) in order that it might transcend philosophy. This frees Buddhist philosophy of religion from the error that the rationalistic philosophy of religion falls into in approaching the essence of religion from the outside—however sympathetically—and overlaying it with an alien gridwork that forces religion into the measures of its own principles and categories until finally religion comes to be reduced to a pure system of rational thought.

In Buddhism religion and philosophy are like a tree that forks into two from its base. Both stem from the same roots and both are nourished by the same sap. To be sure, religion forms the main trunk and philosophy its branch, but the two remain intimately connected to each other. There have been times in the long history of Buddhism in which a pruning of the philosophical branch has helped the trunk to flourish, and other times at which the philosophical branch stood in full bloom while the trunk had become hollowed out. But by and large the two have shared together the common fate of the same tree, through its flower and its decay—two partners locked together in dialogue. Religion reflects on its own essence through philosophy and thereby deepens and renews its vitality. It is like the steady flow of water gushing forth from an underground spring: at the same time as the steady stream of water continues to purify and freshen the water that flowed before it, it also goes on boring its own well deeper into the earth. The life of religion includes philosophical thought as its counterpart, a sort of centrifugal force to its own centripetal tendencies, both moved by the same dynamism. Strictly speaking, Buddhism has nothing like what Saint Paul refers to as the "folly of the cross." This is both its weakness and its strength and has led Buddhist philosophy in a direction different from Western philosophy and theology. That is to say, the religious experience of the "folly of the cross" set philosophy and religion in opposition to each other in the West, establishing the autonomy of reason to criticize religion from the outside; but at the same time this basic opposition led to a new, albeit secondary, relationship between philosophy and theology, a mutuality grounded in a common concern with metaphysics, which Heidegger has referred to as "onto-theology."

Originally philosophy served as an inner principle of religion for Buddhism, not as an outside critic, even though it has often functioned as a means of criticizing the obscurantism of religion. That is to say, philosophy in Buddhism is not speculation or metaphysical contemplation but rather a metanoia of thinking, a conversion within reflective thought that signals a return to the authentic self (or anātman). For Buddhism this "metanoesis" represents the true meaning of enlightenment to the truth of religion. In other words, Buddhist philosophy is a metanoetics. It is not a metaphysics in the Western sense of the term but a philosophy that transcends and overcomes the presuppositions of metaphysics. This is what I like to call Buddhist existentialism: the appropriation through philosophical thought of the Buddhist appeal to awaken to the absolute reality of truth.

But how is one to explain this way of doing philosophy of religion and reconstruct it in terms suitable to the present world when the very idea of philosophy and metaphysics has been usurped by Western models? The question is too big to handle in its entirety here. Let me only try to take a few steps in that direction.

The Buddha's Attitude to Metaphysical Questions

In Buddhism religion and philosophy form a dynamic unity, but a unity that is grounded in opposition. They stand over against each other and therefore cannot simply and without further ado be made the equivalents of each other. The Buddha himself often warned his disciples against confusing the religious search, the "noble quest," with philosophical and metaphysical questions.

In one of the sūtras of the Majjhima-Nikāya, a certain disciple named Mālunkyāputta asks the Buddha for a clear and definite answer to the following questions: whether the world is eternal or not; whether the world is finite or not; whether the vital principle (jīva) is the body; and whether the human soul (tathāgata)[1] exists after death or not. The Buddha reproaches the disciple for having gone astray in the labyrinth of opinions, likening his metaphysical inquisitiveness to the stupidity of a man hit by an arrow whose tip had been smeared with poison. When the man's friends and kin had a doctor sent for, he objected:

> I will not have the arrow drawn out until I know the one who pierced me, whether he is a nobleman or a brahman, a merchant or a laborer. . . . What is his name, and to which clan does he belong?
>
> I will not have the arrow drawn out until I know the type of bow with which I was pierced, whether it is a spring-bow or a cross-bow. . . .

Now, even if a solution were possible to Māluṅkyāputta's metaphysical questions, it would not aid him in his religious quest. Later in the same sūtra we find the Buddha saying:

> In the same way, Māluṅkyāputta, whoever should speak thus: "I will not fare the Brahma-faring under the Lord until the Lord explains to me either that the world is eternal or that the world is not eternal . . . or that the tathāgata either is or is not after dying"—this man might pass away, Māluṅkyāputta, or ever it was explained to him.
>
> The living of the Brahma-faring, Māluṅkyāputta, could not be said to depend on the view that the world is eternal. Nor could the living of the Brahma-faring, Māluṅkyāputta, be said to depend on the view that the world is not eternal. Whether there is the view that the world is eternal or whether there is the view that the world is not eternal, there is birth, there is aging, there is dying, there are grief, sorrow, suffering, lamentation, and despair, the suppression of which I lay down here and now.

The same is then repeated with regard to the other speculations.

What the Buddha means here is that the religious situation (as task and as actuality) belongs to a dimension totally different from that of metaphysics. Moreover, our efforts to resolve such questions do not lead to any conclusion on the variety of opinions possible. We remain stuck in "the path of opinions, the thickets of opinions, the wilderness of opinions, the stage-play of opinions, the cramp of opinions . . ." Hence the disciple is advised merely to accept what the Buddha has taught as what has been taught, and what has not been taught as not taught:

> And why, Māluṅkyāputta, has this not been explained by me? It is because it is not useful for the goal, is not fundamental to the Brahma-faring, and is not conducive to turning away [from the world], nor to dispassion, stopping, calming, super-knowledge, awakening, nor

> to nirvāṇa. Therefore it has not been explained by me, Mālṅkyāputta.[2]

This silence of the Buddha with regard to metaphysical questions has remained a perennial riddle with any number of possible interpretations. In part two we shall explain at some length the viewpoint of Watsuji Tetsurō, who held that the Buddha's rejection of these problems did not stem from a naive distaste for or simple denial of metaphysics altogether in favor of agnosticism,[3] but rather represented a higher and more disciplined insight cautious of being led astray by the antinomies of theoretical reason. This will then provide the basis for Watsuji's interpretation of the doctrine of dependent origination as an attempt to lay out the a prioris of everyday life.

Here we may consider two further explanations, the pragmatic and the contemplative.

Silence as Pragmatic

Perhaps the oldest interpretation of the Buddha's silence is already to be found in the Pali canon:

> Once the Exalted One was staying at Kosambī in Siṃsapā Grove. Then the Exalted One, gathering up a few siṃsapā leaves in his hands, said to the monks:
>
> "What think ye, monks? Which are the more numerous, just this mere handful of siṃsapā leaves I have here, or those in the grove overhead?"
>
> "Very few in number, lord, are the leaves in the handful gathered up by the Exalted One; much more in number are those in the grove overhead."
>
> "Just so, monks, much more in number are those things I have found out but not revealed. And why, monks, have I not revealed them? Because they are not concerned with profit, they are not rudiments of the holy life, they conduce not to revulsion, to dispassion, to cessation, to tranquility, to full comprehension, to the perfect wisdom, to Nibbāna [nirvāṇa]. That is why I have not revealed them."[4]

This explanation of the Buddha's silence presupposes the faith of the disciples in their teacher's omniscience, which led them to conclude that while the Buddha of course knew the solution to all metaphysical questions, he withheld it from them as unnecessary to their "noble quest."

He fitted them with blinders, as it were, in order to spur them on at full gallop to the goal of nirvāṇa.

Another and more modern explanation characterizes the standpoint of the Buddha to the religious question as "pragmatic"[5] or "positivistic,"[6] and for that reason as indifferent to metaphysical problems of all sorts. In one sense the terms are misnomers, since they imply an attitude based from the very outset on the truth of the sensible world and our objective reflection on that world. The notion of utility is forever bound up with finite objects. Consciously or unconsciously as the case may be, objectifying thought always maintains an inner relationship to utility. Objective or discursive thought is interested in objects, and always reckons things in terms of its relation to objects, even in the "disinterested" attempts of scientific method to treat the object in a purely "objective" manner, free of the interferences of private bias. But in Buddhism the point is rather to overcome this underlying notion of utility by sounding to its depths the ground of all our objective thinking (the disjunction of subject and object, the notion of truth as a correspondence between object and representation, the relationship between truth and evidence, the law of contradiction, the notions of good and evil, and so forth), exposing that ground as false, and uprooting the notion of utility. It sees both utility and the ground of objective thinking as stemming from a common "attachment to self," a blind craving of the ego for itself and for things. Accordingly, the first thing Buddhism wishes to eradicate is the pragmatic attitude itself because it obstructs thinking from attaining true peace of mind. The pragmatic standpoint in all its forms may be indifferent to metaphysics and abstain from all interest in the problem of transcendence both in metaphysics and in religion, but there are times when religion runs counter to philosophy and metaphysics precisely because metaphysical transcendence substitutes a conceptual abstraction for authentic transcendence. In such cases, the pragmatic standpoint fails to provide us with any help.

From another point of view, however, the pragmatic or positivistic explanation is not without its basis. First of all, the Buddha not only had the goal of salvation clearly before his eyes but went on to achieve it during his own lifetime, thus providing his disciples with a concrete verification in the here and now, "as if setting upright what had been stooped over, uncovering what had been hidden, returning to the path what had gone astray, kindling a light in the darkness. Thus did the Holy One proclaim his doctrine in manifold ways."

Secondly, looked at in terms of the philosophical issues themselves, the Buddha's resolute silence with regard to God, individual souls, a highest principle, and so forth amounts to a negative answer, a denial of such transcendence.[7] The sharp contrast between his teaching of anātman and the doctrine of ātman found in the Upanishads confirms this.

Finally, the pragmatic point of view is in evidence in the doctrine of the five skandhas, which forms the counterpart to the doctrine of anātman. Buddhist psychology looks on the person as a succession of momentary constellations of five classes of dharmas and does not need the idea of a subjective "ego" to serve as a substrate to personality. This functional approach to the problem of the soul—in contrast to the substantialist conception prevalent in Europe since the time of the Greek philosophers—views the ego as a composite of body or form (rūpa), feelings (vedanā), perceptions (saṃjñā), volitional impulses (saṃskāra), and consciousness (vijñāna),[8] reminiscent of the pragmatic model of the psyche adopted by psychologists at the beginning of this century, as C. A. F. Rhys Davids has correctly pointed out.[9]

Actually these three areas are all interrelated and mutually explanatory of one another.

It is quite correct to say that the Buddha took a positive stance with regard to the immediate, lived experience of religious truth. He presented the Buddhist goal of the salvation and holiness to his disciples concretely, offering himself as personal evidence of its truth. But at the same time this enabled him to provide a critique of the commonly accepted idea of the means suitable to attain that goal. In religion the relation between means and ends is different from the way it is understood in our ordinary, pragmatic standpoint. The end here is nirvāṇa, which is not to say that the goal of salvation in Buddhism is a sheer nothingness that dissolves the need for a determined struggle for salvation. Quite to the contrary, the Buddha and his disciples were convinced that the ideal of enlightenment is something that can be realized in this life, and this consciousness and conviction filled them with the enthusiasm to sacrifice willingly everything in the world in the name of the "noble quest." The quest of the Buddha himself thus stood as a model for his disciples to follow. In spite of this, one still finds predominant in the West the idea that Buddhism is nothing but a form of nihilism.

One must guard against misunderstanding anātman as an atheism or nihilism in the ordinary sense of those words. Friedrich Heiler makes the point explicitly in speaking of the positive, creative value that Buddhism attaches to the notion of nirvāṇa:

> Nirvāṇa is the equivalent of what Western mysticism understands as the "Being of beings," the supreme and one reality, the absolute,

> the divine. . . . Nirvāṇa is the infinite, the eternal, the uncreated, the quality-free, the ineffable, the one and only, the highest, the supreme good, the best, the good pure and simple. And yet Buddha and his followers go to great pains to avoid naming nirvāṇa expressly as "divine" or "godhead" or the "Brahman" that Upanishadic mysticism speaks of.[10]

It is precisely this apparently negative conception of nirvāṇa (or anātman) that envelops within itself a strong and profound feeling for holiness and an unshakable conviction of its realization as the emancipation available to us in this life. As Heiler notes, "Buddhism has merely pursued to its final consequences the ideas of 'negative theology' and squeezed out the full implications of the mystical notion of *epekeina.*"[11] But now something most peculiar happens to our ordinary way of looking at things when mysticism is so radicalized. The needle on our terrestrial compass that points the way to the goal of salvation turns around: one might say that Buddhism seeks the beyond of the beyond (the *epekeina* of *epekeina*) and finds it in the here-and-now immediacy of daily human existence. The enigmatic character of its terms (for example, anātman and śūnyatā) is a result of this reversal of the ideas of holiness and transcendence.

It is interesting to observe here the etymological interpretation that the scriptures of primitive Buddhism offer of the notion of tathāgata. Tathāgata is taken to represent one who has already traversed the way from the near side (this world) to the far side (nirvāṇa) and arrived there, (tathā-gata) but at the same time one who is on the way back to the near side in order to encounter us and guide us on our way to the goal (the Tathā-āgata). The Buddha's doctrine is the path of the Buddha's coming-and-going, on which he meets his disciples and stands before them as a "Thou," a real personality who preaches the way and points it out to them. As we read in the Dhammapada:

> This is the path. There is no other that leads to vision. Go on this path, and you will confuse Māra, the devil of confusion.
>
> Whoever goes on this path travels to the end of his sorrow. I showed this path to the world when I found the roots of sorrow.
>
> It is you who must make the effort. The Great of the past only show the way. Those who think and follow the path become free from the bondage of Māra.
>
> . . . This is the clear path. . . .
>
> A man who is virtuous and wise understands the meaning of this, and swiftly strives with all his might to clear a path to nirvāṇa.[12]

A clue to understanding this Buddhist idea may be found in the philosophy of Hegel. According to Hegel the activity of the Absolute can be circumscribed by the term *egressus est regressus,* and demonstrated in the realm of pure thought through dialectic logic. Through speculative thought the activity of the Absolute as a whole can be contemplated and objectively reflected as such a dialectical movement. This understanding of the concrete activity of the Absolute was interpreted by Hegel through a philosophical adaptation of the Christian Trinitarian model, however, and this meant that he lost contact halfway with the full and authentic significance of *egressus est regressus.*

For primitive Buddhism, in contrast, the concrete truth of the activity of the Absolute is captured in the word *tathatā.* Perhaps tathatā (suchness, the absolute truth as absolute reality) can best be understood by relating it to the idea of the Tathāgata. This would mean that the absolute ground of the entire phenomenal world is not a metaphysical one. The metaphysical understanding of *epekeina* is a false one in that it seeks the ground of reality only in a "beyond." The real ground lies not in a metaphysical background but in the foreground of things, in the here-and-now actuality of transient beings. Nishida Kitarō's idea of the "locus of nothingness" can be understood in terms of this Buddhist notion of "being on the way."[13]

A more relevant comparison to Buddhism's aversion for metaphysical problems may be sought in Western philosophy in the philosophy of Kierkegaard, particularly in his turn against Hegelian speculation as nothing more than an imaginary unity of transient, temporal existence with eternity. Philosophy produces a magnificent harmony between the two, but in fact it leaves our poor existence in much the same condition as before. In spite of all its systematizing we remain wretched and unsaved. The philosopher may be likened to a man who builds himself a magnificent palace only to live in a poor cottage nearby. Were we immortals, we might perhaps indulge ourselves in idle speculation to kill time. But we are transients in this world of impermanency. In becoming absorbed in meditating on things *sub specie aeternitatis,* philosophers indict themselves for having forgotten who they are, for squandering the little time they have and dissipating their Dasein. Imaginary schemes to relate the mortal to the immortal are never of any help to human existence. Thus Kierkegaard speaks of our existence, "our being in finitude which is infinitely interested in eternal bliss." For a long time I troubled over the expression *infinitely interested* (or *passionately interested*), unable to understand it because of my habitual Buddhist way of thinking. To me, interest seemed to be an attitude that one takes to the things of the world, whereas here *interest* and *passion* were being given an eschatological tinge. There is a radical shift in the relationship between the goal and the way to the goal when we shift from our everyday ends to the Buddhist notion of nirvāṇa or the Christian eschatological understanding of the Kingdom of God. The question of salvation that Kierkegaard speaks of is a question that touches the very foundations of our human mode of being. It shakes our Dasein from the ground up and turns it around from a striving after the useful and the comfortable to a *totaliter aliter.* A great eschatological passion infuses our being from its depths. Our quest remains a quest, but at the same time it undergoes a qualitative transformation, as we read in the letters of Paul,[14] a change that is as different from the interests of everyday as love is from mere desire.

Something similar is to be seen in Buddhism, even though the basic attitude it espouses toward the "noble quest" is expressed in negative terms. Yet negative feelings like ennui, world-weariness, and indifference do not correspond to what it means by authentic detachment, the ultimate state of religious emancipation. Like Meister Eckhart's idea of *Abgeschiedenheit,* true detachment in Buddhism (upekkhā) must be constant and unshakable, and yet remain flexible and adaptable to changing circumstances. Only this sort of passion can inspire us on the noble quest of religion. This passion lines the path to our final goal like milestones and guides us every step of the way. It criticizes the things we do and the things we neglect to do from the viewpoint of that absolute goal; it continues to ask how and to what extent our behavior is conscious of our goal.

We may note here in passing that in the answer of the Buddha to Māluṅkyāputta, the Pali text uses the word *na atthasaṁhitaṁ* ("are not useful for the goal"). C. A. F. Rhys Davids paid special attention to the word *attha* in her later works,[15] even though she persisted in her former pragmatist interpretations of the Buddha's silence.

When we translate this into theological language, we may speak of this great passion wrought by the encounter between transient being and eternity as "eschatological" in origin. In ontological terms, I like to speak of it as determined by the encounter of being with nothingness. What draws the sharp line between Christianity and Buddhism here is the different mode in which this encounter takes place. Seen as ideal types, the story of Paul's encounter with Christ en route to Damascus, and the story of the Buddha's encounters with an old man, a sick man, a corpse, and a monk (to which we shall return in part two), have each exerted considerable influence on the shape that the religious spirit took in Christianity and Buddhism respectively. Moreover, the essential differences in the way each views the relationship between philosophy and religion stem from the characteristic way that each poses the question of this encounter of being with nothingness. This issue, which has interested me greatly in recent years, is one I should like to return to later.

Silence as Contemplative

A third way to approach the silence of the Buddha is to see it as a sign of contemplation (dhyāna; samādhi). This, it seems to me, brings us closest to the secret of his silence, though it is not without its own peculiar blend of strengths and weaknesses.[16] Inasmuch as this interpretation is the focal point of the following chapter, I only mention it here in connection with a short legend of the Buddha handed down in the history of Zen:

> One day as the Buddha was sitting down with his disciples he stooped to pluck a lotus blossom. He looked at it and a smile played upon his lips. None of the disciples was able to grasp what it meant. Only Kāśyapa smiled with him. The Buddha noticed this and said, "Henceforth will you be a bearer of the heart of Buddhism."

The smile of the Buddha and his silence are one and the same. Both are an immediate communication that crosses over the greatest distance that separates one existence from another.

Let us leave the lotus blossom as it is. It blooms when it blooms, it falls when it falls. Now it stands up in full blossom under the clear blue sky, and the entire cosmos is reflected in it. Neither the Buddha nor Kāśyapa can touch that—nor can we. It simply greets us in the soft breeze and awaits our quiet and holy smile.

·2·

The Stages of Contemplation

The Problem of the Sāmaññaphalasutta

One moonlit night, as the story goes, it came into the head of King Ajātassatu of Magadha to discuss a metaphysical problem. So off he went to the Buddha, who at the time was living in a mango forest in the regions outlying the regal palace.[1]

Ajātassatu had already brought the same question to a group of enlightened sages and materialist-sensualist philosophers—a group known as the six false teachers, whom the so-called Brahmanistic faith and Buddhist philosophy alike have dismissed as heretics. These six false teachers (Pūraṇa Kassapa, Makkhali Gosāla, Ajita Kesakambalī, Pakudha Kaccāyana, Sañjaya Belaṭṭhaputta, and Nigaṇṭha Nāṭaputta) were among the many sages living at the time in the bustling, up-and-coming city of Magadha. These sages, passing themselves off for philosophers and spiritual masters, collected about themselves numbers of disciples whom they directed in religious discipline, and frequently held open lectures and discussions with other schools, much as one might have found in ancient Athens.

The texts of the Āgama (Hīnayāna scriptures) also tell of philosophies whose doctrines are known even though their founders are not mentioned by name, and, conversely, refer to numerous intellectuals and philosophers whose names have been preserved while their thinking has passed into total oblivion.[2] It seems that new currents of thought circulated freely throughout Magadha, which was quickly developing from a small town or residential district into a lively commercial center for the monarchy. Still, we lack historical certainty as to whether these six philosophers were actually all in Magadha at the same time.[3] True enough, the Suttanipāta does recount how a disciple of the Buddha came before the six false teachers, who happened to be gathered together in a hall, and posed a difficult question that finally only the Buddha was able to answer. And according to the Mahāsakulūdāyisutta from the Majjhima-Nikāya, they were supposed to have lived together in Magadha during the rainy season. But there, as in the case of King Ajātassatu, we apparently are dealing with an editorial device invented by the author who compiled the traditions into textual form.[4]

Now the question that Ajātassatu put to the Buddha was this: What real good do a monk's hardships do him? In reply the Buddha reminded the king that the philosophers (he has in mind the six false teachers) had already answered that question for him, whereupon Ajātassatu proceeded to lay out in broad outline the gist of their replies, and in so doing to present their various systems of thought. But the king was not satisfied with the answers he had received and had therefore repeated the question to the Buddha. The Buddha's answer, which Ui Hakuju has referred to as a set of "general rules for spiritual practice," indicates the most important stages through which the Buddhist disciple progresses in his practice. The various stages of contemplation and the preparations that precede it as laid out in the reply of the Buddha are repeated time and again in various texts of the Sāmaññaphalasutta, but the compiler seems to have singled out this one scene to serve as a preface to the "general rules for spiritual practice" that come to us as a genuine part of the Buddhist tradition.

Over the years the passage on the six false teachers has been accorded painstaking investigation by European and Japanese scholars and found to be a rather reliable description of the details of the philosophical thought of the time, a fact that is confirmed by supplementary material aside from the Buddhist literature itself.[5] While the arrangement of the texts according to individual philosophers is disputed, the presentation as a whole is valued as a good, if one-sided, account of the intellectual tendencies of some of the Buddha's contemporaries.

This might lead us to expect that these "general rules for spiritual discipline" represent a fairly trustworthy picture of what the oldest community of Buddhist believers actually professed, but history contradicts such a conclusion. The "general rules for spiritual discipline" are indeed given such predominance in the Āgama that they overshadow the doctrine of the four holy truths and the noble eightfold path, and the spiritual practices that were deduced from them. Nonetheless, they are only an introduction to the contemplative practices to be advanced later and fully established after the death of the Buddha in the course of the development of the Buddhist community. At any rate, that is the view current among Japanese scholars today.

Frauwallner offers a differing view worthy of note. In his opinion these "general rules for spiritual practice" are to be considered rather as a handbook for the spiritual practice of Buddhists that contains the actual teaching of the Buddha in his final years.[6] While it seems to me he goes too far in several aspects of his argument, there is no gainsaying the validity of certain important points that he makes. It is very probable that the doctrines of the four noble truths and the related noble eightfold path as we find them laid out in the first sermon of the Buddha at Benares were further reflected on and developed in the long course of the Buddha's preaching activity, only later to be rearranged into those "general rules for spiritual practice," at least in their primitive form. For if one takes into account the conservative character of the early Buddhist community, it is hard to imagine that the disciples would simply have altered a scheme of spiritual practices decided on by the Buddha or let its original form go neglected in favor of a new set of rules.[7] What is more, the manner of expression we find in the "general rules for spiritual practice" is more concrete and more thorough in its presentation of the particulars of religious experience than what is contained in the noble eightfold path. Friedrich Heiler seems to have been the first to recognize the religious significance of this text. His penetrating insight into European mysticism has helped him to shed light directly on the core of the experience of contemplation in primitive Buddhism.[8]

Now to return to the preface of the Sāmaññaphalasutta, King Ajātassatu is known to have been the son of Bimbisāras, who had been a close friend of the Buddha and whom his infamous son had killed in order to ascend the throne of Magadha. This story is taken up again and treated exhaustively in the Mahāparinirvāṇa Sūtra as the conversion of King Ajātaśatru (the Sanskrit transliteration of the Pali name). The metaphysical debate with the six false teachers is taken up in this sūtra as part of the story of a king driven by a guilty conscience to search for the truth of salvation. This is all supposed to have occurred shortly before the entry of the Buddha into nirvāṇa. In the Sāmaññaphalasutta, however, the king confesses his sin of parricide *at the end* and begs the Buddha for mercy.[9] The presumption of the compiler throughout, it should be noted, is that the whole background of events is already known to the readers. Something similar occurs in the case of oral tradition, where there seems to be a general consensus among the transmitters that what has already been recounted on another occasion should be passed over in silence. This is the case with this text, which, as it happens, goes back to a very early written account. If one reads this section of the Sāmaññaphalasutta in the light of the Mahāparinirvāṇa Sūtra with the assumption that the king is suffering from pangs of conscience, the teachings of the six false teachers suddenly take on a new significance: the denial of karma, the refusal to acknowledge a life beyond, the glorification of sensuality and hedonism, and the argument based on the indivisibility of the atom that "murder" is really not murder at all but only a case of a sword-passing through a field of atoms. In the end, the argument concludes, there is neither a murderer nor anyone who instigated a murder (the reference clearly being to King Ajātasattu). Seen in this way, the whole conglomerate of teachings no longer looks to be the haphazard arrangement it might have originally seemed to be.

In any case, the intention of the compiler of the text from the very outset seems to have been to present the question of King Ajātasattu in such a way that the Buddha's "general rules for spiritual practice" might be offered as the fitting answer, while the replies of the six false teachers are presented in such a way as to stir up the king's displeasure at having been handed a breadfruit when what he had asked for was a mango. The disposition of the material makes plain the dramatic technique of the compiler.

The General Rules for Spiritual Practice

The Buddha's reply to King Ajātasattu begins with the actual benefits of being a monk, but this section does not concern us directly here. Rather we are interested in the detailed treatment that follows on the process of spiritual practice that leads to salvation. There we find mention of the four noble truths, the tisro-vidhāḥ (the three insights), and the ṣaḍ-abhijñāḥ (six saving powers). Ui argues that the "general rules for spiritual practice" should be considered an alternate system to that of the noble eightfold path, since the latter does not contain the "three core notions" around which the former is structured: śīla, dhyāna, and prajñā.[10] According to Ui, these concepts lack the practical meanings attached to the four noble truths and the noble eightfold path, and are grounded rather in an early form of the Abhidharmic analysis of dharma. Heiler suggests, in contrast, that the system represented by these "three core notions" is in fact common to mysticism East and West insofar as they portray the so-called stages of mystical experience. He lays out the correspondence as follows:

śīla	via purgativa	catharsis
dhyāna	via illuminativa	elampsis
prajñā	via unitiva	henosis[11]

Let us first look at śīla. In the mystical traditions of all times and places, conversion is said to begin with self-purification, with a catharsis of soul. Purification that follows upon conversion stands on a higher plane than what we normally understand as the uprightness of spirit that accompanies mere morality or ethics. As we see in the first conversion of the Buddha (his departure from home into homelessness), such purification is permeated throughout by the problem of the impermanence of all things, by the problem of life and death. The way that all sensible things lose their charm when set under the light of impermanence, or that the experience of impermanence casts a shadow over all of being so that the colors of perception and sense suddenly lose their sparkle, is expressed in the Buddhist scriptures in many and varied forms.

We see this reflected well in the epigrammatic wisdom of the Dhammapada, which shows us how the disciples of the Buddha saw all of earthly reality in the light of transitoriness and impermanence:

> How can there be laughter, how can there be pleasure, when the whole world is burning? When you are in deep darkness, will you not ask for a lamp?
>
> But death carries away the man who gathers the flowers of sensuous passion, even as a torrent of rushing waters overflows a sleeping village, and then runs forward on its way.
>
> And death, the end of all, makes an end of the man who, ever thirsty for desires, gathers the flowers of sensuous passions.
>
> Neither in the sky, nor deep in the ocean, nor in a mountain-cave, nor anywhere, can a man be free from the power of death.
>
> From pleasure arises sorrow and from pleasure arises fear. If a man is free from pleasure, he is free from fear and sorrow.
>
> From lust arises sorrow and from lust arises fear. If a man is free from lust, he is free from fear and sorrow.
>
> He who knows that this body is the foam of a wave, the shadow of a mirage, [is] unseen by the King of death, he goes on and follows his path.
>
> He who has gone beyond the illusion of saṃsāra, the muddy road of transmigration so difficult to pass; who has crossed to the other shore and, free from doubts and temporal desires, has reached in his deep contemplation the joy of nirvāṇa—him I call a Brahmin.[12]

Heiler draws attention here to the fact that this way of looking at things *sub specia mortis* with its admonition of *memento mori* is common to religious personalities East and West, and from there goes on to describe this form of meditation in detail.[13] In an earlier essay I undertook an existential analysis of the "self-consciousness of human finitude," or the problem of "being unto death," as the encounter of being with nothingness.[14] Here I should like to return briefly to the attempt made there to liken the power of negation that grips the totality of all that is (*das Seiende*) out of its ground at a single stroke, which shows up in the religious attitude of "denying life and the world," to the power of negation in morality, which, as an "ought" or moral imperative, contradicts the lusts, the inclinations, and the passions that appear in specific situations.

The experience of impermanence referred to earlier is brought about by some particular event that at one point quite overcomes us and rends our everyday life asunder. This does not of itself imply that the extraordinariness reaches down to touch our innermost core. We often speak of death "taking" someone busy with the things of life—or, as the Dhammapada has it, busy "gathering flowers." This means that we are destined to come to our end without actually being in possession of our end. In order to become conscious of the fact that we are terminal beings, that ours is a "being towards an end," and thus know death and appropriate it, the power of negation that works its way into our lives from the outer experience of impermanence and the breakdown of everydayness has at the same time to come face to face with itself and turn around to become a more intensified negation, a negation of all that is, both of the objects that make up the world as well as of our own Dasein. This intensification of negation occurs because the totality of being is shaken at its very foundations within the consciousness of the experiencing subject—"even as a torrent of rushing waters overflows a sleeping village." The negation is here concentrated within, since it engulfs the experiencing subject itself in the same whirlpool of annihilation in which all of being is caught up, and does not let it remain calmly aloof from the situation. This violent nothingness, which "nullifies" everything and brings under its sway all of being within and without the interiorized sense of impermanence, lies in back of such things as the grim and ghastly "reflections on a decomposing corpse" as a presupposition. Without the *memento mori,* without an accompanying awareness and appropriation of death in the depths of one's own being, those reflections become no more than pathological abnormalities. According to the recipe for meditation in the Satipaṭṭhānasutta,

> "When he [the monk] spends two or three days at a burial grounds, looking at one decaying corpse after the other, swollen, discolored, oozing with foul pus, he compares what he sees to his own body and realizes, 'Surely this is also the nature and destiny of my own body, and there is no making exceptions.' " The image of the decomposing corpse grows more and more ghastly in the sick fantasies of the monk. He sees a cadaver, "devoured by wild animals or torn apart by vultures," a skeleton "with the flesh and tendons hanging from it and

> the blood still dripping," bones "stripped of their flesh and stained the color of dried blood, still held together by the body sinews," dry bones "fleshless and bloodless but still hanging on to one another by their tendons," "a rotting corpse whose bones have let go of one another and lie scattered about on the ground," "bones as white as seashells," bones strewn about in haphazard heaps and washed clean by the wind and rain, "bones rotted and stinking, decomposed to ashes."[15]

The Satipaṭṭhānasutta does in fact lean in the direction of such a sick obsession, as seen in the reflection on one's own body that it commends in this regard:

> And moreover, bhikkhus, a brother reflects upon this very body, from the soles of his feet below upward to the crown of his head, as something enclosed in skin and full of divers impurities: "Here is in this body hair and down, nails, teeth, skin, flesh, sinews, bones, marrow, kidney, heart, liver, membranes, spleen, lungs, stomach, bowels, intestines; excrement, bile, phlegm, pus, blood, sweat, fat, tears, serum, saliva, mucus, synovic fluid, urine."
>
> Just as if there were a double-mouthed sample-bag, bhikkhus, full of various sorts of grain, such as rice, paddy, beans, vetches, sesamum or rice husked for boiling; and a keen-eyed man were to reflect as he poured them out: "That's rice, that's paddy, those are beans," and so forth. Even so, bhikkhus, does a brother reflect upon the body, from the soles of the feet below upward to the crown of the head, as something enclosed in skin and full of divers impurities.
>
> So does he, as to the body, continue to consider the body, either internally or externally, or both internally and externally. He keeps on considering how the body is something that comes to be, or again he keeps on considering how the body is something that passes away; or again he keeps on considering the coming to be with the passing away; or again, conscious that "There is this body," mindfulness hereof becomes thereby established, far enough for the purposes of knowledge and of self-collectedness. And he abides independent, grasping after nothing in the world whatever. Thus, bhikkhus, does a brother continue to regard the body.[16]

There can be little doubt from all of this that the Satipaṭṭhānasutta is considering "things in their origination and in their transiency." But its understanding of impermanency is done in a fully objective manner: it begins with a discriminating consideration of the object that does not engage the subject in self-reflection, and only later calls to mind the fact that everything has reference to the objectifying subject, almost as if thought were being forced to pen its own name into the death announcement!

The same contradiction reappears in its strongest form when, as an observer, one reflects "purely theoretically" on the object without allowing oneself to be shocked by what one sees. This is how the theory of non-ego (the anatta-vāda) has fallen into its current misinterpretation, according to which the ego is nothing other than the sum total of bodily form (rūpa), feelings (vedanā), perception (saṃjña), volitional impulses (saṃskāra), and consciousness (vijñāna), so that there is left no subject that can be called an ego. In my view, Mrs. Rhys Davids is entirely correct in rejecting the propriety of the simile of the wheel, according to which the self is like a wheel, which, once dismantled, is no more than a heap of wood, since there is no wheel to begin with, any more than a self exists except as a mere name. This simile, which is frequently cited, does not in fact originate from the sayings of Gotama the Buddha, but from a nun called Vajirā who twisted the Buddha's teaching poetically in order to set forth her own views on the sorrows of being human.[17] Still, it is a "frightful" misunderstanding on Mrs. Rhys Davids's part to argue that the Buddha would not have been able to harbor such a "frightful" theory of non-ego in concentrating on his theory of an original or authentic self.

The so-called kṣaṇikavāda also stems actually from a later Abhidharmic analysis that cannot be validated by primitive Buddhism. According to this theory, the Buddhist dharmas combine with one another only as momentary constellations that come about, last for no more than a moment, and then pass away to make room for the next constellation. Such thoughts stem from an objectifying manner of thinking that is altogether alien to the explanation of human existence by force of the interiorization of impermanence, and in this way they corrupt the authentic sense of impermanence and non-ego, reducing it to a quantitative particularization of discriminating thought.

In order to avoid such false interpretations, which crept in by way of Hīnayāna commentaries and strayed wide of the right path of understanding quite early on, it is necessary to recover all over again the authentic, original "existential-religious" sense of the experience of impermanence. Here I find the thought of existential philosophers and theologians most helpful for rearticulating the original spirit of primitive Buddhism for the Western intellectual world. From a Buddhist point of view, Heidegger's interpretation of human existence from the starting point of a preliminary resolve (*vorlaufende Entschlossenheit*) with regard to death, and his treatment of the problem of self-transcendence from a viewpoint that is neither anthropocentric nor theocentric but rather anthropo-eccentric, and hence avoids ending up in either theism or atheism, are both of particular significance. Thus may the Oriental tradition of interpreting the Absolute as "nothingness" enter into dialogue with the Occidental interpretation of the Absolute as "being."[18] We shall have occasion to return to this point later.

Returning to the Satipaṭṭhānasutta, let us now look more closely at the religious significance of its recipe for meditation. What Heiler has to say with regard to Western parallels will head us in the right direction:

> Our healthy Western zest for life trembles in the face of those dismal fantasies of the Buddhist mendicant monks. And yet that consideration of the "uncomely, impure, and detestable" (the asubha-bhāvanā, as it is technically called in Buddhism) almost literally reappears in many of the works of later Christian ascetics and mystics, even in the more extensive devotional tracts. One such religious treatise compiled by a Jesuit and reprinted in numerous editions, for example, contains a gloomy meditation on a corpse that is made all the more effective through the rhetoric device of depicting a fresh cadaver: "Today it is the very picture of beauty in full bloom, sweet-smelling, brightly decked out, lovely, enchanting—tomorrow it is mute, simpering, disfigured, foul-smelling, abhorrent, and repulsive. Today the fresh picture of youth—tomorrow shriveled, aged, a deformed picture of death, an eerie and hollow frame. . . . Pale, twisted, cold, motionless is the corpse that in but a few weeks will be no more than a scattering of bones with a skull." The mentality so harsh and grating to our sensitivities that centuries before Christ lay deep in the hearts of those lonely Buddhist ascetics even today finds its echo in the Christian soul given over to asceticism.[19]

Now, if we go a step further beyond this contrast of today and tomorrow, or the "savory" (assāda) and the "unsavory" (ādīnava), we are able to elevate their polar opposition to the mysterious inner bond that links them together in enlightened consciousness. According to Nishitani Keiji, this is how we are to understand the words of the New Testament:

> And as he came out of the temple, one of his disciples said to him, "Look, Teacher, what wonderful stones and what wonderful buildings!" And Jesus said to him, "Do you see these great buildings? There will not be left here one stone upon another, that will not be thrown down." (Mark 13:1–2)

Jesus is here bringing the past and the present together. In his famous poem, *The Waste Land,* T. S. Eliot writes:

> Unreal City,
> Under the brown fog of a winter dawn,
> A crowd flowed over London Bridge, so many,
> I had not thought death had undone so many.

The people streaming across the bridge are also being viewed *sub specie mortis*. Bashō catches in a single poetic breath the terrifying sight:

> Lightning flashes—
>   Close by my face,
> The pampas grass!

It is the sorrowful vision of a skull in the wilds, lighted up for a moment by a flash of lightning that breaks the dark of night amidst the rustling meadow grasses. Bashō was inspired to the poem by seeing the painting of a Noh play with skeletons as the actors depicted on a sliding door, but one might as well interpret it as the image of a woman player smiling coyly with eyes that peek out from behind a fan she has raised to her face. When present and future, or past and present,[20] are the same, the streets bustling with activity become no more than a Golgotha: death roams about the crowd and clutches people one by one away from those with whom they joke and laugh together.[21]

In the West as well as in the East there are a multitude of attempts to treat this contrast between the savory and the unsavory in terms of a dialectic of two principles. Indeed, there is an inner dynamic presupposed at the ground of this dialectic, as we see it clearly presented in the forms of meditation of primitive Buddhism. It is really a characteristic shift that occurs within the religious mind like the swing of a pendulum back and forth, and that enables the mind to ascend to a higher, exponentialized synthesis. What Buddhism understands as the relationship between assāda and ādīnava in the five skandhas and as nissaraṇa (the escape or release from them), constitutes the three elements of the inner dialectic of the religious mind. As for the role of the sense of impermanence in this dialectic, it is only in this light that the savory and the unsavory in the five skandhas are able to come to expression. Just as the assāda of the five skandhas is realized essentially through the experience of its opposite, the ādīnava of the five skandhas—for only through the shock of seeing the unsavory quality of things is the savory quality of everydayness uncovered

for the vital problem that it is and eradicated from the ground up—so also is the ādīnava of the five skandhas only completely recognized for what it essentially is through the escape from the five skandhas.[22]

Religious feeling that has been permeated with anxiety about nothingness must be surmounted to the will to nissaraṇa, to religious resolve. The commonplace individual's standpoint of everydayness that binds the subject fast to the variety of objects that surrounds it becomes a true religious consciousness through the experience of the successive changes from one scene to another, as if on a darkened stage. Thus the sudden change of heart—what was colored becomes black, and then what was black becomes white—can be called the first conversion. The negation of sensuality lies, in this case, one stage beyond the negation of perception and desire that takes place in moral awareness. While morality negates sensible drives one by one, the negation of sensuality we are speaking of here is a method of extirpating the roots of willful drives or perception all at once. What this means will become clear by and by. Let us only note here that this purification of everyday life begins in the first place with poverty and asceticism, both of which are, one might say, the living expression of that purification, its lived realization. But the first disengagement is not yet perfect disengagement. The first conversion is still far from being the final end of conversion, which is enlightenment. It is to the intervening stages that we next turn our attention.

In speaking of stages or steps, it is obvious that the latter step must always follow upon the former, which is the case with the so-called stages of mysticism. What have been called here the "three core notions" of śīla, dhyāna, and prajñā are depicted in terms of a progression—from śīla to dhyāna and from dhyāna to prajñā—as stages of consciousness on the way to enlightenment. While this is certainly the case, at the same time the three are in fact one from the very start. They only have force and meaning when they entail one another. Thus the Buddha teaches that dhyāna has no meaning without śīla, just as prajñā has no meaning without dhyāna; and that the three purify one another, like one foot rubbing the other. Strictly speaking, all three moments are already present in the first conversion when this is brought about by the dynamic relationship among assāda, ādīnava, and nissaraṇa. By means of the first conversion the purified world is opened up so that worldly life replete with sensuality turns into a dim and colorless panorama languishing of unsavoriness, and hence recedes into the background. (This experience, as we shall explain later, represents an encounter with the spirit of śīla, but at the same time already entails dhyāna and prajñā.) This does not mean, however, that the sensible world is simply wiped away with a single stroke. Quite the contrary, it works an enchantment of its own over the monk, blinding him demonically at the same time as it fills him with a sense of abhorrence and disgust. The soul of the monk becomes the scene of a fierce struggle. The legend that tells of the Buddha being pursued by Māra just before his enlightenment—leaving aside all questions of historical veracity here—shows the form that this bloody skirmish takes in the arena of the spirit. Basically, the entire śīla complex presents this struggle for self-denial and self-overcoming.

The commandments were first proclaimed in Buddhism in response to certain errors that crept in through particular disciples who entered the community in order to follow the teaching of the Buddha but were unable to overcome themselves and thus withdrew from spiritual practice. This is what we are wont to call the "Pātimokkha," which is oriented to specific concrete circumstances. In the Sāmaññaphalasutta these community commandments are treated as the fruits of asceticism or monastic performance from which those monks who had fallen into decline are shown in some detail to have strayed. These commandments are of historical interest in that they touch on particular, concrete questions that show us the actual situation that obtained at the time in the monastic community through their detailed divisions and subdivisions.

The main concern, however, centers about the "five commandments," or pañca-śīla. The Sāmaññaphalasutta divided the commandments systematically into minor, middle, and major, beginning with the five minor commandments. Frauwallner describes their content as a normal, mundane ethic, in contrast to the middle and major commandments, which form the ethic of a severe asceticism and poverty for the monk. As Hermann Beckh points out, however, the minor commandments continue to hold true for the monk as they do for the laity, the difference lying in their meaning and method of application. The five commandments are as follows, though we should note that in the Sāmaññaphalasutta, the fifth, which treats of shunning intoxicating drinks, is not included:

> Putting away the killing of living things, the Bhikshu holds aloof from the destruction of life. He lays the cudgel and the sword aside, and ashamed of roughness, and full of mercy, he dwells compassionate and kind to all creatures that have life. . . .
>
> Putting away the taking of what has not been given, the Bhikshu lives aloof from grasping what is not his own. He takes only what is given, and expecting that gifts will come, he passes his life in honesty and purity of heart. . . .
>
> Putting away unchastity, the Bhikshu is chaste. He holds himself aloof, far off, from the vulgar practice, from the sexual act. . . .

> Putting away lying words, the Bhikshu holds himself aloof from falsehood. He speaks truth, from the truth he never swerves; faithful and trustworthy, he breaks not his word to the world.[23]

As Beckh explains—and Frauwallner follows him here—these five commandments are nothing other than the disciplines, or yama, spoken of in the Yoga Sūtra, where they are viewed similarly as the preliminary stages of Yoga.[24] From the Upanishadic philosophy through the time of the early doctrines of Yoga and up to primitive Buddhism, meditation seems to have been bound up already from an early period with one or the other of the five commandments. Most important, though, is that religious sensitivity was deepened through the commandments and through meditation both in Yoga and in Buddhism, so that the connection between the commandments and meditation grew ever more intimate while, conversely, the recognition of this connection worked positively in both. The contents of the five minor commandments, distinct from the middle and major commandments in the Sāmaññaphalasutta, comprise the fundamental rules of humanness.

The first commandment, not to harm any living thing, for example, was taught from ancient times in Indian religions as ahiṃsā. We find it already in the Bṛhadāraṇyaka Upanishad.[25] But the commandment not to harm any living thing is restricted to those times when Brahman enters into all living things, and hence not for all times. Thus in such cases as the offering of sacrifices for divine service, it does not come into the picture. It does not represent a compassion that puts all beings, everything that lives, on a par with oneself. In order to evolve into a general, universal love, the feeling of love must rise to the level of a soul free from everything that "closes" it off, restricting it to a particular people or tribe, to the standpoint of a general love for humanity in an "open soul." For that to happen, the *popular religion* of the Veda and Brāhmaṇa, which up to that point had merely set its sight on the welfare of one people or tribe, needed to orient itself to the interiority of personality and shape itself into a *world religion* of a more free and compassionate outlook wherein the whole of the human race and indeed the whole of being could be viewed in the mirror of the inner world of one's own personality. Buddha and Jesus were the first to have experienced this love at its highest level, and world religions in general can be said to be based on this experience of their founders.[26]

The injunction not to harm any living thing can apply *in general* or can be narrowed down to apply *in particular* to those who happen to belong to the same people or tribe, which presents us with a qualitative difference between a "specific" ethic and a "generic" ethic. The sages of the Upanishads were already on the way to the development from the former to the latter. There is no difficulty with supposing that Yoga had already promoted this development prior to primitive Buddhism, though it is of course not clear from the textual material at our disposal. How did the individualistic tendencies and magical traits of later Yoga look at the early period? And how might these tendencies in Yoga tie in with the contemplation of compassion and with the four sublime states of brahma-vihāra? These questions remain open. But according to a later commentary on the Yoga Sūtra, ahiṃsa—the maintaining of an upright and peaceful relationship between oneself and the outer world—represents one of the indispensable conditions for entering into the contemplative state. The Yoga Sūtra itself may already imply this idea in its consideration of the injunction against harming any living thing as an outer command (yama). Perhaps we should suppose this idea to be an inheritance from a previous age that Jainism and Yoga share with Buddhism, namely, as a doctrine stemming from early Yoga.[27] At the time of the Buddha the idea filtered through by way of the notion of a universal, compassionate love that one should completely abstain from religious sacrifice and from eating fish and meat. The underlying religious spirit of this period achieved a breakthrough in the personality of the Buddha and there reached its high-water point. With primitive Buddhism we see the first flowering in the spiritual history of India of an "open" ethic of compassionate love, namely, in the experience of the Buddha with its manifest mysticism of compassion and its compassionate meditation. It is in contemplative experience that the similarity of all living things first comes to consciousness in a pervasive "non-differentiating love" (upekkhā) that extends to everything without discrimination, like the sun and the rain. The contemplation of catvāry apramāṇāni, or the four infinite states of mind (the samādhi of the four brahma-vihāra referred to earlier),[28] in primitive Buddhism will be taken up later. The injunction against harming any living thing belongs among the fundamental principles that set the religion and ethics of primitive Buddhism free from its particularizing limitations, from the narrow confines of an application to some specific people or tribe, and widened it out to embrace a universal humanity. We shall soon see how the mutual influence and mediation of śīla and dhyāna served to define this motivating force of love at its deepest and innermost point.

Something similar can be said with regard to the third commandment to chastity, or brahma-cariya. Unchasteness in general, even at the earlier period of the Upanishads, was taken to mean engaging in improper or extramarital sexual relations. The same understanding is to be found in the primitive Buddhist doctrine of chastity, which is taken as one of the minor commandments, intended principally for the laity (as we see in the Dhammapada). The situation is different for the monks, on whom are imposed greater demands. There brahma-cariya was understood by primitive Buddhism to entail a life of complete celibacy through seclusion in the forest or a life of wandering in homelessness, corresponding to the final stage of the older Hindu life-style. In the case of the latter, however, the holy conduct of brahma-cariya clearly presupposed that one had lived for a time as a householder.

Those who belong to the Brahman caste are required as a matter of duty to lead a normal sexual life, while chastity is viewed as a duty that belongs to a *specific period of time.* In primitive Buddhism, on the other hand, celibacy represents a permanent state for monks and nuns, and a monastic life of seclusion is seen as the authentic mode of being human. From the very start Buddhism has often been accused of obstructing the prosperity of family or clan. Why has a monk to keep chaste? The answer is simplicity itself: because chastity is a necessary condition for contemplation. As we read in the Dhammapada: "As long as lustful desire, however small, of man for women is not controlled, so long the mind of man is not free, but is bound like a calf tied to a cow."[29] Here we have a possible instance of how the doctrine of chastity takes on a different significance and also a different stringency for the laity and the monks. But if we take a closer look, we see that the first commandment, the injunction against harming any living thing, also takes on a different meaning according to whether one merely follows it formalistically or understands its original underlying spirit. The former is open also to the laity, but the latter requires the cultivation of samādhi through its higher stages (which we shall come to later). It is possible only in the fourth dhyāna, where one reaches the upekkhā of nirvāṇa, which, as the concentration of benevolence, compassionate mercy, and compassionate joy, represents the complete escape from the world of illusion. Thus in primitive Buddhism all five commandments have a different meaning for the laity and the monks. If one takes into consideration the historical background against which these commandments came into being, the process by which certain virtues ascended from a "closed ethic" to an "open ethic" also becomes clear. Here we have only been able to touch on one or the other of these commandments.

Vigilance, Right Mindfulness, and the Custody of the Senses

The notion of the custody of the senses (indriyesu guttadvāro) enables us to see at a glance the relationship between śīla and dhyāna in primitive

Buddhism and the way the two developed further. The Sāmaññaphala-sutta explains this concept in a stereotyped form of expression similar to that found in the treatment of the five commandments, and after the whole śīla complex is detailed in all its sub-groupings. The dry, matter-of-fact style suggests that we have something close to the form of a direct oral transmission:

> And how, O king, is the Bhikshu guarded as to the doors of his senses?
>
> When, O king, he sees an object with his eye he is not entranced in the general appearance or the details of it. He sets himself to restrain that which might give occasion for evil states, covetousness, and dejection, to flow in over him so long as he dwells unrestrained as to his sense of sight. He keeps watch upon his faculty of sight, and he attains to mastery over it. And so, in like manner, when he hears a sound with his ear, or smells an odor with his nose, or tastes a flavor with his tongue, or feels a touch with his body, or when he cognizes a phenomenon with his mind he is not entranced in the general appearance or the details of it. . . . And endowed with this self-restraint, so worthy of honor, as regards the senses, he experiences, within himself, a sense of ease into which no evil state can enter.[30]

The custody of the senses is based here on the spirit of Yoga. If we attempt to trace its sources still further back, we find it already present in the older sections of the Upanishads. From a logical point of view, this thought represents the reverse side of the emphasis that the mysticism of the Upanishads puts on the unity of Brahman and ātman. Simply put, the knowledge of the Absolute in the Upanishads comes down to this: *whoever knows Brahman becomes Brahman.* Behind this idea lies another: whoever knows sensible objects becomes a sensible object, that is, becomes a transient, impermanent, unreal being liable to death. Accordingly, the first step to emancipation is to draw self-consciousness away from the objects of sense perception and center on oneself, within oneself. The heart of Yoga consists in liberation from the fetters of sense objects and in the return of the soul to itself.[31] This seems to be of still greater importance in primitive Buddhism, where the liberation and "escape" from sensation already implies an element of ethical negation; while in early Yoga, which stands closer to the tradition of the Upanishads, emancipation from sensation remained strongly speculative in character, and it was stressed that the process of centering, or concentration on one's own interiority, was immediately united to the knowledge of and therefore also to the being of the Absolute. The custody of the senses is therefore envisaged as an indispensable first step on the way to contemplation. It is otherwise with primitive Buddhism, where the task of guarding the senses is important not only for the initiation into contemplation or the start of the process of contemplation, but remains true as a basic principle that holds sway over śīla as a whole. Moreover, the custody of the senses joins with vigilance and right mindfulness to form a fundamental principle of life that runs throughout śīla, dhyāna, and prajñā.

In order not to break the commandments, it is best, where śīla is concerned, to set a yoke upon the organs of sensation, which are the direct cause of avidity. This subjugation does not mean that we begin by trying to recover the senses that have gone astray after objects, but that we put them under a yoke from the very start to protect them from setting their sights on sensible things. It is far more advantageous if the appeal is absent from the beginning, rather than waiting to try and hold the senses back later and reacting defensively in the face of the charm of objects. We have already touched on the dynamic of the savory, the unsavory, and the escape from the world of illusion in upekkhā from the viewpoint of impermanence. There we saw that the disgust resulting from the sense of impermanence operates differently from ethics, where elements of sensation are rejected one by one in specific instances; it is rather as if the roots of sensation were torn out from their ground at a single stroke. In the custody of the senses, this disgust or abhorrence that occurs at the level of feelings urged on us by outer realities is fused with reflection on the relationship between sensation and the subject to forge an attitude of willed restraint proceeding from within. By coming to a realization of the feeling of disgust and interiorizing it, that feeling constellates into a posture of the will.

Thus constituted, this resolve or activity of the will represents a much stronger rejection of the workings of the element of sensation at the center of the subject than that found in ethics. We saw how the standpoint of śīla exponentializes negation to the power of infinity until at last it steps outside of the social realm of ethical order altogether and takes the radical form of a withdrawal from the world—asceticism and poverty—that is almost inhuman in form. Corresponding to this external life-style of the commandment is an internal rigor in the emotional life. A monk, by detesting the "outer man," turns completely inwards and is transformed into an "inner man" who needs only to follow the inner voice of conscience: "Do not what is evil. Do what is good. Keep your mind pure. This is the teaching of a Buddha."[32] As originally a subject of śīla, the human person is basically pure, but in allowing oneself to be exteriorized one takes evil karma upon oneself, just like iron that rusts because it has been left exposed to the elements. That evil karma then rusts the subject to the core, like a rust corroding the iron. It is something that takes place from without and yet penetrates within unhindered to corrupt the core of the subject. The fault here lies completely and totally with the subject:

> By oneself the evil is done, and it is oneself who suffers: by oneself the evil is not done, and by one's Self one becomes pure. The pure and the impure come from oneself: no man can purify another.
>
> Only a man himself can be the master of himself: who else from outside could be his master: When the Master and servant are one, then there is true help and self-possession.[33]

This is how the self-sufficiency and autonomy of the śīla-subject come to be emphasized without restriction. In this regard the consciousness of śīla in primitive Buddhism, which rests on the consciousness of dharma, is close to the moral rigorism of Kant. The connection between commandment and contemplation, between morality and religion, lies in the fact that contemplation sublates the standpoint of the commandment, raises it up and maintains it in its truth by negating it.

Hence the śīla-subject, by plunging headlong into the depths of moral consciousness, permeated by the sense of impermanence, is likely to experience a hitherto unprecedented sharpening of conscience. Through moral conscience, self-examination and self-reproach for one's own deeds arrive at a much deeper realm of consciousness, indeed at the very ground of consciousness (karma and saṁsāra). The same problem that grips us in the Kantian doctrine of radical evil is encountered here in its Buddhist version. The deepening of conscience has its first phase in the sense of impermanence, goes on to will the radical elimination of ingrained moral evil through the desperate battle over śīla, and finally the interiorized encounter that occurs in contemplation breaks through the wall of the habitual moral consciousness of good and evil. The intermeshing of these deepenings and denials leads one at last to a consciousness of original avidyā and at the same time to a salvific awakening by the very self-consciousness of avidyā. The darkness of ignorance (avidyā) turns into the light of knowledge (vidyā). "Unknowing turns around to knowing!" When things proceed in this fashion, the consciousness of śīla itself brings to fulfillment the threefold dialectic process from śīla to dhyāna to prajñā. Here, however, we restrict ourselves to a concern with the custody of the senses.

The custody of the senses, then, is the feeling of antipathy deepened so as to reach all the way down to the subjectivity of the will and to provoke a reflective analysis of the inner constitution of the subject. This led in turn to the Buddhist doctrine of the ṣaḍ-āyatana, or six senses, which in fact represents a further clarification of the process we have been discussing. We shall have occasion to return to this doctrine in chapter 6 and take a closer look at its underlying epistemology. What we need to see at this point is that this is closely connected with the doctrine of Yoga and further attempts to get beyond the subject-object dichotomy in order to arrive at a more authentic, original religious existence.

The practice that accompanied Yogic doctrine was an attempt to turn the mind away from the outer world to the inner world, to relieve the continued tension in the mind between subject and object by replacing its "outward-looking" attitude with an "inward-looking" one. The aim of early Yogic thought was indeed interiorization, but it still sought to effect this concentration of the mind on the side of the object. The so-called kasiṇa method, which is still employed in Buddhism, provides us with a good example of how this works.

In the kasiṇa method the meditator enters an empty house or a still place, puts some object—red or blue or green or some other color—before the eyes and looks at the color, concentrating the mind for a period of time until the object has become impressed on it. Heiler describes it this way:

> The subject fixes the gaze intently on one object until such time as the afterimage, the "inner reflex" that remains after closing the eyes, is as clear as the perceptual image. What we have here is a sort of pathological prolongation of a common perceptual experience according to which the afterimage that normally lasts only for a moment is made to last by autosuggestive or hallucinatory techniques. If the ascetic attains self-mastery through this Yogic practice of "inner reflex," the kasiṇa object can be eliminated and the inner image can be observed in another place and concentrated on until it leaves another afterimage, a second-level reflex image. In abhidharmic terminology this is called paṭibhāganimitta ("equivalent depicting"; or, according to Nyāntiloka, "artistic brand"), in distinction to the original afterimage, the uggahanimitta ("apprehended sign," or what Seidenstücker calls "apprehensive reflex").
>
> If the contemplating monk stares for a long time at this shadowy secondary image of the kasiṇa object, it gradually evaporates and in its place arises an imageless notion of an infinite realm. In this way the first stage of arūpa is achieved.[34]

What Heiler has called "abstract contemplation"[35] may in later developments have been accompanied by more concrete religious feeling. We know, for example, that this method of observation was employed—of course, in the time of Mahāyāna Buddhism—to view the splendors of paradise in its rich and colorful diversity, as we see in the gazing at the sun and the water in the Amitāyūrdhyāna-sūtra.[36] In that sūtra the believer is invited to undertake a particular form of contemplation: first one turns oneself to the setting sun and stares at it until the image is still clearly present even after the eyes have been closed. Then one must look at a river, gazing through its translucent waters down to the riverbed at its bottom. After that, one is to see the sight as if it were a great frozen piece of lapis lazuli, veined with sparkling golden threads that shine like so many setting suns. This is the way that one views the earth of the Pure Land in contemplation. The flowers of the Pure Land, the trees, the clear ponds with lotus blossoms of every color, and so forth come into view, until at last Amida Buddha himself and the two bodhisattvas that serve him become visible. The connection between this form of contemplation and the kasiṇa method, which was well known from the time of primitive Buddhism, is not hard to see. According to the Amitāyūrdhyāna-sūtra, however, contemplation through observation, beginning with its simpler objects, brings the whole complex structure of the Pure Land to light in a process of gradual unfolding.

When the kasiṇa method is considered as a technique of meditation, it is found to be far removed from the experience of impermanence and the doctrine of the six senses that concerned primitive Buddhism. As described above, it is in early Indian Yoga a form of, or aid to, mystical union with the All, which, in accord with the Upanishadic tradition, was still viewed "noematically." There is no disputing the point that this method of observation has assumed a variety of forms in Buddhism as well. Earlier I discussed the difference between the meaning of the "custody of the five senses" in Yoga and in primitive Buddhism.[37] The same holds true for the notions of vigilance and right mindfulness (sati-samyagjñāna). The Sāmaññaphalasutta defines vigilance and right mindfulness in the following terms:

> And so also in looking forwards, or in looking round; in stretching forth his arm, or in drawing it in again; in eating or drinking, in masticating or swallowing, in obeying the calls of nature, in going or standing or sitting, in sleeping or waking, in speaking or in being still, he keeps himself aware of all it really means. Thus is it, O king, that the Bhikshu becomes mindful and self-possessed.[38]

In short, the "custody over the gates of the senses" and "vigilance and right mindfulness" need to come together in a mind that upholds consciousness of its origins. To withdraw from the senses does not therefore mean that one shuts out objects, as it were, by shutting one's eyes, but rather that the way of seeing itself is changed even as one continues to look on objects. It is a question of rising above the dichotomy between subject and object by shutting out the burning desire that is its cause. Indeed, the mind liberated in meditation permeates the whole of life. Frauwallner rightly stresses that the ideas of vigilance and right mindfulness did not represent a prelude to a distinct contemplation in primitive Buddhism, but affected all the stages of contemplation, beginning with the preliminary steps. It is, one might say, a preeminently ethical idea.[39] The Sāmaññaphalasutta, as we noted, describes in straightforward and dry language how we need to maintain vigilance and right mindfulness in all the things of life, in our going and our coming, our sitting and our sleeping; while the poems of the Suttanipāta portrays such a life-style in fresh and living terms.

The Four Stages of Contemplation

The Sāmaññaphalasutta considers a monk to be prepared for true contemplation when he follows the rules of ethical propriety, lives a life of speech and action beyond reproach, and earns an honest living, and further when he is vigilant and alert in his activity and full of contentment. Wherever he goes, he is to take along a garment to protect his body and a bowl for receiving alms, "like a little bird that takes its whole coat of feathers with it wherever it flies." He is to lead a life of contentment in a forlorn place, in solitude—at the foot of a tree, on a mountain, in a gulley, in a grotto, on a burial ground, in a hidden wood, under the open sky, or on a haystack. There he is to set himself down with crossed legs and body erect, center himself, and thus pass through the four stages of contemplation. A Buddhist disciple has extolled this life of contemplation in the following poem:

When in the lowering sky thunders the storm-cloud's drum,
And all the pathways of the birds are thick with rain,
The brother sits within the hollow of the hills,
Rapt in an ecstasy of thought—no higher bliss is given to men than this.

Or when by rivers on whose banks together crowd
Garlands of woodland blossoms bright with many a hue,
With heart serene the brother sits upon the strand,
Rapt in an ecstasy of thought—no higher bliss is given to men than this.[40]

The poem naively exalts the joys of contemplation and needs no lengthy explanation of itself. I should like to take it as an initial indication of the elements that make up the inner structure of contemplation. We are being given here a picture of the rainy season in India, with the dark clouds that cover the mountains and the valleys, the wind and the rain that beat against the earth. The dark clouds represent the darkness of ignorance, the avidyā that embraces all living things; from there comes the cloudburst of "burning thirst" that rains down and is whipped about by the winds of impermanence. In this storm everything gets drenched to the bone. The thunder rolls follow one after the other with their frightening roar, just as all living things are gripped by the fear of death and have no recourse against it. In the midst of this the monk remains alone in his mountain grotto, far from the winds and the rain, where the bellowing of the thunder cannot reach him. His habitat lies close to the summit of a mountain that towers high above the level ground below. But, it should also be noted, this cave lies deep in the bowels of the mountain, so that it might just as well be said to lie in the depths of the earth, or at the ground of the earth. Insofar as the monk has left everything worldly and renounced the everyday life, he both ascends to the heights and descends to the depths; he transcends life and returns to its original ground. The custody of the senses has to do with stepping beyond everyday experience, both rising above it and penetrating beneath it, in order to open up within oneself an inner world protected from the fear we spoke of. The heart of this transcending, which results in the self-subsistence of existential freedom, is nothing other than an awakening to the self-conscious relationship between samudaya (origination) and nirodha (extinction) in dependent origination. On this we shall have more to say in later chapters.

In the second stanza of the poem we see a complete shift of landscape. The first stanza showed a distressing sight of living things exposed to the wind and rain of impermanence, while the condition of the soul of the meditator was only mentioned briefly at the end by way of contrast. But in the second stanza we see depicted the feelings that develop within the monk: joy, good fortune, peace, quiet, and so forth symbolized in the blossoming flowers and trees in all their color and variety. A monk who wishes to cultivate contemplation must seek out for that end a quiet and yet particularly beautiful natural setting. In Indian belief the experience of salvation and deliverance is always effected in the beauties of nature.[41] The woods near the town of Senā in Uruvelā, where the Buddha reached enlightenment, must have been such a place. The Ariyapariyesanasutta (Discourse on the Holy Quest) depicts it in these terms:

> There I saw a delightful stretch of land and a lovely woodland grove, and a clear flowing river with a delightful ford, and a village for support nearby. . . . So I, monks, sat down just then, thinking, "Indeed this does well for striving."[42]

To the meditator who sits on the quiet shore, the winds transport a host of fragrances from flowers blooming in distant fields. These fragrances borne far and wide on the wind may serve as a simile for the bliss of contemplation. The monk hears the rush of a river nearby. The flowing of the stream is immediately identified for him with the flow of consciousness. His quest is to pursue that stream of consciousness back to its source. En route to the source of consciousness, he will soon recognize the beautiful flowers reflected in the water and the deep blue in the midst of the quiet wood with its colorful garlands. But the one on the quest for the soul has to pass all this by until arriving at the source where the river ceases its flow. It is precisely this sort of quest for the source of consciousness that the doctrine of the four stages of contemplation attempts to show with its differentiation between religious and mystical consciousness:

> And gladness springs up within him . . . and joy arises to him thus gladdened, and so rejoicing all his frame becomes at ease, and being thus at ease he is filled with a sense of peace, and in that peace his heart is stayed.
>
> Then estranged from lusts, aloof from evil dispositions, he enters into and remains in the *First Rapture*—a state of joy and ease born of detachment, reasoning and investigation going on the while.
>
> His very body does he so pervade, drench, permeate, and suffuse with the joy and ease born of detachment, that there is no spot in his whole frame not suffused therewith. . . .
>
> Then further . . . the Bhikshu suppressing all reasoning and investigation enters into and abides in the *Second Rapture,* a state of joy and ease, born of the serenity of concentration, when no reasoning or investigation goes on—a state of elevation of mind, a tranquillization of the heart within.
>
> And his very body does he so pervade, drench, permeate, and suffuse with the joy and ease born of concentration, that there is no spot in his whole frame not suffused therewith. . . .
>
> Then further . . . the Bhikshu, holding aloof from joy, becomes equable; and mindful and self-possessed he experiences in his body that ease which the Arahats talk of when they say, "The man serene and self-possessed is well at ease," and so he enters into and abides in the *Third Rapture.*

> And his very body does he so pervade, drench, permeate, and suffuse with that ease that has no joy with it, that there is no spot in his whole frame not suffused therewith.
>
> Then further . . . the Bhikshu, by the putting away alike of ease and of pain, by the passing away alike of any elation, any dejection, he had previously felt, enters into and abides in the *Fourth Rapture,* a state of pure self-possession and equanimity, without pain and without ease.
>
> And he sits there so suffusing even his body with that sense of purification, of translucence, of heart, that there is no spot in his whole frame not suffused therewith.[43]

The experience of these four stages of contemplation appears in nearly the same form in the Yoga Sūtra as well as in the texts of Jainism. However, it is in fact discarded in the Brahmajālasutta (The Net of Encompassing Knowledge) mentioned above, where it is considered to belong to the sixty-two-fold heteredoxy and is thus rejected as a heretical philosophy. According to that sūtra, the doctrine of the four dhyānas deals with a false mysticism belonging to the categories of diṭṭha-dhamma-nibbāna-vāda. We cannot fail here to take into account the view held by the majority of Japanese scholars that the four dhyānas are to be excluded from primitive Buddhism. But numerous Buddhist texts, including the Sāmaññaphalasutta, link the attainment of Buddhahood and enlightenment with the doctrine of the four dhyānas and do not only consider the experience of contemplation as the foundation of the religious experience of the Buddha, but take the four dhyānas as the core of the samādhi of the Buddha as a whole, a fact not less worthy of note. Ui considers one particular view of contemplation—that of contemplation for its own sake—as a heretical element in Buddhism, or a diṭṭha-dhamma-nibbāna-vāda. In contrast, it is his view that the proper centering of the self in the noble eightfold path is the only path to enlightenment. The experience of samādhi often brings with it an enchanted, ecstatic feeling, and those who experience this only very rarely persevere in a commitment to the quest. In that case, overpowered by ecstasy, one necessarily forgets the final goal or ends up surrendering oneself to a religious passion that mixes up ends with means, just as avarice does. But when we look at things from the standpoint of the final state of religious experience, it is very doubtful whether such a rational way of thinking geared to ends and means and the like can be elevated into a principle for the critique of religion. But we may leave this question to one side and turn to the doctrine of the four dhyānas once again to see what each of these stages of contemplation might mean in itself.

The Sāmaññaphalasutta provides a fitting image for each of the four dhyānas. By means of these analogies, we are able to see with perfect clarity the direction that this text takes in its exposition of the doctrine. In what follows I would like to analyze the religious experience of each of the stages of contemplation, taking those images as a starting point.

The image for the first dhyāna reads:

> Just . . . as a skillful bathman or his apprentice will scatter perfumed soap powder in a metal basin, and then besprinkling it with water, drop by drop, will so knead it together that the ball of lather, taking up the unctuous moisture, is drenched with it, pervaded by it, permeated by it within and without, and there is no leakage possible. This . . . is an immediate fruit of the life of a recluse, visible in this world, higher and sweeter than the last.[44]

The experience of the first dhyāna sets up the first, free, and powerful self-consciousness achieved by the mind in its nissaraṇa, the state reached in the consideration of the "savory" and "unsavory" in the five skandhas and their extinction referred to earlier. This catharsis is likened to a bather getting a thorough scrubbing in a tub of soapy water. In the still of a mind and body that has been purified, the hold that earthly things have over one is washed away. This is not something that takes place only at the level of an imagined ideal but is an actual achievement wrought through training and hard work, a veritable cleansing of the entire mind and body that leaves not one single spot of one's essence untouched. Being is impermanent, and so long as we adhere to impermanent being our human existence is set upon by fear. But here the peaceful joy and happiness that are awakened through escaping fill mind and body to the brim and permeate them.

"Reasoning and investigating going on the while" (vitakka-vicāra) is how this first dhyāna was characterized. It means that the mind is centered fully on the inquiry into truth. In the Suttanipāta the word *vitakka* or *takka* is used to describe the thoughts of a wanderer wondering what he will eat this evening and where he might pass the night.[45] The word *vicāra* is often used jointly with *vitakka,* the two mostly being used as specific expressions for the thinking that goes on in samādhi. A later commentary describes them in these terms: "vitakka is the rough work, vicāra the fine craftsmanship;" "vitakka is thought fixed firmly on the object, vicāra is the uninterrupted continuation of vitakka; vicāra follows upon vitakka as an ongoing movement of refined thinking, like the reverberations that follow the first strike of a gong."[46]

Not only in primitive Buddhism but also in the Yogic system and Jainism, *vitakka* and *vicāra* describe particular functions of thought in contemplation—albeit with different meanings and a different relationship to the dhyānas themselves. In Jainism, for instance, vitakka is only present in the first and second stages of contemplation but not in the third and fourth, while vicāra is supposed to have been already sublated by the second stage, as it is in Buddhism.[47] Similarly, in Yoga the words have distinct meanings all their own. If we compare this with primitive Buddhism, we are better able to locate the difference between the consideration of the doctrine of the four dhyānas as diṭṭa-dhamma-nibbāna-vāda and the authentic standpoint of primitive Buddhism. I shall not dwell on the point here, however, but concentrate rather on an analysis of the image given above.

To add only one further comment, it should be noted that vitakka and vicāra are considered both in primitive Buddhism and in Yoga and Jainism to be the proper method for pursuing the truth of knowledge; but at the same time, they are to be sublated and overcome as the experience of contemplation deepens. As acts of knowing, they signify discriminating thinking and inference, argument and dialectic. *Vicāra* (investigation) is related etymologically to *vicarati* (to wander about), calling to mind the etymology of the word *dis-cursive.* It may be helpful here to think of the meaning of the word in a sense closer to its origins, as we find it in the passage from the Suttanipāta referred to above. The initial meaning is a kind of self-troubling or self-concern for the object. The monk is indeed taken up with "reasoning and investigating," but his mind is already on the way to centering and is caught up in the process of elevation and integration.[48] In seeking to arrive at its own elevation and integration, and to be interiorized, the mind no longer pursues the outer world. But in this inward quest a residue of the outward quest still remains. In the experience of contemplation the mind fixes itself on metaphysical objects and becomes enraptured in probing those objects. The concern with life and the earthly world turns into a concern for religious and absolute truth. But even in such a case, the element of concern is still present. In order to state the relationship between these two concerns in simpler form, it might be best to introduce a comparison between sensation and perceptual judgment, or in Buddhist terms, between rūpa (form, corporeality) and saṃjñā (representation, name, idea). One point of affinity is that the notion of saṃjñā can both be defined through the interiority of the world achieved in contemplation, and yet can also yield a judgment, such as "this is blue," or "it is red." Similarly, we see a connection in that saṃjñā on the one hand occupies a general, abstract, infinite realm distant from rūpa; and yet on the other hand is judged to be a delusion, since in meditation at this level, the opposition between the subject and the object has not yet been fully overcome, and the residue of this opposition adheres to the meditator as a personal delusion, since the unconscious roots of the longing for truth are poisoned by that residue. Thus saṃjñā has to be negated by a continuing deepening of the experience of contemplation. It is the same with vitakka and vicāra. In one of the sūtras of the Dīgha-Nikāya, vitakka and vicāra are aligned with saṃjñā, cetasika (thought), and taṇhā (burning thirst), all of which point to a grasping after the things of the world. They are nothing other than the attachment to the "savoring" consideration of the five skandhas, which continues to bring forth suffering in the world.

Joy comes when the body and mind of the meditator have come to rest and been grasped in an act of elevation and integration. This joy is a strong movement of one's disposition, while in comparison happiness is not as intensive but embraces one's entire being as a permanently instated "feeling." Like vitakka and vicāra, joy and happiness follow one from the other and yet are distinct from one another, like the beat of the gong and its after-reverberations. Happiness is a highly spiritual feeling that echoes quietly in the depths of interiority. Earlier we referred to the contentment of the meditator achieved in poverty as a preparatory stage to contemplation. If he had it to choose, the monk would consider his condition as a good fortune better than that to befall any king. After the experience of release in contemplation, this feeling of happiness becomes still more clear.

The prosaic image of a bather getting a good scrubbing, the bathing assistant, and the soap to exemplify the first stage of catharsis is interesting but almost a bit comical. Still, the comparison is fitting in that the first dhyāna entails the negation of the stain of things earthly, but at the same time because of that negation the worldly spirit is still involved. While the first dhyāna is likened to the bather, the image used for the second dhyāna strikes out in a completely different direction and reaches more deeply:

> Just . . . as if there were a deep pool, with water welling up into it from a spring beneath, and with no inlet from the east or west, from the north or south, and the god should from time to time send down showers of rain upon it. Still the current of cool waters rising up from that spring would pervade, fill, permeate, and suffuse the pool with cool waters, and there would be no part or portion of the pool unsuffused therewith. This . . . is an immediate fruit of the life of a recluse, visible in this world, and higher and sweeter than the last.[49]

When one arrives at the second stage of contemplation, there is no longer any vitakka and vicāra. Vitakka and vicāra represent the resound of the outward-directed quest that keeps returning to reason. So long as vitakka and vicāra remain, interiority needs to seek a still higher elevation and integration, and the unrest that vitakka and vicāra bring needs to arrive at a more profound peacefulness. The image likens this peacefulness that is sought for to a deep pool on a mountain plain. No rivers flow into this pool, which means that the mind no longer receives any influence from the conditions of the outer world. On the contrary, cool water gushes up inexhaustibly and fills the pool. As the passage says, the god sends a rainshower from time to time. Perhaps the rainshower that waters the surrounding plain feeds the source of the pool with water. In the first dhyāna joy is awakened by extinguishing the five hindrances (pañca-nivaraṇāni). It is a situation in which one resolutely negates and dismisses the outer world and yet because of that very negation is still bound up with the world. Thus in the first rapture happiness originates from out of joy. This joy, the secondary state of mind, is indeed mediated through negation but still remains "external." It screens and covers the primary interiority (the disposition of happiness) and determines it from without.

In the second dhyāna, however, joy and happiness well up from out of the interiority of contemplation like cool water gushing from its source underground. Bright and clean, joy and happiness permeate the mind throughout like cool water that remains clear and fresh in every part of the pool. The statement that the god grants a rainshower from time to time may mean that the pool of the meditating subject is showered in that interiorization of the joyful religious spirit with a holy rain sent from time to time by a transcendent reality. Or perhaps it means that the cool water that gushes up within the pool only indirectly belongs to the water that has fallen into the surrounding plain, so that the spirit cannot remain forever in relationship to the gods but only from time to time.

The image for the third dhyāna reads as follows:

> Just . . . as when in a lotus tank the several lotus flowers, red or white or blue, born in the water, grown up in the water, not rising up above the surface of the water, drawing up nourishment from the depths of the water, are so pervaded, drenched, permeated, and suffused from their very tips down to their roots with the cool moisture thereof, that there is no spot in the whole plant, whether of the red lotus, or of the white, or of the blue, not suffused therewith. This . . . is an immediate fruit of the life of a recluse, visible in this world, and higher and sweeter than the last.[50]

In this third stage of contemplation the joy (pīti) of the second dhyāna is sublated, just as the vitakka and vicāra that showed up in the first dhyāna had been. The mind is cleansed of joy and arrives at a state of indifference, or non-differentiation (upekkhā). This state, it is said, is nothing other than vigilance and right mindfulness. Joy is not the goal, in spite of the strong upswing of religious feeling that it brings about. The unswerving spirit of vigilance and right mindfulness is considered something far nobler. In this third dhyāna a holy rainshower could in no sense be taken any longer to signify a grace come from without that operates from time to time, for, as is made clear, a state is achieved like that which the holy sages spoke of as "indifferent, vigilant, and happy." The image for the third stage of contemplation likens it to blue, red, and white lotus blossoms that have grown up in a pool fed with cool water. In the third dhyāna the pool forms the setting, just as it had for the second. The lotus blossoms represent the interior of the pool, that is, interiority. Perhaps they take root in the bottom of the pool and rise up to bloom on its surface, thus forming a vital link between the deepest reaches of the pool and its surface. The outer and the inner are shown here as one in their fresh and vibrant activity. Thus the divine rainshower mentioned earlier is no longer needed. The rainshower sent by the god is replaced here by the lotus blossoms in full bloom. If one represents joy pictorially as a movement occurring on the surface of the mind's pool, the floating blossoms will be stirred slightly by it but their roots will not be disturbed. The unswerving mind is rooted deep in the bottom of the pool. The mind that has cleansed itself of joy and become indifferent yet remains permeated by the deepest happiness. The pure blessedness that embraces all of being and enlivens it like the cool of clear and fresh water that embraces and enlivens the lotus in its entirety—roots, stem, and flower—is the state of mind that rises quietly into consciousness in the third dhyāna as a bright happiness.

The image for the fourth dhyāna reads:

> Just . . . as if a man were sitting so wrapt from head to foot in a clean white robe, that there were no spot in his whole frame not in contact with the clean white robe—just so . . . does the Bhikshu sit there, so suffusing even his body with that sense of purification, of translucence, of heart, that there is no spot in his whole frame not suffused therewith. This . . . is an immediate fruit of the life of a recluse, and higher and sweeter than the last.[51]

In this fourth stage of contemplation, the happiness (sukha) present before is now absent. Sorrow follows happiness as its contrary the way shadows follow the light. So long as happiness remains happiness, that is, so long as happiness affirms itself, however deep and joyful it be, there is still one final unfreedom remaining. The fourth dhyāna, where the mind is further cleansed through indifference and vigilance, represents the final state of complete release and escape, a complete freedom that has elevated itself beyond the opposition of happiness and sorrow. This freedom is what Buddhism calls nirvāṇa. Appropriately, Heiler has likened this fourth stage of contemplation to what Eckhart calls *Abgeschiedenheit.*

The prosaic image of the bather in the first stage is discarded in the second in favor of the image of the pool on a mountain plain, and in the third colored lotuses were seen to bloom in the pool. In the fourth stage these blossoms are transformed into a purified human form clothed from head to foot in a white robe. The one in white (odātavattha) clearly portrays a person cloaked for a religious ceremony (a baptism or sacrifice).[52] We may suppose that the white robe signifies something like the clothing adopted in the initiation rites of mystery cults. The man in white is a new man. We are given here the image of that newly perfected holiness with which one appears when one has resurrected to a new religious life, when one has become a truly free mind and pure heart.

In primitive Buddhism the purified spirit of such a monk is revealed in compassion. Compassion is seen as the consummation of contemplation, and contemplation as the realization of compassion. We need to have a closer look at the relationship between these two, and to that end to approach contemplation as the catvāry apramāṇāni, the four immeasurables. Here we can be served by a comparison with Eckhart's idea of *Abgeschiedenheit.* The doctrine of the four dhyānas and the contemplation of the four immeasurables are like twin mountain peaks crowned with upekkhā. Just as the mysticism of Eckhart reaches its summit in *Abgeschiedenheit,* so does primitive Buddhism arrive at its summit in "indifference," and it would not be going too far to insist that in judging primitive Buddhism everything hinges on whether or not one has understood this state of indifference.

Contemplation and Compassion

If one has passed through the four dhyānas, one has gone through a step-by-step renunciation without reserve of everything earthly, including finally all joy and all happiness of a religious nature. Arriving at the summit, the mind thus released from all human and worldly-minded feeling reaches the state of the fourth dhyāna: upekkhā. At this point we may feel the urge to ask what is left for the mind that has, so to speak, retreated into its innermost solitariness to do. Arrival at the state of upekkhā means that one has likewise become a new person, clothed in white. One steps into the world all over again. The mystery of this upekkhā mind consists in the fact that there are two contradictory tendencies, that the innermost is able suddenly to turn around and function externally. Following Heiler, we suggested that this upekkhā can be compared to Eckhart's *Abgeschiedenheit.* Note the following passage from Eckhart's sermons:

> As I have often said, if a person were in such a rapturous stage as Saint Paul once entered, and he knew of a sick man who wanted a cup of soup, it would be far better to withdraw from the rapture for love's sake and serve him who is in need.[53]

In the same way one might say that for a Buddhist consciousness that has passed through the four dhyānas, even the contemplative attitude itself can abandon itself and turn to those who suffer the sorrows of the heart, all the while maintaining its highest religious bliss. This final summit of contemplation, which, while remaining in itself, yet exhibits continual movement and affects the other is what Buddhism calls compassion or compassionate contemplation. For the highest and most solitary peak of religious mind represents a state where one mind and another affect each other like mountain peaks greeting one another. Indeed, consciously or not, this heavenly height is the homeland of the soul for every person.

In Buddhism human love is likened to a thirst drenched with the moistness of sorrow. One is to forsake even religious love insofar as it is tinged with the human, as we have already seen in reference to the need to transcend joy and happiness. But at the highest summit in its rarified air, sparks spring directly from mind to mind as if in a vacuum. Earlier we spoke of kasiṇa contemplation, and there touched on the experience of a universal sympathy for all things; we saw a form of contemplation in which one first fully centers the self on its own interiority, turning to the infinite so that the microcosm harmonizes directly with the macrocosm. Here that contemplative state is seen realized in compassionate contemplation. The rays that strike forth here have none of the warmth of earthly love and yet seek to spread out to reach every corner of the world.

Compassionate contemplation is described in terms as terse as those used for the four dhyānas that had been transmitted orally in customary terms. To begin with, obedience of the rules of morality is treated as a preliminary stage, as it had been in the Sāmaññaphalasutta; thus compassionate contemplation, the contemplation of the four immeasurables, is presented in the Tevijjasutta from the very same starting point from which the first dhyāna began in the Sāmaññaphalasutta:

> And how . . . is his conduct good?
>
> In this . . . that the Bhikshu, putting away the killing of living things, holds aloof from the destruction of life. . . .
>
> . . . And being thus at ease, he is filled with a sense of peace, and in that peace his heart is stayed. . . .
>
> And he lets his mind pervade one quarter of the world with thoughts of Love, and so the second, and so the third, and so the fourth. And thus the whole wide world, above, below, around, and everywhere, does he continue to pervade with heart of Love, far-reaching, grown great, and beyond measure.
>
> Just . . . as a mighty trumpeter makes himself heard—and that without difficulty—in all the four directions; even so of all things that have shape or life, there is no one that he passes by or leaves aside, but regards them all with mind set free, and deep-felt Love.
>
> Verily this . . . is the way to a state of union with Brahmā.
>
> And he lets his mind pervade one quarter of the world with thoughts of pity . . . sympathy . . . equanimity. . . .
>
> Verily this . . . is the way to a state of union with Brahmā.[54]

The contemplation of the four immeasurables reaches over into the spirit of benevolence (mettā), compassionate mercy (karuṇā), compassionate rejoicing (muditā), and indifference (upekkhā); and it extends the bliss that comes from this state of mind after the model of kasiṇa, reaching a universal sympathy for all living things, indeed for everything that exists. With regard to the first stage of mettā, we find the following verses in the Suttanipāta, which have a somewhat more vibrant ring than the earlier description:

> This by one ready for the goal must be,
> As nigh unto that born of calm he draws:
> He must be able, straight, yea, truly straight,
> Gentle in speech and mild, without conceit:
>
> And he must be content, soon satisfied,
> Be of few needs and frugal in his ways,
> Calm in the faculties of sense, and apt,
> Not coveting, nor bold within men's homes:
>
> And he must never in a mean way act,
> So others who are shrewd may censure him.

May beings all be happy and secure,
And come at last to happiness-of-self!

And all in whom the breath of life exists:
The feeble and the strong, the tall and large,
The short and middle-sized—omitting none—
The little creatures and the very great!

All creatures who are seen, all those unseen,
Those that dwell far away, those that dwell near,
Those that are here and those that seek to be:
May all come unto happiness-of-self!

Let not another e'er mislead another,
Nor anyone despise in any place:
From quarrel or from enmity let none
Wish ill to any other one whate'er.

Like as a mother wardeth her own son,
Her only son, as long as she doth live:
So, verily, for every creature here
Quicken a heart to boundless thoughtfulness.

Quicken a heart of boundless amity
For all things and creatures in the world,
Upwards and downwards and athwart the world.
Unhindered, free of hate and enmity.

And as one stands or walks or sits or lies,
Till overcome by drowsiness, let him
Devote himself unto this mindfulness:
"Godly abiding" here this state is called.

And when man takes not to himself a view,
With virtue dwells, with insight is endowed,
And hath all greed for pleasures here expelled.
Then goes he to the bed-of-womb no more.[55]

"May beings all be happy and secure, and come at last to happiness-of-self!" Schopenhauer once heard this blessing of love (mettā) filled with benevolence towards all of life recited in the final act of an Indian drama; and from that moment on, it became for him the most beautiful and sublime of all prayers.[56] The spirit of contemplation is, from the very start, universal in its renunciation of human passion.

But these cool rays of benevolent love that extend over the totality of being must at the same time have an opposite pole for the current to flow. On the field of love-energy, the contemplation of merciful compassion (karuṇā) and compassionate rejoicing (muditā) appear as still higher concretizations of love. Karuṇā is a compassion that is grounded on this contemplative experience. In Buddhism, however, muditā is still more greatly esteemed than is karuṇā. Our experience, too, teaches us that it is easier for us to show compassion in mercy for another who has met with misfortune than it is to rejoice with another over success. The contemplative effort needs to go further to eradicate the vestiges of resentment and hatred that remain lodged in the subconscious mind, and Buddhists rightly regard pure benevolent love free of all attachment (mettā), merciful compassion free of all enjoyment at seeing another's misfortune, and pure compassionate rejoicing without resentment as properly one with the experience of contemplation. In this way the spirit of mercy and rejoicing can in turn be incorporated into a universal sympathy and into the totality of being. Like a pebble tossed into a pond that ripples into ever wider circles, so does Buddhist love surrender itself to an object in order to become concrete in a particular situation as compassionate mercy and compassionate rejoicing; and at the same time it embraces the other, grows beyond it, and goes on to permeate the whole of being—the interiority of every existing thing—and expand itself infinitely and without limits. Thus is its "concrete universality" realized.

The fourth stage of the four immeasurables, like the fourth dhyāna, is upekkhā. Love and compassion are already both released from mere human feeling and possess, as it were, the diaphanous quality of a crystal, stemming from the centering on oneself. The "concrete universality" of the merciful and rejoicing compassionate mind reminds us of the small sapphire in which the entire blue expanse of the heavens comes to rest, or the piece of red ruby that reflects the "red sea of God" (to draw an image from Indian myth) at the outbreak of creation, the morning sky where light has not yet penetrated the darkness. The mind in upekkhā here is higher than the opposition between compassionate mercy and rejoicing. If one takes mettā as the essence of contemplation (*an sich*) and karuṇā and muditā as its ex-istence (*für sich*), then upekkhā can be taken as the realized unity of the two (*an und für sich*). As Eckhart says, detachment stands higher than love.[57] So too, here, does upekkhā rise above mettā, karuṇā, and muditā. Regarding the remark that Jesus makes when he is about to take leave of his disciples, "It is to your advantage that I go away, for if I do not go away, the Counsellor will not come to you" (John 16:7), Eckhart says that it contradicts true religious consciousness to make visual images of God.[58] The apostles would only receive the freedom of the Holy Spirit once Jesus had gone from them. In primitive Buddhism the meditator similarly judges the religious experience of joy and happiness. For many religious thinkers of the West, other than mystics like Eckhart, it is extremely difficult to understand how the heart of Buddhist love can reside in upekkhā. It is for such a reason that even someone like Albert Schweitzer, for all his deep appreciation of mysticism, could not appreciate the love of the Buddha.

For Schweitzer, love is manifest in the concrete, social, mutual love of one for another (love of neighbor) and is irreconcilable with a "denial of the world and life" that renounces everything earthly. If the work of love is to be effected at all, a direct "affirmation of the world and life" is unavoidable for him. Of course, he had high praise for the Buddha as the first person through whom true religious love made its appearance in Indian thought and as the one who directly or indirectly imprinted all later Indian religions with the spirit of love. But at the same time Schweitzer lamented the fact that the love of the Buddha had almost become a force powerful enough to break down the traditional world-negating and life-negating spirit, but in the end remained bound to that tradition.[59]

By way of illustration, Schweitzer cites the example of the Buddha faced with a mother sorrowing over the loss of her child and only offering the counsel that "All is impermanent," when Schweitzer thought she might have rather needed words of reassurance and consolation. But for the Buddha, who looks at things from the standpoint of upekkhā, only the highest love contained in these apparently cold words is true religious love.

Nygren's *Eros and Agape* explains the difference between eros and agape as two forms of spiritual love and sees caritas as a compromise between these two contradictory positions that arose respectively in Hellenistic thought and in the Middle Ages. In my view, however, the love of caritas has a completely different origin from that of eros and agape. Caritas is forever bound up with the mystical experience of infinity. It is this type of love that has found typical expression in the upekkhā of the Buddha. To be sure, we find in Buddhism a certain opposition between love and contemplation, and this indeed incited the development of the Mahāyāna tradition, as we see more clearly in the notion of praṇidhāna, or sacred vow. In the personality of the Buddha, however, the two opposing tendencies are fused together into a dynamic unity and crystallize into the very archetype of mystical love.[60]

·3·

Centering and the World Beyond

Eschatology and the Stages of History

To locate the origins of eschatological thought and belief in Buddhism we have to go back to the early period of Indian Buddhism. In the Pali canon there are already a few indications of the later developments this belief would undergo, a fact that comes out particularly clearly when we compare the Pali texts with the corresponding Chinese translations. The Chinese texts even show coincidences of terminology here and there with later teachings, though hardly with the same rigor of definition.

In general, Buddhist eschatology includes three periods. First is the era of *correct dharma,* which is to last for some five hundred—or, according to alternate traditions, for up to one thousand—years after the death of the Buddha. During this period the doctrine of the Buddha would be followed perfectly, and his disciples would be able to reap the fruits of saving wisdom in this world.

After this first era of five hundred or a thousand years such saintly discipleship would disappear. There would be many disciples of the Buddha who would in fact follow their master's path and perfectly carry out religious practice as had once been done, but they would no longer be able to reap the fruits of saving wisdom. This era of *falsified dharma* would last another five hundred (or one thousand) years.

Finally would begin the era of the *final dharma,* the time of the last things. This is to continue until the year 10,000, a period in which neither redemptive enlightenment nor genuine religious practice would be found. Deprived of their spiritual vitality, the sūtras would become mere corpses, until finally with the year 10,000 the whole world would go up in flames in the great kalpa-fire, and the sūtras would sink into the bowels of the earth or the depths of the sea.

Another method of reckoning eschatology proceeds more according to historical events. Here the duration of the various segments of time is about five times longer than actual historical reality itself. In the Mahāyāna text known as the *Ta-chi-yüeh-tsang-ching,* we also find predictions of the Buddha that speak of five basic eras to follow his death. According to that text, in the first phase, the disciples would be able to attain wisdom with steadfastness; in the second phase, they would be able to attain contemplation with steadfastness; in the third, to hear and see many things with steadfastness; in the fourth, to erect stūpas, virtue, and bliss and to arrive at penitence with stability; in the fifth phase, however, the pure dharma would become hidden and cease to function, which would be the cause of great strife and leave behind only a few good ones. This account goes on to tell of events that would wreak havoc on the period to follow.

These two methods of reckoning time, when combined, produce numerous predictions, as we see particularly in those times of persecution when schisms proclaimed the end of the "falsified era."

The sūtras in which these eschatological ideas were used were soon translated into Chinese and caused a great flare-up of anxiety in China, leading people to believe that the world had entered into its third era, the time of the last things. (All of this occurred around the middle of the sixth century of the Christian era.) Actually, Chinese Buddhism after a time experienced the same fate as had befallen Indian Buddhism. After the flowering of Buddhist philosophy in China, a period of persecution suddenly broke out, and it was then that the predictions of the horrible events to occur in the eschaton and their descriptions in the sūtras became a pressing problem for all Buddhists. A Chinese emperor, inspired by Confucianism, banned Buddhism from his realm, forbidding the people to believe in Buddhism and decreeing that all monks return to the lay state. But in spite of all the misery that this persecution brought, Chinese Buddhism did not die out. Quite the contrary, it became purified and took to reflecting once again and with firm spiritual intensity on its true aims.

Thus after the golden age of theoretical Buddhism, when cities had invariably been preferred as the center of teaching, a new orientation came about: the existential and practical religion of Buddhism. The two important representatives of this new orientation are Zen and Shin (or Pure Land) Buddhism.

From an eschatological standpoint, Shin Buddhism is the more important. It is instructive to note that in most cases its predecessors were those very scholars who had previously devoted themselves to writing commentaries on the sūtras. But under the influence of the words and deeds of their religious leaders, and profoundly gripped by the temporality of human being, people turned themselves to belief in the Pure Land.

The temporality of human existence here has to be seen in the sense of a general destiny that affects the human in each particular period of time. Precisely how this belief in the Pure Land developed its own existential problematic is something we shall not pursue in detail here. I would rather restrict myself to the final phase of this development, the religious efficacy of Shin Buddhism in Japan, and in particular the influence of Shinran (1173–1262).

Shinran and the Phenomenology of Religious Consciousness

According to Shinran, the three periods of eschatological history—the rise and fall of the sūtras as spiritual forces—correspond to the transformations of the spirit that religious individuals must each pass through in their own inner experience. Furthermore, these three transformations of the spirit are intimately linked by Shinran to three vows that Amida Buddha, out of his great and merciful compassion (karuṇā), made on behalf of sinful humans in order to lead them into the Pure Land. The triad that this sets up of the threefold vow, the threefold movement of eschatology, and the threefold transformation of the religious individual represents a central relationship that we may, without exaggeration, liken to the Hegelian triad of the absolute spirit, the objective spirit, and the subjective spirit. There is such a dialectic method of a "phenomenology of the religious spirit" at work in the way Shinran develops the final part of his major work, the *Kyōgyōshinshō* (The Teaching, Practice, Faith, and Enlightenment).

The first stage of the religious spirit, according to Shinran, is aesthetic and ethical. The nineteenth vow of the Buddha is cited:

> After I have attained Buddahood, there will be sentient beings in the ten quarters who raise the Bodhi-Mind, practice various meritorious acts, and desire to be born in my land with sincere aspiration; if, on the eve of their death, I should not appear before them surrounded by a host of [sacred] beings, may I not attend the Perfect Bodhi.[1]

In Shinran's interpretation, this vow corresponds to the religious observance that the Amitāyurdhyāna-sūtra (The Meditation Sūtra) urges on neophytes. The Sūtra requires a particular form of contemplation of believers, whom we have alluded to in the previous chapter: the kasiṇa meditation on the setting sun, and river, and the lapis lazuli that culminates in a vision of the Pure Land in all its splendors and including the figure of Amida Buddha himself. Together with these thirteen stages of contemplation, which proceed from the easy to the difficult, the Meditation Sūtra urges the believer to perform meritorious deeds, but the list of virtues laid out here proceeds in the opposite direction, beginning with the highest good and proceeding to the lower forms of virtue. Even for those who throughout their entire lives have done nothing good, the promise of future redemption through the grace of Buddha is held for the one who, instructed by a good master, will confess his sinfulness on his deathbed and pronounce the name of the Buddha ten times.

A certain confusion appears at this point in the way the Meditation Sūtra has been constructed, and Chinese and Japanese Buddhists have tried to explain its meaning in numerous ways. Many argue that the Pure Land, into which all—saints, fools, and wicked alike—can be taken up, cannot be the real realm of the highest salvation, since the highest must always be the most difficult and therefore the most rarely attained. Moreover, they go on, the assertion that one can be saved by pronouncing the name of the Buddha ten times should be taken in an indefinite sense, as a way of animating neophytes to set out on the path to nirvāṇa.

Those who view the matter from an eschatological consciousness come to a different understanding. For them no person in the present—that is, in the eschaton—can become a saint or enlightened one by his or her own powers, since the power of time necessarily and unavoidably conditions the sins of all people. Only the grace of Amida Buddha can bring redemption in this time. The idealism of a theoretical Buddhism that abstracts from time cannot understand how the essence of Amida Buddha can be achieved powerfully in the midst of time, and how in this achievement of the essence of Amida Buddha the reality of the Buddha is accomplished through karuṇā. For Shinran, calling on the name of the Buddha is not only our deed, but much more the original essence or essential achievement of the Buddha himself. The pronouncing of the name *is* the Buddha; it is nothing other than the fulfillment of his vow. This is how the pronouncing of the name of Amida Buddha becomes the source of salvation. The achievement of the essence of the Buddha is thus at the same time our own achievement. It is our appropriation of the essence of the Buddha.

Hence we see in the Meditation Sūtra a duality of a "revealed" and a "concealed" sense. *Revealed* refers to what is clear and true for a *given consciousness,* while *concealed* refers to what is clear and true only for *genuine belief.* (In this regard, Hegel also uses the two notions of *für das Bewusstsein* and *für uns*—or *für den Philosophen*—in his phenomenology.) What consciousness first and directly believes to be true and good collapses with the experience of failure, and in its place what had first been at work in hidden fashion gives rise to an achievement of our innermost heart.

For Shinran, kasiṇa contemplation stands for contemplation in general. It is also the easiest form of contemplation because it is centered on a specific object. Furthermore, the virtues that are listed are in turn easier than contemplation, since the good of virtuous deeds is the good of an extraverted, *scattered* consciousness, while the good of contemplation is the good of an introverted and *centered* consciousness.

But one who lives in the latter days is no longer able to center the mind as the holy sages of old were able to do. The ardent longing for salvation means that one forever experiences an inner dividedness at the ground of one's being and that zeal for the highest good always sees radical evil as one's essence. But it is precisely at the point of this dividedness and doubt within consciousness that we are able, under the right circumstances, to encounter the name of Amida Buddha, who "comes like a great ship from the yonder shore over the sea of life and struggle to help humanity."[2]

According to Shinran, this encounter with the name of Amida Buddha represents the second stage in religious consciousness. He cites the twentieth vow of the Buddha:

> If, after I have attained Buddhahood, beings in the ten quarters who, having heard my Name, direct their thoughts towards my land, plant various roots of virtue, and desire to be born in my land by sincerely turning their merits [towards it], should not ultimately attain Birth, may I not attain the Perfect Bodhi.[3]

In Shinran's explanation, this vow signifies the religious decision to direct oneself with one's whole being to the Pure Land. It is a decision that one arrives at only by trodding the path of despair, only through confessing one's own finiteness and sinfulness. It is here that for the first time one is able to experience the powerful grace from the beyond and to belong to that Pure Land. Shinran often speaks of his experience of religious decision, as we read in one of his conversations with his disciples:

> When we believe that we are to be born in the Pure Land being saved by Amida's inconceivable Vow, there rises up within us the desire to utter the Nembutsu [name of the Buddha]. At that moment we share in the benefit of "being embraced and not forsaken."

> We should know that Amida's Original Vow does not discriminate whether one is young or old, good or evil, and that Faith alone is of supreme importance, for it is the Vow that seeks to save the sentient beings burdened with grave sins and fiery passions.
>
> Therefore, if we have Faith in the Original Vow, no other good is needed, because there is no good surpassing the Nembutsu. Nor should evil be feared, because there is no evil capable of obstructing Amida's Original Vow.[4]

Shinran here puts his religious decision in intimate relationship with the root of all virtues, namely, with the name of the Buddha. The contrast between virtues and their root is set up still sharper in another passage:

> Even a good person is born in the Pure Land, how much more so is an evil person! However, people in the world usually say, "Even an evil person is born in the Pure Land, how much more so is a good person." At first sight this view seems to be reasonable, but it is contrary to the purport of the Original Vow, of the Other-Power. The reason is that, as those who practice good by their self-power lack the mind to rely wholly on the Other-Power, they are not in accordance with the Original Vow of Amida. However, if they convert their minds of self-power and trust the Other-Power, their Birth in the True Land of Recompense is assured.
>
> Amida made his Vow out of compassion for us who are full of evil passions and who are unable to set ourselves free from saṃsāra by any practice. Since the purpose of His Vow is to have evil persons attain Buddhahood, the evil person who trusts the Other-Power is especially the one who has the right cause for Birth in the Pure Land. Hence the words, "Even a good person is born in the Pure Land, how much more so is an evil person."[5]

In still another passage he says to his followers:

> The aim of your visit to me, after crossing over the boundaries of more than ten provinces at the risk of your lives, is solely to ask me the way to Birth in the Land of Utmost Bliss.
>
> However, if you find something unfathomable in me and suppose that I know a way to Birth other than the Nembutsu, and that I am well-versed in the Buddhist doctrines, it is a grave mistake on your part. If so, then there are many distinguished scholars in the Southern Capital and on the Northern Mountain, whom you had better call upon and ask, to your satisfaction, about the essentials of Birth.

> As for me, Shinran, there is nothing left but to receive and believe the teaching of the Venerable Master—that we are saved by Amida merely through the utterance of the Nembutsu.
>
> I am entirely ignorant as to whether the Nembutsu is really the cause of Birth in the Pure Land, or whether it is the karma which will cause me to fall into hell.
>
> I will have no regrets even though I should have been deceived by Hōnen Shōnin,[6] and, thus, by uttering the Nembutsu, I should fall into hell. The reason is that, if I could become Buddha by performing some other practice and fell into hell by uttering the Nembutsu, then, I might feel regret at having been deceived. But since I am incapable of any practice whatsoever, hell would definitely be my dwelling anyway.
>
> If the Original Vow of Amida is true, then Sākyamuni's sermons cannot be untrue. If the Buddha's words are true, then Zendō's[7] comments cannot be untrue. If Zendō's comments are true, how can Hōnen's sayings be false? If Hōnen's sayings are true, what I, Shinran, say cannot possibly be false, either. After all is said, such is the faith of this simpleton. Beyond this, it is entirely left up to each one of you whether you accept and believe in the Nembutsu or reject it.[8]

The passage has the ring of Pascal's *logique du pari.* In his own way, Shinran was seeking a relationship between evidence and risk in the decision to faith. In a poetical work he writes:

> Be it that the great chiliocosm be aflame,
> He who dares to pass through the fire
> To hear the Sacred Name of the Buddha,
> Will attain the Non-retrogressive Stage forever.[9]

The fire of the great chiliocosm is the fire of the end of the world. The eschatological confession of Shinran concerning our human existence arrives in the second stage of religious awakening at its highest seriousness. How one is able to awaken the root of virtue (the name of Buddha) he explains thoroughly and with dialectical clarity.

Just as the first stage corresponds to the Meditation Sūtra, so the second corresponds to the short Sukhāvatī-vyūha-sūtra (also called the Amida Sūtra), where we find the following description:

> If a believer centers himself and calls on the name of Amida Buddha for one or two days or for as many as seven days, the Buddha will certainly appear to that believer on his deathbed and receive him into the Pure Land.[10]

To hear this and confirm it in oneself is for Shinran the repetition of decision. The utterance of the name of Buddha ten times is the same as the affirmation of the name for seven days. Indeed, to utter the name once on one's deathbed in all resoluteness to convert, and to utter it repeatedly throughout one's entire life, mean the same thing.

But in this very repetition of the name the step from the second stage to the third, which is always certain to reach the goal, since it means being escorted by Amida Buddha himself, is achieved. The way from the second to the third stage involves the contradiction within us between our pride on the one hand, and our will to surrender totally to dependence on the Buddha on the other. The first encounter, which seems to us already to be an absolute experience of the other—of the transcendent itself—is in fact at first only our own experience, our own egoistic reaction. What is concealed to consciousness becomes clear to it through the repetition of the religious decision, that is, through adherence to the name. One might also say that the proximity and the distance of the Pure Land to our world opens up for the first time dimensions in which our believing minds and hearts are able to experience in a real sense the event of transcendence. This means that the eschatological destiny of our human existence is for the first time able to be consciously appropriated through the achievement of the step from the second to the third stage. Only one who has walked this path can recognize the genuine reality of eschatology, just as only one who has awakened can gain insight into the dream.

Conversely, Shinran defines the second stage of religious consciousness, in which one considers oneself to have surrendered utterly and completely to the name of the Buddha, as the "misappropriation of the name" (the gift of the Buddha) on our part. The believer's intention to surrender to the name of the Buddha actually entails the acceptance of this name not as a pure gift from the yonder shore but rather as one's own merit for one's own profit. This perversity of consciousness, which lies hidden deep in the ground of our human existence in the form of the principle of ego, is the very thing that the classical school of Indian Buddhism known as the Vijñānavāda referred to as the mano nāma vijñāna. In Shinran, however, the problem of effecting a reversal of the perversion at the ground of our being (āśraya-parāvṛtti) is put in terms that connect it intimately with the utterance of the name of the Buddha and thus make it at once more concrete and phenomenologically more perceptive than the merely abstract and hence difficult-to-comprehend speculation of the Vijñānavādin.

Let us not forget, though, that awakening from the dream is not enlightenment and the achieving of saving wisdom. In eschatological terms the absolute knowledge we are speaking of is what the saint is able to accomplish as the fruit of individual effort during the first stage. It is also the ideal that religious individuals in our own day aim at when, viewed from the vantage point of the believer, they walk the path of "self-redemption." In contrast, for the believer the proximity and distance of the Pure Land maintains its significance permanently on the way to that Land. The realization of the name of Amida Buddha in the world (the vow of Amida Buddha) renders possible a faith-transcendence in a double sense: as a transcending that occurs by way of a transdescending, and a transcending that always occurs at once with a transdescending.

The correlatedness of transcendence and transdescendence is not only something essential for the believer but points to a double meaning of the Buddha himself: Tathāgata, the one who has trod the path from this world to the world beyond (nirvāṇa), and likewise the one who has come to the path of this world from the world beyond. The name of Amida Buddha is precisely the way on which the Buddha, as the coming-and-going one, can encounter the believer for the first time as a person. We saw in the first chapter how Hegel described this characteristic of the Absolute with the term *egressus est regressus*. But Shinran sought to characterize these two movements in closest correlatedness with the essence of the name of Buddha as the duplicity of the Buddha. Here we cannot enter into detail on his theological thought. Instead, some concluding remarks should be made on Buddhist eschatology in its transcending and transdescending characteristics in terms of two other aspects, the subjective and the objective, since this double meaning of the eschaton is always present for the believer.

The eschatological age is repeated again and again in its particulars. Of course, we do not possess in everyday life the fruit of saving wisdom, as do the saints, but, like them, we are free of anxiety and doubt in this sea of sin and death because we are blind. We become aware of the real bottomlessness of life only when we feel the pressure of their affects. Only then are we driven to the quest of the true self and of true being as something completely different from this impermanent world. In all earnestness we strive for the ideal of the theoretical and the ethical. But this idealistic rein on life turns out in fact to be in vain, and the truths that accompany it to be only imaginary truths. Thus our striving, with all its intensity and seriousness, eventually drives us to the point of shipwreck. Our existence loses that quiet and freedom from anxiety that seemed to correspond to a saving wisdom at the first stage. It comes to despair of its own activity and in so doing repeats the first and second eras of world history. At the very abyss of the essence of our existence we encounter the

name of Buddha. Yet even on the path of encountering this name of the Buddha we must be led to a further despair, since we have yet to learn how deep the abyss of nihility of ego is, how absurd our own pride is in entering onto the path for the first time. Only in the repetition of the religious decision do we experience the difficulty (and at the same time the simplicity or, one might say, the simple difficulty) of preserving the essence of the name. It is like someone excavating a well who has to bore through the layers of earth one after another until reaching the real, richest underground watercourse, in order then to let the water gush forth from its inexhaustible source. In the same way, one must wander perseveringly through the many torments of the heart so that the genuine achievement of an encounter with the name of Buddha (the steadfast utterance of the name) can take place in one's innermost being. Just as in the well the whole pressure of the earth is concentrated at one point in the flow, so too in the genuine utterance of the name of Buddha is the entire power of the eschaton centered on the utterance of the name and the power of depression is transformed into the power of ascension, of freely gushing forth. The greater the depression, the greater the force of the spring upwards. This is what we described above as the correlatedness of transcending and transdescending. In this way the essence of the eschaton is recalled and repeated in us when we have experienced how to encounter the name of the Buddha authentically and confirm it in ourselves. In this experience we perceive the sense of what is contained in the eschatological myth:

> All the sūtras of the Buddha will sink into the bowels of the earth or the depths of the sea except for those that preach the Pure Land, which will remain for a hundred years after the time of the final kalpa-fire in order to save humans burdened with affliction.

The survival of the sūtras here means the workings of the name of the Buddha. These sūtras represent the total working of the Buddha, which, as an object of encounter, is qualitatively different from what is meant by the usual sūtras of "self-redemption." As a vow, it calls out to us entirely on its own, without our having any part in it insofar as we are capable of learning the correct correspondence and making a decision with regard to it. What Karl Barth had to say regarding revelation and religion, and what Paul Tillich was later to say in opposition to Barth's position, calls to mind the problem of religions of grace that Rudolf Otto has characterized as the difference between the way of the cat and the way of the monkey.[11] One ought not, however, confuse Tillich's position with a synenergism. The grace of God alone is active insofar as the believer has arrived ek-statically (transcending-transdescending) on the way of encounter, but not like a car bumping into a careless pedestrian on the street. Even reason can become ek-static of itself if it reaches its own ground through the contradiction of itself and, reassuming its activity from there, allows itself to enter into communication with the transcendent—in a word, insofar as it is authentically dialectical.

The Return to Primitive Buddhism

As we have already stated above, from the very outset the appraisal of the first two eschatological eras is very ambiguous, since the first era of pure dharma is also at the same time the flowering of Hīnayāna, while the second era of falsified dharma must be seen as the flowering of Mahāyāna; and also because this way of reckoning time in general has come into India from Mahāyāna. As we read clearly in the Mahāmāyā Sūtra, Nāgārjuna and Vasubandhu themselves belonged to the second, false era.

For the Chinese and, in particular, for the Japanese Pure Land sects the problem is perfectly clear. The Chinese Pure Land sect first became conscious of the meaning of the third era, whose beginning was the setting for their own time of tribulation. On Shinran's reckoning, Japanese Buddhism entered into the third era with Prince Shōtoku's decision to lead a life according to the later principles of the Pure Land sect.[12] The extreme temporal and geographical distance of Japan from primitive Buddhism stimulated the yearning for a return to authentic Buddhism precisely at the end of ancient times and the onset of the Middle Ages with its movement "back to the spirit of primitive Buddhism" and its profession of an eschatological point of view infused with a sense of the philosophy of history. One of the outcomes of this event was that Shinran became aware that the time of the greatest distance from primitive Buddhism could correspond in an authentic sense with the fulfillment of the vow of Amida Buddha, which is what Gotama the Buddha was really preaching.

Nishitani Keiji has expressed himself on this problem, and I rely on his views, at the same time complementing them with my own, for the remaining pages of this chapter.

The impact of the reformation that took place in Japanese Buddhism during the Middle Ages was so rich, so radical, and so forward that in the entire history of Japan only the Meiji Restoration can be likened to it in significance. The Meiji Restoration, however, lacked religious underpinnings and hence the medieval reformation remains for Japan the only substantial achievement of a cultural synthesis and a firmly grounded unity of life that is rooted deep in the religious consciousness of the Japanese.

Prior to this time Japanese Buddhism stood at the "aesthetic" stage. One can ignore here the philosophy and speculations of the monks of the time, since that was the work of only a few intellectuals functioning independently of the popular beliefs of the age. In contrast, the great masses of the people believed in a Buddha who would bestow on them the gift of happiness and who was supposed to aid them in avoiding danger. Through Buddhist teachings and through their own experience, they knew of the impermanence and untruth of everyday life, even though they continued to depend on it, hoping that the Buddha would provide them with benefits in their perils. They depended on the proof of miracles that, in their minds, would only occur rarely and under extraordinary circumstances. They believed in the charism contained in things and persons and did not take the significance of a true Buddhist life all that seriously. The splendid, romantic ceremonies of the Tendai sect and other sects of Japanese Buddhism of the time were enough to satisfy what the people needed. Their preference for the proof and witness of the rare miraculous event (which are nothing other than another form of the "fruit of saving wisdom" taught by the six heretical teachers mentioned in the previous chapter) shows us that Buddhism in Japan had not at the time effected a complete unification of religious life with profane life.

This spiritual relation is intimately bound up with the fact that at the time Buddhism was believed in *aesthetically*. One would marvel at the beauty of the paintings and statues of the Buddha and stand in awe of the magnificence of the Pure Land. This attitude betrays a mixture of the sense of "denying world and life" and "affirming world and life," two poles charging each other through mutual mediation. We can refer to this attitude as "aesthetic" in that the pole of affirmation, while seasoned with the negative pole, was positive and strong, leaving people so much the more dependent on enjoying the things of life.

As the setting sun brings to the fore the colors of the foliage and sharpens the outline of things on earth, even as it projects a lustrous shining of colors in the sky as if in the Pure Land, only for the whole brilliance of the scene to disappear quickly back into darkness, so is life seen only in terms of the contradiction of this world and the world beyond, of the negative and the affirmative, only a fantasy-unity of beauty in which no more than a fleeting, apparent harmony of the two is achieved. It only covers over the contradiction without really sublating it into a higher order. Only with eschatological belief is this Buddhism made conscious, in unconditional clarity, of the radical incompatibility between the profane world and religious truth. Viewed in its authentic sense, the dharma of the Buddha is eternal and there should be no such thing as an eschatology in Buddhism. But this unity of "is" and "ought" is not really able to rule over the whole reach of the profane world. It only comes about rarely—pure and beautiful, but fading—quickly to melt away again like snow on a sunny day. In order to save oneself in this disunity, one has to preserve a "beautiful soul" untainted by the outer world. The aesthetic posture of this belief finds a strong expression in the painting and poetry of the period.

Eschatology first brought to the fore clearly and in its entirety the gap between the everyday and the religious that is perpetually with us. Yet through the sublation of this contradiction in life the religious truth contained in the concreteness of everyday life becomes realized and our life on earth is made holy and religious. The mutual interpenetration of the spiritual and the earthly was first established in Japan through the reforms of Zen and Shin Buddhism. Genuine eschatological belief is thus necessary for the purification and practice of a Buddhist way of life.[13]

·II·

FREEING

·4·

The Problem of Dependent Origination

The notion of dependent origination is the root and trunk of Buddhist thought. However luxuriant the branches and leaves that flourished in later Buddhist philosophy, however fragrant their flower and sweet their fruit, everything finally hangs on this central notion and draws upon its life-giving sap. It is therefore necessary that we begin by understanding correctly the basic thrust of what primitive Buddhism had to say about dependent origination (its doctrine of the twelvefold causal sequence) and that we reflect from within on what the doctrine is aiming at in speaking the way it does (the meaning of its "symbolic" logic), in order then to set out ourselves, sympathetically, along the path that leads to deeper realization.

Given the current intellectual climate, such a task is not quite as straightforward as it might seem. All too frequently in our own day the outcome of literary criticism on the sacred texts of primitive Buddhism has developed into an impediment to understanding the fundamental spirit of primitive Buddhism. Eventually the time will come for this sort of oversight to be corrected, but for the time being prospects look dim. A closer look at the matter suggests that such a mistaken approach to the notion of dependent origination is not something restricted to our own day. In one of the canonical texts treating the doctrine we already find a disciple voicing his doubts to the Buddha: "Whereas this doctrine of events as arising from causes is so deep and looks so deep, to me it seems as clear as clear can be!" To this the Buddha comments in reply:

> Say not so! Deep is this doctrine of events as arising from causes, and it looks deep too. It is through not understanding this doctrine, through not penetrating it, that this generation has become a tangled skein, a matted ball of thread, like to munja-grass and rushes, unable to overpass . . . the Constant Round [of transmigration].[1]

The text to which this passage belongs cannot be considered very late, since, as we shall explain further on, it expounds a theory of dependent origination that adopts a ninefold causal sequence beginning with lust, or the burning thirst of desire.

Why the "so deep" should have seemed clear and on the surface to the disciple is not apparent from the text. The Pali word *gambhīra* is used to refer, for example, to the translucent depths of a lake, the point being that things exceedingly deep are sometimes made to look as deep as they are (like the waters of the ocean), while at other times the translucence can make what is deep look shallow.[2] The disciple's remark seems to be an instance of the latter.

From the Āgama scriptures to the Mahāyāna scriptures, the expression *so deep* is often used to refer to the essence of dependent origination. In the main, it carries the sense of something that looks deep because it is so, although there are also cases like that just cited in which dependent origination is referred to as the sort of idea that looks at first glance to be simple and clear. Nearly all contemporary scholars, both in Japan as well as in Europe and America, display a consistent bias to such simple interpretations. But it is like a man who looks down into a riverbed, whose bottom floats up through the limpid waters to the surface, and neglects to keep his own stature in mind: all too readily such a one falls prey to the reckless temptation of trying to walk across.

The History of Dependent Origination

As Ui Hakuju has shown in his late work,[3] the history of India, China, and Japan presents us with a variety of understandings of the fundamental spirit of the primitive Buddhist doctrine of dependent origination. Each country developed its own characteristic approach in conformity with its own ethnic background, resulting in the formation of the principal well-known schools and sects. To begin with, the evolution from Theravāda to Mahāyāna Buddhism in India received a great deal of its impetus from the Abhidharma theory of the twelvefold chain of dependent origination. In opposition to the Theravāda notion of the three temporal worlds and its dual causality—which Ui takes as "embryonic"—and critical of the Theravāda standpoint on the self-nature (svabhāva) of dharmas, a new dialectic emerged with Nāgārjuna's view of dependent origination as emptiness (śūnyatā). That is to say, on an interpretation of the Theravāda doctrines of the four noble truths, the five aggregates (skandhas), the six senses (ṣaḍ-āyatana), and the twelvefold chain of dependent origination, along with the general Abhidharma theory of dharma that was based on them, Nāgārjuna's standpoint of emptiness wrought its critique with the aim of clarifying once again the fundamental spirit of primitive Buddhism's doctrine of dependent origination.

After Nāgārjuna the philosophical speculations of Indian Mahāyāna Buddhism evolved further into an opposition between the ideas of śūnyatā and idealism. This latter, the consciousness-only philosophy, can be taken in turn as another dialectical unfolding of the notion of dependent origination. For while the relationship of polar opposition between the two standpoints of śūnyatā and idealism can be said to represent the high-water mark in the development of Indian Buddhism, the viewpoint of the consciousness-only theory itself—that is, the foundations for the teachings of Asaṅga and Vasubandhu (c. 350), whose approach to dependent origination differs somewhat from Nāgārjuna's—took as its point of departure a new interpretation of what primitive Buddhism meant by *dependent origination.*

Still, the opposition between these two standpoints planted a contradiction within Indian Buddhism that could not be resolved. Things are somewhat different when we come to Chinese Buddhism. Fa-ts'ang's (643–712) commentary on the Śraddhotpāda Śāstra shows that Chinese Buddhism took up this problem and pursued its solution along the lines suggested by the text but gradually evolved a unique framework of its own. Through Fa-ts'ang the literary expressions of Indian Kegon (Avataṁsaka) thought came to take the form of a new philosophical theory, the dependent origination of the dharma-realm, which was able to translate the negative character of the dependent origination of avidyā (the darkness of ignorance) into a positive doctrine. In the consciousness-only theory, aside from the theory of the "twelve nidānas," thought had already been given to the idea of "self-origination."[4] The former doctrine adopts a *forward progression* to elucidate how human existence comes to be filled with suffering as a result of the various sorts of karma that come through avidyā; and then, through a *backward progression,* the doctrine of dependent origination is shown to outline the journey to enlightenment, the process of conversion by which consciousness, which begins from the sorrows of a life sunk to the level of the everyday, secular world, through self-negation and self-transcendence, gradually shakes free of self-love (ego attachment) and everydayness, traversing the way of denial and ex-stasis (dropping off of the self) until at last it arrives at absolute truth (nirvāṇa). The notion of self-origination shows these two aspects, the forward and backward progressions, as the working of store-consciousness, or ālaya-vijñāna (as dependent origination). But in Chinese thought the theory of the dependent origination of the dharma-realm goes further to bring to the fore the concrete working of this absolute truth itself (the revelation of the dharma-realm), and makes manifest the true reality (truth *sive* reality; i.e., truth as reality, reality as truth) of dependent origination in a positive and affirmative manner that bears on the praxis of the religious subject. The Tendai and Kegon sects were both attempts to sublate and synthesize the contradiction between the approaches of consciousness-only and śūnyatā they had inherited from India. In viewing dependent origination from a practical standpoint (as a way of "observance"), each was able to bring its own characteristic interpretation. The creative form that religious awakening took, based on this sort of transmission of Buddhist history, brought about a process of synthesis and analysis that, even in its reflective phase, was backed up by experience. Yet insofar as this thought took the form of commentaries on the scriptures that were written down, their lofty speculations turned into comprehensive accounts and failed adequately to satisfy that purity and subjective intensity that are essential elements in religious existence. That is why in China we find Zen and Nembutsu (calling on the name of Amida Buddha) rising up in opposition—to perfect the concentration and condensation of the existential subject through religious observance.

The distinctive characteristics of Japanese Buddhism are to be seen first of all in esoteric Buddhism. The esoteric tradition originally came by way of India, whence it passed over into China only at a relatively late stage, while the transition from China to Japan came about very quickly. Moreover, it was through Saichō (767–822) and Kūkai (774–835), first-class thinkers in the history of Japanese Buddhism, that this took place. The special character of Japanese esoteric Buddhism, and in particular the lasting impact on the future that Kūkai secured for this body of thought, can be seen as an existential orientation in that it seeks to restore to the logic of Kegon its basis: the immediacy of religious life. Japanese Zen and Nembutsu, as inquiries into the existential reality of Buddhism that reached their peaks in the figures of Dōgen and Shinran, drink from the deep wellsprings of primitive Buddhism that in our own day only they can reach down to. The path they clear for bringing to light the profound significance of the doctrine of dependent origination is an indispensable one.

What I have described above, while following the lead of Ui, represents my own view. It has been my intention to make it clear at the outset that I consider an understanding of the doctrine of dependent origination in primitive Buddhism normative for fathoming and evaluating the history of Buddhism as a whole. I would even go so far as to state that when seen from the vantage point of the philosophy of religion, Buddhism and the whole question of its future (which we shall take up presently) are intimately bound up with the interpretation of that primitive Buddhist doctrine. Those who are familiar with recent research on primitive Buddhism may have their doubts about this. It may be objected that primitive Buddhism is extremely unsophisticated, that the Buddha did no more than voice, in fragmentary fashion, a commonsense morality. One may arrive at such a conclusion from the standpoint of contemporary literary scholarship or appeal to the time-worn view that ascribes the Theravāda Buddhist interpretation of the doctrine of dependent origination to primitive Buddhism without further ado—which is where great numbers of contemporary western European scholars seem to have stopped. From either of those standpoints, what I am doing must surely appear to involve overlaying the modes of thought of a later, more mature period on conditions that obtained at the earliest beginnings without giving those conditions their rightful due, like a fool trying to graft flowers and fruits onto mere sprouts and seedlings.

But does not the greatness of founders of world religions like Buddha and Jesus lie in the fact that the truth of their teachings, rather than merely possessing a validity that transcends space and time, is a source of inspiration and an impetus to new solutions to the serious questions that trouble the human spirit at various times and in various spiritual environments? In the case of Shinran and Dōgen (or of Augustine and Luther), the words and deeds of the Buddha (or of Jesus) came to shine with a brilliance previously unknown and to echo among those who heard and saw them with a resonance never before experienced, precisely when they were offered as a response to questions that had ripened from out of their own religious existence in the here and now as the true questions for their age and their world. Is not this the authentic way religious truth is transmitted? I sense in the Buddha a far deeper and more fundamental, a more purely constellated form of religiosity, one that abrogates and surpasses the various opposing positions that grew up in later Buddhist philosophy and that we touched on earlier. It will no doubt be thought presumptuous of me to call upon Dōgen and Shinran to illustrate the approach I have in mind and seem only to testify to my ignorance of the limits of my own resources. I can hardly disagree—and yet insofar as these figures represent models for the philosophical understanding of primitive Buddhism, there is no avoiding the comparison. Ui, lamenting the fact that in the end access to primitive Buddhism is circumscribed by the powers of its interpreters, has humbly to admit, "The crab digs its hole to the size of its shell." My sentiments exactly. I prefer digging holes to my own measure over stepping into rented quarters.

With certain notable exceptions, nearly all European and American scholars of Buddhism do not share in the Buddhist faith, and therefore, quite naturally, assume that the interpretations they work out with literary methods are the only correct ones. On the other hand, even though it shares this interpretative bias, a work like Albert Schweitzer's *Indian Thought and its Development,*[5] born from youthful sentiments of affinity with Schopenhauer, Nietzsche, and Kant in an author nurtured in Christianity but of a free spirit and broad outlook, does give off a certain religious fragrance in its accounts. Seen from the vantage point of the present, there may be much to fault in Schweitzer's work in terms of its literary and historical materials. But its true merit is that it is a masterpiece that only in the light of his various investigations on primitive Christianity and his arguments for a religious ethic of respect for life reveals its great value. Or again, the influence of Schopenhauer in H. Oldenberg's *Buddha,* and the depth of erudition in Kant and Western religious thought that we find in H. Beckh's *Buddha und seine Lehre,*[6] envelop both these works with a sort of religious atmosphere. Research done by later scholars in the West may have been more literary-critical and more academic, but one would not necessarily call it religiously or philosophically superior. If I may be allowed a personal impression, while I respect the scholarship that is being done, somehow I cannot escape the feeling that something is missing. And I ask myself, might this not perhaps be because when primitive Buddhism is taken only as one chain in the spiritual history of India and the voice of the Buddha as the founder of a world religion fails to reverberate (I am thinking here in particular of certain scholarly authorities on India), the unique appeal of Buddhism to the soul that is open to it is being passed over?

In the case of Christianity one frequently finds that literary considerations are taken as the counterpart of theological considerations—at first merely as co-existing or in opposition, but eventually as mutually complementary. For some, no doubt the word *theology* still has the ring of the medieval about it. But in the Western intellectual world, especially in the realms of religion, dialectical theology and existential theology have exerted a powerful influence throughout the twentieth century and right up to the present (or at least for the last half century). Even in the matter of the literary criticism of the Bible, there has been a methodological awakening—particularly in the case of existential theology—to the need for the mediation of theological and philosophical reflection and for an integration of the results into the subject as the seat of the confession of faith. It seemed a matter of course that literary interpretation proceed in this manner in order to arrive at a deep understanding of the meaning of religious symbolism.[7] Put the other way around, when religious consciousness assigned to theological reflection a mediating role in opening the self up to the contemporary world, it was incumbent on faith, directly or indirectly, to presuppose research into objective historical sources. This meant that faith, in establishing this tie, was able for the first time to become a guiding principle for life concretized in historical fact.

Let us look again, by way of example, to literary-historical research on the Bible (whose methods may at some future date reach over and influence researches on primitive Buddhism, a view, incidentally, that Bultmann once told me he shares). In advancing from "source criticism" to "form criticism," the methods of recent literary studies have shown how the words of Jesus and the events surrounding his life, which we find in the Bible as a series of stories, first appeared as short literary pericopes; and going still further back, the attempt has been made to reduce these stories to an oral tradition preserved in form by the first small ecclesial community around Palestine. In this way progress is made in studying the general rules operative in developmental changes of pattern that occur when transmissions are transformed—either by expansion or simplification—through oral tradition, as well as in the elucidation of specific details of content. From there investigations naturally flow into questions of influences stemming from the various regional religions of the time to which primitive Christianity had connections. Moreover, at several key points in such reflections and interpretations, the perspective of existential theology is inserted, its existential hermeneutic functioning like a well-meshed axle that sets all the gears in motion. Thus with existential theology literary research on the Bible shifts around to a here-and-now subject awareness of faith, a faith evoked as a decision made in response to the word of the living God mediated through the Bible. The way in which thinkers like Bultmann or those of the post-Bultmann strain of theology have closely interwoven the opposing orientations of literary research and subjective reflection into a single whole is well known.

In the case of Buddhist studies, and in particular where primitive Buddhism is concerned, the existential subjectivity capable of playing the role that theology plays in Christianity will have to be provided for the present in Japan by the philosophy of religion. Building on the foundations of Ui's studies on the source materials of primitive Buddhism, Watsuji Tetsurō's *The Practical Philosophy of Primitive Buddhism,* published in 1926, marks the first important watershed of this sort of undertaking in Japan.[8] While Watsuji drew on the literary researches of Ui, his understanding of primitive Buddhism's notion of dependent origination was later in turn to have its influence on Ui. The dominant standpoint in *The Practical Philosophy of Primitive Buddhism* consisted of the theory of values and epistemology of neo-Kantian idealism, which was in the mainstream of Japanese philosophy at the time. Insofar as this current of thought took natural science (in particular, Newtonian physics) and mathematics (differential and integral calculus) as an academic model for grounding a scientific theory of knowledge, it was in accord with Kant's original critical spirit. Thinkers like Hermann Cohen found it necessary to go beyond Kant in order to recover the original Kant and thus came to radicalize his epistemology in the direction of an idealism closer to logicism. Ernst Cassirer, proceeding by way of Wilhelm Windelband and Heinrich Rickert, Cohen and Paul Natorp, upheld the correctness of this approach right up to his final years, and in so doing can be said to have championed the essential and indispensable role that the problem of providing a basis to science plays in philosophy. Watsuji's neo-Kantian interpretation of Kant also lays the main stress on getting beneath the details of Kantianism to its fundamental spirit, from whose understanding he then turned his attention to the fundamental attitude of the Buddha and the spirit of primitive Buddhism.

What seems to have caught Watsuji's eye as highlighting the heart of primitive Buddhism was the silence of the Buddha (avyākata). The oldest texts in the Pali canon record that the Buddha did not pronounce on such religious and philosophical questions as: Is the world finite or infinite? Are body and mind one and the same or are they distinct? Does the soul exist after death? According to Watsuji, the numerous disparities contained in the relevant texts that have been handed down to us make it difficult to ascertain just what the teaching of the Buddha himself was. What is certain, however, is that in deciding to collate metaphysical questions in the form of antinomies, and thereby acknowledge the limits of human reason (discrimination) and keep argumentation within its legitimate bounds, a standpoint of an extremely high level of philosophical and speculative refinement was forged. Here one cannot fail to make the connection in modern Western philosophy with Kant and his predecessor Pascal.[9] Thus, he goes on, for primitive Buddhism to have secured such an eminent critical standpoint, it cannot simply have dismissed philosophical thinking outright as meaningless so as to return to a crude and prephilosophical standpoint of common sense.

To this view of Watsuji's we may perhaps add that it is the same with the Buddha's denial of the ego (ātman), which had been the metaphysical principle of the Upanishads, in order to stress non-ego (anātman). This does not represent a shift from the affirmation of the self to its simple negation by placing it between the poles of an antinomy but rather proceeds from a higher standpoint that transcends both affirmation and negation (translated into the terms of contemporary existentialism, we might refer to it as the standpoint of the "conquest of metaphysics"), so that even in coming to the doctrine of anātman there is no question of simply rejecting everything metaphysical in the name of "positivism" or "utilitarianism."

The fundamental spirit that Watsuji sees permeating primitive Buddhism is a critical spirit akin to Kant's, although the mathematics and physics that Kant took up in his critique of pure reason as indicative of the science of a realm of universal knowledge did not exist in the age of the Buddha. The a priori categories of human existence accessible to the Buddha were those of everydayness. The doctrine of the five skandhas and the ṣaḍ-āyatana can thus be interpreted as aiming at the pursuit of universally valid laws (dharmas) for human, understood as practical, everyday, existence. According to Watsuji, as later commentaries on the Abidharmakośa Śāstra and the Vidyā-mātra-siddhi Śāstra have amply demonstrated, Vijñaptimātratāsiddhi primitive Buddhism's notion of dharma was one of "upholding selfhood, understanding the constitution of things." That is, it carried the sense of a conceptual unity, permanently maintaining its own essential provisions in a self-identical way, these essential provisions in turn serving as a norm to make other things (phenomenal existence) intelligible.[10] Accordingly, even though the fact of impermanence is accepted and thus all phenomena subject to the law of impermanence are transient and liable to change, the law of impermanence itself is taken as eternal, unperishing, and constant. (This is particularly conspicuous in the Abhidharma interpretation of impermanence. Whether in fact this can be said of primitive Buddhism is another question.)

Even in his late writings Watsuji continued to stress the same point. For instance, at the time that later Mahāyāna Buddhism was elevating the standpoint of śūnyatā as the acme of prajñā (wisdom) and Nāgārjuna was developing his logic of śūnyatā, if the five skandhas had not been established *as dharma,* it would have been meaningless to speak as they do of "five skandhas—all are empty." The law of the five skandhas comprehends the flow of the coming to be and passing away of phenomena in their infinite diversity by understanding it as dharmic at its very ground. By combining the five categorical concepts of form, feelings, perceptions, volitional impulses, and consciousness, it seeks to embrace the entire realm of relationships negotiated between human beings and the world. Thus the path that brings to conceptual unity the ever-changing and ever-shifting modes of everyday human existence is first made clear in terms of the doctrine of the five skandhas, which then serves as a presupposition for the argument that "all are empty."[11] If we look carefully at the historical transition and temporal sequence from Theravāda to Mahāyāna, things certainly seem to be as Watsuji would have them. But if we base ourselves on the way things actually are, it would rather be the opposite. It seems to me that Watsuji's understanding of the dharma is Abhidharmic and does not represent the original notion of dharma found in primitive Buddhism. Both in primitive Buddhism and in Mahāyāna Buddhism dharma is not a svabhāva (existence as self-nature, *für sich*). It is a symbolic notion (a "cipher" in Jaspers's sense of the term) that takes self-negation and self-transcendence as its fundamental principles but is never an objective a priori. Dharma is a flexible principle for the conversion or change of heart that occurs within self-awareness only then to turn right around and do away with all foundations. It entails an elucidation of foundations that at once turns the foundations upside down. To say that the five skandhas are constituted from the standpoint of śūnyatā means that when they are constituted their unity takes a leap into emptiness in a self-transcending way. As we shall see later, impermanence must also be understood in the same way.

According to Watsuji, the categories that go into making up everyday life were to be seen in the five skandhas, and the doctrine of dependent origination arose from a further theoretical pursuit of the basic relationships that obtain among them. Even if we grant this to be the case, namely, that such categories and their grounding are able to explain the constitution of everydayness, still in their present form they are not directly connected with the fundamental aim of primitive Buddhism, which is the *overcoming* of everydayness. This is probably the reason that in Watsuji's explanation of the twelvefold causal chain of dependent origination the final stages of avidyā and saṃskāra (ignorance and volitional impulses) are so particularly difficult to understand and full of problems. In short, Watsuji's work on dependent origination is an epoch-making achievement that far exceeded the level of Buddhist studies in Japan during the half century previous to it. But at present it has become something of an anachronism not to advance beyond his understanding of primitive Buddhism and to interpret the Buddha's standpoint as a kind of critical philosophy (in the sense of neo-Kantianism) or idealism, or, with a slight shift, to identify it with utilitarianism or pragmatism, or to comprehend dependent origination merely as an epistemological theory.

In Western philosophy and theology, thanks both to dialectical theology and to existential philosophy and theology, neo-Kantianism—along with the liberal theology based on it—has already long since been radically and exhaustively criticized for its lack of existentiality; it has been discarded as an abstract, theoretical idealism fettered to the immanentism of human reason and hence incapable of relating to the true dimension of transcendence that religion aims at, indeed, only impeding our view of that abyss of death and sin and nihility that opens up under our very feet as the fate of being human. Of course, Buddhism and Christianity from the very outset took different attitudes to the relation between immanence and transcendence, which has come to represent a fundamental point of divergence between the two traditions. It follows as a matter of course that these recent deliverances of the European and American philosophical and theological world, therefore, cannot be inserted directly and without further ado into the Buddhist world. But why should Buddhist research—which prides itself on the remarkable progress it has made in the study of primitive Buddhism through recent achievements—by and large have failed to advance beyond the interpretations of Ui and Watsuji in its appreciation of the spirit of primitive Buddhism? Of course, one can point to the exceptional nature of what Watsuji has achieved with his tough-minded and elaborately detailed theory and the highly polished eloquence of his prose. Among his many representative works, *The Practical Philosophy of Primitive Buddhism* has surely to be singled out as a work of the first rank, and we can only consider ourselves blessed to be in possession of such a masterpiece of Buddhist philosophy. But to rest there is to stagnate.

The Future of Dependent Origination

Since the middle of this century new light has been shed on Watsuji's field of inquiry, the a priori of everydayness. In his last work, *The Crisis of European Sciences and Transcendental Phenomenology,*[12] Husserl sought to comprehend the *Lebenswelt* (everyday world) from just this sort of standpoint. There are a number of reasons why Husserl came to this problem in his later years. With the publication of *Being and Time* in 1927, Heidegger arrived at a viewpoint different from that of his teacher. For his part, Husserl made continued efforts to persuade his disciple to return to his own transcendental phenomenology, and undertook a deliberate and meticulous study of *Being and Time,* as we know from the marginal annotations in the copy he left behind in his library. The margins are almost entirely filled with Husserl's jottings, which show how intensely he concentrated his attention in coming to grips with the work. The result, we are told, was that Husserl himself was influenced by the existential analysis that Heidegger had worked out, by viewing human existence, or Dasein, as a "being-in-the-world," and this gradually turned him back to the realm of the *Lebenswelt,* to a more immediate and elemental form of existence that not only goes beyond the natural attitude of science and common sense but even surpasses the phenomenological perspective of noetic intentionality. It was the locus of the ordinariness of primary life, the locus of the reciprocal mediation of the world and the human subject. Husserl's shift to these concerns that began with the *Cartesian Meditations,* and his new interpretations of the body, the other, and the historical *Lebenswelt,* have had considerable impact on recent developments in philosophy.

Through the efforts made by French existentialists (Merleau-Ponty, Paul Ricoeur, and others) to trace Heidegger's existential philosophy through to the final developments of his final years, and then to effect a synthesis with the thought of the later Husserl, existentialism has opened up new horizons of great relevance to the philosophy of religion. An outstanding illustration of this is Merleau-Ponty's extension of Husserl's phenomenological reduction in order to reach the primary realm of experience in all its immediacy and fullness (including what Lévi-Strauss has described as *pensée sauvage*), anchoring his speculations in the mystery of the deep recesses of truth. He presents us with the world of experience as a whole, a harmonious unity of art and religion and everydayness.

The a priori of everydayness is disclosed here at a point that far surpasses the viewpoint of subject and object, or the intentional domains of neosis and noema. Here the fullness of the religious sensitivity of the uncivilized heart is fused with contemporary existential speculations. This is the same thing that takes place within the fundamental experience of artists and poets. Let us say I am in the middle of a woods painting on a canvas I have set before myself and I suddenly become aware of the fact that it is I that am being looked at by the trees. Through the perception of the interfusion, the mutual mediation, and the structure of co-dependency between an I and a thou (an other)—and thus achieving a more primary, elementary, and immediate perception of reality than the standpoints of commonsense or science or the philosophy I had hitherto espoused were able to provide—I experience an immediate embodiment of the dynamism of the world of body, other, and life prior to the distinction of subject and object.

To turn our argument back to Husserl and Heidegger, Husserl's concern with the *Lebenswelt* was actually gestated within a complicated relationship between the two thinkers. Unless one happens to be in possession of firsthand, intimate details of the nature of this contact, the transformation that took place in their academic views can only appear to be teeming with hidden factors that are difficult to put one's finger on. In his 1969 book, *The Matter of Thinking,*[13] Heidegger once again speaks with high praise of the significance of Husserl's phenomenology and takes another look at the meaning of the line of thought proceeding through Descartes, Kant, Hegel, and Husserl down to himself. His manner of speaking in that book suggests that when he himself studied under Husserl he already knew the material in the Paris lectures (*Cartesian Meditations*) that would become important in the thought of the later Husserl. Or again, already in 1928, the year after the appearance of *Being and Time,* Oskar Becker had observed in his review of the book that "Heidegger's transcendental analysis of Dasein belongs to the camp of the hermeneutics of *Lebenswelt* within the program of Husserl's transcendental phenomenology."[14] These things make it hard for me to surmise what might have taken place around the year 1930. Perhaps Heidegger's Dasein analysis had ended up leaning more heavily on Husserl than he had anticipated; perhaps the notion of *Lebenswelt* itself was already in common use in Husserlean circles.

Whatever the case may be, as the last major work of Heidegger, *The Matter of Thinking* gives the appearance of being once more intimately in touch with Husserl's thought. One of the reasons, of course, might be the resurgence in Heidegger's late years of affectionate memories towards his master. (There has been a good deal of loose talk to the contrary, but reports indicate that even when Heidegger was taking a stance in opposition to Husserl's phenomenology, his academic criticisms did not obstruct the personal respect that he harbored for Husserl, whom he considered a rare example of a true philosopher.) But more important, it seems to me, is Heidegger's concern for the speculative matter itself and the issues it poses. For him, *matter* is here taken in accord with the German words *Sache* and *Strittige* to point to the polar opposition and interdependency implied by the "matter at issue," as when accuser and accused engage in debate in a litigation. For Hegel the central matter and issue in thought is the law of identity. But A = A points, in an elemental sense, to the self-identity of the ego; it shapes the behavior of the ego in terms of a creative synthesis of a transcendental ego. Ever since the *cogito* of Descartes, the self-identity of the ego in modern philosophy has been the source of clear evidence. From Hegel's "certitude" of absolute knowledge to Husserl's "original *selbst-gebende* intuition," the standard of truth has been the realization of the subjectivity of the ego, and this represents, as it were, the convergence of modern attempts to base truth on logical coherence and on standpoints that appeal to the clarity and distinctness of intuition as unshakable foundation. Hence developments and amplifications that might be thought to lead to a complete and mutual opposition between the transcendentalism of Hegel and that of Husserl end up to be bound to the same *Sache* (the matter of greatest issue) of thinking.

When Heidegger dealt with the *Sache* of Hegel's philosophical speculations in his 1957 work, *Identity and Difference,*[15] he took up division, opposition, and contradiction in Hegel in a more elemental way than Hegel himself had, interpreting them as ingredients in a debate. This enabled him to turn his thoughts to the *Sache* of the co-dependency and correlatedness within divisiveness, to arrive at something like a creative synthesis that goes beyond the still self-identical dialectic movement of thesis, antithesis, and synthesis. In similar fashion Heidegger made use of this notion of co-dependent correlatedness to shed new light on the significance of the word *Sache* in Husserl's phenomenological appeal *"zur Sache selbst."*[16] In this way even Hegel and Husserl, who are as opposite as opposite can be, seem clearly to be concerned with the identical *Sache*—the guarantee of transcendental subjectivity—and it is from this standpoint that Heidegger must once again have reevaluated the significance of Husserl's phenomenology. But for Heidegger this perspective opens up to other speculations that differ from the whole of recent philosophy. The co-pertinence (*Zusammengehörigkeit*) of opposites requires that the fundamental interdependency of the world and human beings, of existence and thought, be made clear in the realms of a truth that has cracked the shell of the law of identity that lies at the ground of the dialectic. When he wrote *Being and Time,* Heidegger interpreted the *da* of (human) Dasein from the standpoint of the human as a being-in-the-world. But after the Second World War, at least to judge from what we know of his thought, the *da* was made to open up under the light of *Sein.* In the final stage of *Sein* (at the time of *On Time and Being*), the "light of *Sein*" was reinterpreted in the sense of "within the open sky." The open sky—as is also the case with the Zen saying, "Light and dark, each at bottom the other"—indicates the point at which both light and darkness are given their elemental possibility. This is the proper sense of what Buddhism means by *true suchness* and *open emptiness* (*sky*). This must be the reason that Heidegger spoke of the affinity of this idea to the East Asian way of reasoning, but if we take the standpoint of Heidegger's final years as a whole, it seems to me closer to the standpoint of dependent origination as it is found since the time of primitive Buddhism.

In Heidegger's final period, the idea of returning *Sein* to the elementary state of time—as we find it in *Being and Time*—was deepened into the idea of a co-dependency between time and space. That is, time as time enjoys a unique and elemental opening (the opening of the past, the future, and the present), and space a unique and elemental opening as space; but in addition, time is ex-static of itself in space, and space ex-static of itself in time, which together result in a locus of epochal time (*Weile*) that is the time-space of the historical world. This leads to the realization that the provenance of *Da-sein,* whose fate it is to bear the burden of the historical world at that locus, represents the "event-aspect" (*Ereignis*) of the principle of śūnyatā.

Prajñā Buddhism says, "Form *sive* emptiness, emptiness *sive* form." Heidegger's notion of event as *Ereignis* has to do with the workings of the copula *sive* (a somewhat archaic rendering of the Sanskrit word *anantaram,* but not as misleading as the word *is* would be) in "emptiness *sive* form." It is not clear just what the connection is between the event-aspect as we find it in Heidegger's argument on "time and being" and elsewhere, and the aspect of dependent origination as we find it in *Being and Time.* That is, it is not clear how he understands the sive of "form *sive* emptiness." He speaks of "the end of Western metaphysics," but only because he remains forever locked into a standpoint that limits philosophy to a Western affair; whereas the prospects of negotiating an encounter between a Western metaphysics of being and an Eastern (particularly Buddhist) metaphysics of nothingness might open up a different standpoint, a philosophical *Weile* reaching from the present into the future.

For Heidegger's part, drawing the understanding of truth close to the standpoint of true suchness and śūnyatā meant passing beyond the tradition of modern Western philosophy and out into the future. It meant turning around to a different sort of speculation from that which has characterized philosophy up to the present. At the same time, he saw that developments in cybernetics and applied technology, together with the dizzying changes and transformations that they have brought to the human environment, have effected a metamorphosis in the way human beings themselves think and reason. His notion of *Ge-stell* was that of a giant chain of manufacturing, as for instance we find in industrial complexes in which the managerial manufacturing process has become cut off from human craftsmanship and largely reduced to the automated manipulation of machinery. As a result, working relationships between one manufacturing process and another are established automatically, as we see for example on the conveyor belt, where space and time are brought together in automation. Accordingly, wherever such a chain of manufacturing links has been established, the gigantic planning and arrangement of machines and apparatus is more important than the actual work of manufacturing itself and the human element that it involves. Indeed, this kind of management and disposition (*Bestand*) of apparatus—especially if we consider things from the viewpoint of the capital invested—is even more gigantic than the raw materials and resources being worked on.

In order for the process of production to be set up as this sort of *Ge-*

stell, the machinery of production has to become more important than the production itself; machines become the "center" of production. It is as if a road constructed to get people from one place to another were to assume a self-existence all its own—like one of those underground shopping malls that we find so common in Japan—and then jerk itself free of the human hands that made it to walk off uncannily on its own. This is the sort of managerial metamorphosis that has become our own uncanny fate in letting the manufacturing processes walk by themselves, oblivious to the working of individual reason.

In the gigantic manufacturing process, human knowing has assumed a form that not only would have been impossible for education in an earlier age, but that would have been considered undesirable. Universities have been reorganized around the idea that "bigger is better" and are no longer able to give attention in what they teach to the fullness of the human, to a harmonious balance, in a word, to "general education." Up until the first half of the twentieth century, the object of knowledge for science was the laws of nature, only indirectly tied in with applications to human technology and manufacturing. But the object (*Gegenstand*) has since become the planned disposition (*Bestand*) of things, and the role of the worker has been usurped by the machine—subject and object changing places. In addition to this, production has far exceeded that sort of manufacturing process involved, for instance, in squeezing the thermal power out of coal and leaving coke as a residue (which is already the exact opposite of the give-and-take of natural production: receiving *from* nature, returning *to* nature) to become a form of *exploitation,* as when atomic power is wrenched from matter by smashing the atom.

I live near an industrial complex, and night after night I watch the flames of petrol being spit up into the sky and the glow of factory lights that gives the complex the eerie appearance of a castle that never sleeps. Little wonder that Heidegger's analysis of *Ge-stell* has made such a profound impression on me, and perhaps even biased my interpretation in the direction of a *re*interpretation.

Faced with the violent abuses that humanity has wrought on nature—and this includes *human* nature—culminating in the *Ge-stell,* and with the apparent spasms and writhings of nature trying to shake free of those abuses through a sort of counter-insurgency against that *Ge-stell,* Heidegger turned his thoughts to the destiny towards which the human race seemed to be heading in an eldritch and unearthly manner. By concentrating on the interdependency of reasoning and being, of the world and the human, he gouges out the infected flesh from under the skin of the contemporary world. Translated in terms of the doctrine of dependent origination, what we have here is a genuine, undisguised instance of the arising of avidyā. On the whole, however, the *Zusammengehörigkeit* that Heidegger stresses belongs rather to what Buddhism would call an exposition of the positive and affirmative dependent origination of the dharmic realm.

For Heidegger, the elemental ground of truth is reached through obedience (*ob-audire*) to what the ancient Greeks called *a-letheia*. (Following the criticisms of Paul Friedländer, Heidegger later abandoned the idea that the ancient Greek philosophers were fully aware of the true significance of *a-letheia,* observing that while traces of this awareness are to be seen in the philosophical poetry of Parmenides, when philosophy arrived at the stage of grounding itself as philosophy, it had already of necessity disappeared from the face of their consciousness, and hence its most profound contents were not grasped in their originality.) His idea that there is a side to the primacy of *a-letheia* closed off to philosophical reasoning is also characteristic of Merleau-Ponty's appeal to "archaic, primary experience." Like Merleau-Ponty, he approached the concrete fact of the "world of truth" rather from the side of the arts of poetry and painting, and sought to bring reason as close as possible to the fullness of intuition. In the previous pages I have tried to come to grips with the work of contemporary thinkers, taking Husserl's notion of the *Lebenswelt* as a pivot. The whole issue of *a-lètheia* surely merits more attention in its own right than we have given it, but such questions will have to be skirted in deference to the argument we are pursuing here.

For Watsuji, as noted earlier, the law of the five skandhas represents the a priori of everyday life, and the fundamental intent of the doctrine of dependent origination was seen as the ordering of things on the basis of the five skandhas. There are, however, a group of sūtras that elucidate a most peculiar form of correlatedness between the ninth and tenth links in the chain of twelvefold dependent origination: vijñāna (consciousness) and nāmarūpa (name-form). (We shall return to this point in some detail in the following chapter.) In effect, the chain of dependent origination is here reduced to nine or ten links ending with an explanation of the relationship of those two terms, which is expressed in the following manner: "Where there is vijñāna, there is nāmarūpa; where there is nāmarūpa, there is vijñāna. Without vijñāna there is no nāmarūpa; without nāmarūpa there is no vijñāna." This leads us to ask what sort of correlatedness is involved here and what is implied by the terms *vijñāna* and *nāmarūpa,* both questions to which we will return in the next chapter. For the present, let it suffice to note how an understanding of vijñāna and nāmarūpa can be aided greatly by getting a better hold on what we have already had to say with regard to the question of the *Lebenswelt* and its correlatedness to the survival of the subject of consciousness.

In the first place, the definition of *nāmarūpa* is put in the highest philosophical language in the Rig Veda's doctrine of cosmogenesis,[17] although the texts that accord a central place to the notion of nāmarūpa and take it into their accounts of cosmogenesis do not belong to the mainstream of the Rig Veda. Still, this representation found widespread application, from India to the West, and carries with it a most profound meaning that points to the depths of intuition to which archaic thinking (myth) was able to penetrate. Nāmarūpa represents the primary mode through which the world reveals itself. It shows us the whole of existence that wraps itself about the subject of consciousness in the form it assumes prior to division of subject and object. This idea was later to influence the Gnostic idea that would serve in turn as an archetype of the Christian Logos (in the gospel of John).

In the Rig Veda nāmarūpa appears at the initial stage of the world's manifestation from the Absolute, taking the form of a primitive, androgynous human (or cow) or as a cosmic tree. The same meaning is still unmistakable in the older Upanishads. When primitive Buddhism points to the state of enlightenment, it employs nāmarūpa as a very ancient technical term, as for instance in the Suttanipāta and the Itivuttaka, where we read "Here there is neither being nor nothingness, neither consciousness nor name-form [nāmarūpa]" or "Water and earth, fire and wind do not abide, the stars do not give off light, the sun and the moon do not shine, and the darkness does not linger." The world in its primordiality, while remaining an archaic form, is forever encountered in Yoga and contemplation (samādhi) as that very primary world itself. This world is also present when vijñāna is imagined in contemplative experience as a subject at one with the "place" (the world as the realm of experience) where contemplation is said to be "located," as in "the place of consciousness without limits" (vijñānānantyayātana), "the place that is no place" (ā-kiṃcanya-āyatana), "the place where there is neither thinking nor not-thinking" (naiva-saṃjñā-nāsaṃjñā-āyatana). That is to say, in that world—to the extent that it has not yet been seen as itself an interpretation, however lofty the heights of contemplation one may otherwise have reached—there is still present a subjective existence with a mode of being bound to saṃsāra and that is the vijñāna that is set up in a correlatedness with nāmarūpa.

Just like the silkworm that ties itself up with its own rope as it spins its cocoon about itself, the subject that, seen from the world, is part of the world, constructs its own being-in-the-world co-dependently and correlatively with the world and yet does so as its own activity. In this sense, volitional impulses (saṃskāra), while already produced, labor the while to extend themselves farther and increase. The subject of this labor is vijñāna. The correlatedness of vijñāna and nāmarūpa is at the same time the co-dependence of the coming-to-be and the passing away of both together. We may liken it to dreaming: when we dream, we live in correlatedness with the world of the dream and, through the phenomenal identity of dreamer and dream, keep the dream alive; but as soon as we become aware of this correlatedness, we have already awoken. Or again, it is like the knob on the door that serves both to close the door and to open it: correlatedness constitutes the dark room of ignorance (avidyā) and locks us up inside but through its reversal also leads us out into the light of knowledge (vidyā).

·5·

Dependent Origination and Co-dependency

Co-dependency and the Tenfold Causal Chain

Dependent origination, or paṭicca-samuppāda, consists in a relatedness (idapaccayatā) between one thing and another such that, as Nāgārjuna says, through this there is that, and through that there is this. This idea of co-dependency or correlatedness (paraspara-apekṣā) has its elemental ground in primitive Buddhism's doctrine of the twelvefold chain of dependent origination. Canonical texts from the Buddhist scriptures that describe this causal chain generally show how the twelve links are connected one to another, often in terms of the typical formula referred to earlier: "Where there is this, there is that; when this is born, that is born. When this is not, that is not; when this passes away, that passes away." This may also be expressed in the more general terms of the problem of dependent origination as such:

> What, brethren, is causal happening? . . . Whether, brethren, there be an arising of Tathāgatas, or whether there be no such arising, this nature of things just stands, this causal status, this causal orderliness, the relatedness of this to that [idappaccayatā]. Concerning that the Tathāgata is fully enlightened, that he fully understands. Fully enlightened, fully understanding he declares it, teaches it, reveals it, sets it forth, manifests, explains, makes it plain, saying "Behold!". . .
>
> Thus, brethren, that which here is such wise [tathatā], not elsewise, not otherwise, the relatedness of this to that—this, brethren, is what is called causal happening.[1]

The problem is that this sort of correlatedness does not characterize all the relations between the various items that constitute the twelvefold chain in the doctrine of dependent origination. The primitive scriptures give us a number of explanations, but perhaps the simplest is the following:

> What, brethren, is the causal law [paṭicca-samuppāda]?
>
> Conditioned by [12] ignorance [11] volitional impulses come to pass; conditioned by volitional impulses [10] consciousness, conditioned by consciousness [9] name-form, conditioned by name-form [8] the six senses, conditioned by the six senses [7] contact, conditioned by contact [6] feelings, conditioned by feelings [5] lust, conditioned by lust [4] clinging, conditioned by clinging [3] being, conditioned by being [2] birth, conditioned by birth [1] old age and death, grief, lamenting, suffering, sorrow, despair come to pass. Such is the uprising of the entire mass of ill. This, brethren, is called [causal] happening.
>
> But from the utter fading away and ceasing of [12] ignorance [comes] ceasing of [11] volitional impulses; from ceasing of volitional impulses ceasing of [10] consciousness; from ceasing of consciousness ceasing of [9] name-form; from ceasing of name-form ceasing of [8] the six senses; from ceasing of the six senses ceasing of [7] contact; from ceasing of contact ceasing of [6] feelings; from ceasing of feelings ceasing of [5] lust; from ceasing of lust ceasing of [4] clinging; from ceasing of clinging ceasing of [3] being; from ceasing of being ceasing of [2] birth; from ceasing of birth [1] old age and death, grief, lamenting, suffering, sorrow, despair cease. Such is the ceasing of this entire mass of ill.[2]

In this text we do not find a *mutual* relationship set up between one link in the chain and the next in terms of which we could speak of A being tied to B at the same time that B is tied to A. Instead we find a *unilateral* relationship in which the higher (the ground or cause) defines and qualifies the lower (the grounded or caused) along a chain that reaches from avidyā at the top to old age and death at the bottom. What is more, further along in the text the process that leads to the accumulation of all sufferings and skandhas as a forward progression (anuloma) is distinguished from the reverse process that leads to their passing away via a backward progression (paṭilomam).

In addition to those texts in the Pali canon that deal merely with a twelvefold theory of dependent origination, there are other sūtras that speak of ten, nine, five, and even fewer links in the causal chain, from which we may probably surmise that the twelvefold theory came about through a gradual increase of these more simplified theories. Accordingly, the relationships of dependent origination that we find in the twelvefold theory include nearly all the other teachings that seek to elucidate dependent origination, and may be said to represent well the essence of the doctrine in general. But in order for contemporary scholarly research to understand the doctrine of twelvefold dependent origination, it seems preferable to give due consideration to the construction of these various earlier doctrines as well.

In the Nagara Sūtra of the Saṃyutta-Nikāya, in a section entitled "The City,"[3] the Buddha, prior to his enlightenment and while he was still a bodhisattva, is recorded to have thought to himself:

> Alas! this world has fallen upon trouble! There is getting born and growing old and dying and falling and arising, but there is not the knowing of an escape from suffering, from old age and death. Oh when shall an escape be revealed from suffering, from old age and death?

In this introductory statement we see set out in simple form the motivation behind the speculations that led to the doctrine of dependent origination.

From there the bodhisattva Siddhartha Gotama went on to reflect: "What now being, does old age and death come to be? What conditions old age and death?" At that point, by means of right thinking and wisdom, he arrived at this enlightenment: "Where there is birth, old age and death come to be; old age and death are conditioned by birth." The question is then carried a step further: "What now being, does birth come to be? What conditions birth?" And the corresponding enlightenment is then that "Where there is being, birth comes to be; birth is conditioned by being." In this way a causal progression is set up in ten stages: (1) old age and death → (2) life → (3) being → (4) clinging → (5) lust → (6) feelings → (7) contact → (8) the six senses → (9) name-form ⇄ (10) consciousness.

In this text the final relationship between name-form (nāmarūpa) and consciousness (vijñāna) is first posed as the question, "What now being, does nāmarūpa come to be? What conditions nāmarūpa?" and is answered, "Where there is vijñāna there is nāmarūpa; nāmarūpa is conditioned by vijñāna." The further question then follows, "What now being, does vijñāna come to be? What conditions vijñāna?" with its accompanying answer, "Where there is nāmarūpa there is vijñāna; vijñāna is conditioned by nāmarūpa." This is what is implied by depicting the final two links in the chain by two arrows pointed in opposite directions. It means that the entire process is reversed through a backward progression that explains the passing away of all sufferings and skandhas. In this way the doctrine of dependent origination in such texts arrives at a tenfold or ninefold causal chain instead of the usual twelvefold doctrine.

Something similar to this tenfold explanation appears in the Mahāpadānasutta,[4] but there the reflections of the Buddha when still a bodhisattva are not those of Gotama the Buddha but of a former Buddha called Vipassin. The sūtra contains a detailed account of the life of Vipassin the Buddha before he left home, while he was in the palace of his father the king, living the life of a prince. It tells how he came to be confronted with the questions of old age, sickness, and death, and how he left home in order to seek an answer. The doctrine of dependent origination is then presented as an answer to those questions, which fits in well with the way the doctrine was introduced in the selection from the Nagara Sūtra mentioned earlier. The Mahāpadānasutta portrays in striking and dramatic fashion the process followed as these questions are pursued and traced back until they arrive at the final ground of the suffering of human life and then, through a breakthrough, are inverted into answers that eventually lead to the stage of enlightenment. We shall have more to say of this later, in the concluding section of chapter 6.

The section of the Mahāpadānasutta dealing with dependent origination is inserted as a whole into the Saṃyutta-Nikāya, where we find reflections on the doctrine of dependent origination repeated through each of the seven Buddhas—beginning with Vipassin, Sikhin, and Vessabhū, and continuing all the way up to Mahā Sakyamuni Gotama—as a way that leads to enlightenment.[5] But the specific doctrine used to transmit the story of the enlightenment of this group of former Buddhas does not use a tenfold causal chain but a twelvefold one. That is, the relationship of nāmarūpa ⇆ vijñāna is altered to give us two additional links in the chain:

> "What now being, does consciousness come to be? What conditions consciousness?" . . . "Where there are volitional impulses, consciousness comes to be; consciousness is conditioned by volitional impulses" . . . , "What now being, do volitional impulses come to be? What conditions volitional impulses?". . . . "Where there is ignorance, volitional impulses come to be; volitional impulses are conditioned by ignorance."
>
> "That is, in that volitional impulses are conditioned by ignorance, and consciousness by volitional impulses . . . so too grief, lamentation, ill, sorrow, and despair come to pass. Such is the coming to be of this entire body of ill."

> "Coming to be, coming to be!" At that thought, there arose to . . . the boddhisattva a vision into things not called before to mind, and knowledge arose, wisdom arose, light arose.[6]

This is followed by the reflections of the bodhisattvas on the passing away of all sufferings and skandhas, which are laid out in similar order and may be omitted here. This manner of developing the question according to the twelvefold doctrine of dependent origination flows more naturally than the earlier tenfold explanation, which is why Ui refers to it as the "natural order" (in contrast to the previous "logical order"). There are certain problems with this, but for purposes of convenience we may follow his terminology.

Now, when we compare the tenfold doctrine of dependent origination from the Mahāpadānasutta with the parallel section on the seven former Buddhas, it becomes clear that the latter is a later development of the former. Oldenberg also bases himself on the tenfold doctrine from the Mahāpadānasutta and argues for the same conclusion. From there he has gone on to consider what new sorts of problems and what new forms of religious awakening accompanied the development of the ninefold or tenfold theory of dependent origination to its twelvefold form. For the time being, let it suffice merely to note his conclusions without going into further detail.[7]

We have said that an evolution from the tenfold theory to the twelvefold theory can be inferred from the passages on dependent origination that show a "natural order," and that this order is explained as the course that the seven former Buddhas followed to attain to Buddhahood. The intimate connection between these two statements becomes clearer in the light of the allegory of "The City" alluded to earlier in passing. The story itself goes like this:

> Just as if . . . a man faring through the forest through the great wood should see an ancient path, an ancient road traversed by men of former days. And he were to go along it, and going along it he should see an ancient city, an ancient prince's domain, wherein dwelt men of former days, having gardens, groves, pools, foundations of walls, a goodly spot [but no one living in it].[8] And that man should bring word to the prince . . . and the prince . . . should restore that city. That city should thereafter become prosperous and flourishing, populous, teeming with folk, grown and thriven.

The commentary appended to the allegory observes:

> Even so have I [Gotama the Buddha], brethren, seen an ancient path, an ancient road traversed by the rightly enlightened ones of former times.
>
> And what, brethren, is the ancient path, that ancient road traversed by the rightly enlightened ones of former times?
>
> Just this noble eightfold path. . . . Along that have I gone, and going along it I have fully come to know old age and death, I have fully come to know the uprising of old age and death, I have fully come to know the ceasing of old age and death. . . . And going along it I have fully come to know birth, yea, and being and . . . name-form, and consciousness. Along that have I gone, and going along it I have fully come to know volitional impulses . . . I have fully come to know the way going to the ceasing of volitional impulses.[9]

In the latter half of the allegory of "The City" it is clear that the ancient path is taken as *the process by which the former Buddhas attained to Buddhahood;* and the tenfold theory of dependent origination that appears in the first half is expanded to a twelvefold theory, with each of the relationships that link the chain together being explained in terms of the doctrine of the four noble truths. (An exception is made in the case of avidyā, probably because the explanation of the coming to be and passing away of dependent origination through the four noble truths requires a differentiation that is not possible for avidyā.) Further, an intimate relationship is established between the doctrine of dependent origination and the noble eightfold path, which is also defined as the ancient path. (This point is extremely important, though we shall have to pass over it in this context.) Thus to follow the lead of the allegory, it seems quite natural that, on the one hand, the tenfold theory of Vipassin should appear in the Mahāpadānasutta and on the other that the twelvefold theory should come about in the corresponding section from the Saṃyutta-Nikāya on the seven former Buddhas. I have argued previously for an evolution from a tenfold to a twelvefold theory of dependent origination, taking my lead from the Chinese text of "The City" (entitled "The Castle"), but it now seems to me that the key element in this evolution, both in a literary and a speculative sense, may be located more precisely in this allegorical portion of the sūtra.

In addition to "The City," there are only two other sūtras in which we find a tenfold (or ninefold) chain of dependent origination with name-form $\rightleftarrows$ consciousness as the final link in the causal succession. Both are extremely important; in particular, the sections explaining the meaning of dependent origination through allegories display a profound self-awareness based on religious symbolism.

In its explanation of a tenfold theory of dependent origination, the section of the Saṃyutta-Nikāya entitled "The Sheaf of Reeds" begins by asking whether suffering be one's own doing or the doing of another, whether it be the doing of both oneself and another, or whether it be the doing of neither oneself nor another. Thus the problem of whether suffering originates in the self or the other is treated in the tetralemmic form. "Suffering is one's own doing" seems to stress that suffering is what one receives oneself as the result of what one has done oneself (or that it consists in the self as such: when we become aware of ourselves as acting and proclaim, "I myself am a self," that "being a self" invariably ends up as a suffering). "Suffering is the doing of another" seems to stress that "suffering is what the one receives through what the other has done," that it is the result of activity that takes place outside of oneself, and from there reaches the self (who, from the point of view of the acting self, is another self).

With the doctrine of dependent origination we come to a problem of wider dimensions and more profound significance than the problem of self-acting and other-acting with its four-faceted differentiation. When the theory of dependent origination asks the question of suffering it is not concerned with who is inflicting suffering on whom, or with who is actually doing the suffering. Neither does it make an issue of "what" the cause of suffering is, in the sense that A might be taken as an objective cause of the suffering of B. Nāgārjuna, as is well known, took the position with regard to the roles of self and other in suffering that "because of dependent origination, they are empty (śūnya)," and from there went on to develop the problem into one of the central issues of his dialectical method.

"The Sheaf of Reeds" treats this problem as a prelude to its presentation of a tenfold doctrine of dependent origination, in the course of which we find the actual analogy from which the passage takes its name:

> It is just as if, friend, there stood two sheaves of reeds leaning one against the other.
>
> Even so, friend, name-form comes to pass conditioned by consciousness, consciousness conditioned by name-form, the six senses conditioned by name-form, and so on—even such is the uprising of this entire mass of ill.
>
> If, friend, I were to pull towards me one of those sheaves of reeds, the other would fall; if I were to pull towards me the other, the former would fall.

> Even so, friend, from the ceasing of name-form, consciousness ceases; from the ceasing of consciousness, name-form ceases; from the ceasing of name-form sense ceases, and similarly is there ceasing of contact, feelings . . . and of this entire mass of ill.[10]

The point of the analogy of the sheaf of reeds is the mutuality of nāmarūpa ⇄ vijñāna, and talk of correlatedness or co-dependency in dependent origination involves just this sort of connection, while the line of causality from old age and death → life → being and so forth up to contact → the six senses is given as uni-directional. The question of whether primitive Buddhism considered the relationship of co-dependency in this causal chain as this sort of uni-directional succession or whether its doctrine involved a reciprocal mediation is a matter of debate among Japanese scholars that has continued up to the present, with arguments being presented on both sides. The uni-directional interpretation was held by Watsuji, while Ui is a representative of the reciprocal-mediation interpretation. Watsuji stresses the point that if one grants a complete reciprocity to all the relationships in the causal chain, there is no way that any order of succession could have been generated. Ui offers the contrary view of an order of mutual reflection, arguing that in the primitive Buddhism understanding of dependent origination, each of the chains reflects the entire twelvefold succession into the self like so many monads each mirroring the world. In this way an interpenetration takes place based on a pre-established harmony between one link in the chain of dependent origination and another. In a word, what Ui's interpretation does is to extend the principle of reciprocal mediation found in the Kegon philosophy as the "mutual interpenetration of phenomenal forms"[11] (which presupposes a world view according to which "All is One and One is All") to the co-dependency of primitive Buddhism's theory of dependent origination.

If, however, we focus on the tenfold doctrine of dependent origination, a succession like that described above is neither simply a uni-directional grounding of one link in the causal chain by another, nor is it simply a reciprocal mediation. It is, rather, actually the combination of both of these, or some sort of reciprocal mediation of both emerging from a level deeper than either of them. That is, the succession of dependent origination is a theory of conversion, of metanoia, according to which the uni-dimensional chain of causes eventually gives way to a deeper reciprocity of co-dependent causes, which then in turn serves as a springboard for the attempt to leap free of causality altogether.

If we stop to think about the analogy of the sheaf of reeds, we see that the sheaves lean against each other, the first as mainstay for the second, the second as mainstay for the first. But if one should fall, the other will fall as well. The analogy thus shows the workings of a "co-dependent phenomenal identity," according to which a sheaf of reeds is both set up into being and collapsed out of being. Not only is the accumulation (coming-to-be) of all sufferings and skandhas grounded in correlatedness and co-dependency, but so is its passing away (collapse). In this sense, the correlatedness and co-dependency obtains between the coming-to-be and the passing away of dependent origination—as it obtains between the setting up and the collapse of the sheaves of reeds.

That is, the very principle that brings about the appearance of all sufferings and skandhas turns around and effects their disappearance. We see at work here a dynamic principle that makes the turnabout of religious conversion possible, a principle that the consciousness-only school refers to as āśraya-parāvṛitti, the reversal of depending, the turning over of the ground. But now even if we grant that the doctrine of dependent origination has in fact unearthed the ultimate ground of our human liability to limits and sufferings in avidyā, or lust, obviously this is not the same as uprooting ourselves from the ground and overcoming their power over us. Take the problem of contemporary nihilism. We may liken its symptoms to a cancer in that a step-by-step diagnosis of the illness and identification of its etiology does not imply that we have thereby cured the illness or removed its causes. In this sense the two are similar. The difference is that someday medical science may overcome the obstacles that currently impede our diagnosis and cure of cancer, whereas nihilism—insofar as we may take this as a contemporary translation of the meaning of avidyā and suffering—does not admit of such a possibility. The reason is that the two operate on different levels. To follow Max Scheler's distinction between technical knowledge and essential intuition, medical science is an instance of the former in teaching us how to cure illness. But when, faced with illness, one has felt one's own finitude and, as if by fate, been made to open one's eyes to that elusive solitary interiority of being an individual that only illness can teach, then, says Scheler, we come to a new and essential knowledge of what illness is.

Now the Buddhist concept of suffering—our encounter and clash with the liability of human existence to limits and suffering—starts from A and seeks after its root causes by proceeding A → B → C → D → E → F so as to arrive at F as the basic cause. But even if F is a cause *productive* of A, that does not be itself mean that it can work to *extinguish* A. The root cause of old age and death may be said to be the attachment of lust, but this knowledge does not at once make the lust recede from the picture. Even if one judges the suffering and torment of some disease to be caused by something called F, the problem remains how to dispose of F.

The problem of existential causes is different, then, from the problem of curable diseases. It is like sleep. One can only become aware of sleep as sleep by waking up; at the moment one awakens, the various sufferings that troubled the world of sleep are awakened to in the realization, "It *was* only a dream; I *was* sleeping." One passes beyond such things even as one realizes them. In much the same way, the basis on which the entire accumulated complex of sufferings and skandhas is turned around and dissolved is the co-dependent correlatedness of nāmarūpa ⇄ vijñāna. In the twelvefold doctrine of dependent origination, avidyā and saṃskāra are known as something that *was;* they are but the occasion of their own extinction as a self-negation, and in this sense may be designated as what Hegel (with different intentions) calls *Gewesen,* past essences. In the sūtra of "The Castle" (the Chinese version of "The City"), in the first part the causal chain by which all sufferings and skandhas accumulate ends with the co-dependent correlatedness of nāmarūpa and vijñāna, while the second half, which shows the passing away of all sufferings and skandhas, links the chains together in such a way that "by extinguishing avidyā saṃskāra is extinguished, by extinguishing saṃskāra, vijñāna is extinguished, by extinguishing vijñāna nāmarūpa is extinguished. . . ." The sūtra of "The Castle" makes clear how dependent origination consists in a process of transformation from a tenfold causal chain to a twelvefold one; and how when the accumulation of all sufferings and skandhas is turned around in the direction of their extinction, avidyā and saṃskāra are introduced into the twelvefold causal chain as necessary moments for a proper denial and conquest of dependent origination. In other words, avidyā and saṃskāra are only grasped in their primary sense when their essential determination is sought in terms of their extinction, when they are seen as past essences, as things that *were.*

As Heidegger has shown in his 1957 work *Der Satz vom Grund,* the word *Satz* (proposition, principle) carries the sense of a *Sprung* (leap), so that when rationality focuses on an investigation into the principle of causal grounding (*Grund*), it can only come to term by effecting a "leap from the ground." When the principle of sufficient reason (the proposition that states that nothing exists without a sufficient reason) is transferred from the domains of theory to a locus of praxis (where the problem of fundamental evil arises), the Buddhist notions like "karma" or Nietzsche's "eternal return" are suddenly brought to life like fish returned to the water. Both karma and eternal return are resilient and internally vibrant concepts. When they define Dasein or human actuality as radically determined on the level of responsible activity in the endless flow of time from past to present, when they see the self as being woven together with the various threads of destiny and stretched out in all directions like an endless reticulation woven about a single center, it is precisely at that moment that one realizes an ex-static freedom from that destiny.

In order to take this leap, one needs to understand the trick of turning the wheel of saṃsāra and karma. One of the sages of the Upanishads likens it to a snake looking at the skin it has just slipped out of. We may compare it to a swimmer who uses a diving board to get into the water and away from the board. The motion of setting one's feet firmly on the diving board is made in order directly thereafter to leap free of the board, and in fact it is at the point that one grips the board most firmly that the moment of leaping takes place. Through avidyā and saṃskāra (karma), the instant that fundamental human evil is concentrated at one point of the present within existential time is the very instant of the turnabout of the heart in metanoia. This is the sense of existential grounding referred to above.

Hegel argued for a self-caused substance (svabhāva) in his theory of the essence in his *Science of Logic,* and clarified the relationships between such substantial essence and phenomena (and their various modes of being). To translate this into Buddhist terms, it is the problem of the relationship of body, form, and function as found in the "Awakening of Faith."[12] His doctrine of essence is converted into the doctrine of the concept (*Begriff*) of "Absolute knowledge" through the mediation of a dialectical reflection on the interchangeability (*Wechselwirkung*) of cause and effect. If we take the basic point of his theory of essence—the movement "from causality to existence"—as a pivotal point for comparing the standpoints of Hegel and Schelling (in his *Essence of Human Freedom* and so forth), and if we further allow ourselves to be led by what Heidegger has to say with regard to both of them, we might succeed in bringing to light a theory of "from essence to existence" that would combine on the one hand Heidegger's theory of causality and his late thoughts on co-pertinence (*Zusammengehörigkeit*), and on the other Hegel's theory of essence and concept based on subjective freedom—which would probably come very close to the fundamental spirit of primitive Buddhism's idea of dependent origination. In so doing, we might well bring to birth a new logic for fusing together the history of Western metaphysics and Oriental thought.

Co-dependency and the Ninefold Causal Chain

The theory of a ninefold dependent origination is arrived at by eliminating from the tenfold causal chain the eighth link of saḷāyatana (the six senses), though in terms of content there is hardly any difference at all. Among the sūtras dealing with the doctrine of ninefold dependent origination and concluding with the co-dependency of nāmarūpa ⇄ vijñāna is the Mahānidānasutta (The Doctrine of Natural Causation). Worthy of note in this sūtra is, first of all, that it accords separate commentaries to each of the links in the chain of causality; and, secondly, that it ends with an explanation of the stages of contemplation, arriving finally at samāpatti, wherein all saṃjñā is eliminated.[13] Nowadays the relationship between the co-dependency of nāmarūpa and vijñāna and this ultimate stage of samādhi is scarcely paid any attention. But during the time that commentaries on the text of ninefold dependent origination from the Mahānidānasutta were being composed, we may suppose that both for the monks who chanted this sūtra as well as for the compilers who put the text together, it was accepted as a matter of common sense; and that it was understood at the time that the concrete meaning of the co-dependency of nāmarūpa and vijñāna must be grasped in accord with the context surrounding the experience of contemplation (as transmitted by tradition). In a word, it was held that the conversion of dependencies in nāmarūpa ⇄ vijñāna was completed and the realm of perfect enlightenment opened by passing through the last four of the twelve dhyānas into the cessation of all mental activity. This, it seems to me, was the view of this one school of thought that took the ninefold doctrine of dependent origination from the Mahānidānasutta as its point of departure. In the Suttanipāta we find conversion based on the contemplation of nothingness known as ākiṃcanya-āyatana (which is in fact the most effective explanation) and also on the tetralemmic discrimination of the affirmation and negation of thought. Both of these advocated an ultimate stage of samādhi tnat could be analyzed in terms of the co-dependency of nāmarūpa and vijñāna. Later we shall have occasion to return to these questions.

It is in the introductory section to the Mahānidānasutta that we find the passage in which dependent origination is referred to as "so deep," which we cited at the outset of chapter 4. There the phrase "so deep" is used to describe the essence of canonical texts on dependent origination as a whole, but in the Vinaya-Piṭaka[14] it is used to speak of the co-dependency of dependent origination. Let us take a closer look at the actual mode of transmission of the theory of dependent origination by focusing on this notion of co-dependency.

Once the doctrine of dependent origination had evolved to a twelvefold chain of causal succession and this change was accepted as orthodox, we may suppose that the tenfold and ninefold versions largely disappeared from the scene, inasmuch as the amendment did not entail any particular difficulty for those who had advocated the alternate explanations. But whenever the focus was on the *co-dependency* of dependent origination, it was invariably accompanied by a grave concern over the co-dependency between name-form and consciousness. In the case of the consciousness-only school, in addition to the analogy of the bundle of reeds cited earlier, which illustrates the principle of "reciprocal cause forever joined to reciprocal effect," we may also mention the simile of the oil, the wick, and the flame, which appears in the concluding section of the sūtra, entitled "fetters." There we read:

> It is just as if, brethren, because of oil and because of wick, an oil-lamp were to be burning, and in it from time to time a man were to pour oil and to adjust a wick. Verily such an oil-lamp so fed, so supplied with fuel would burn for a long while.
>
> Even so in him who contemplates the enjoyment [assāda] that there is in all that makes for enfettering, lust grows, and is the condition of clinging; so being, birth, old age and death follow; . . . suffering comes to pass. Such is the uprising of the entire mass of ill.

On the other hand, the sūtra goes on:

> In him, brethren, who contemplates the misery [ādīnava] that there is in all that makes for enfettering, lust ceases, clinging ceases, so also being, birth, old age and death, grief, lamenting, suffering, sorrow, despair cease. Such is the ceasing of this entire mass of ill.[15]

The passage does not make the co-dependency of the flame and the oil and the wick all that clear. But that aside, the Mahānidānasutta presents a fivefold causal chain that proceeds from lust → clinging → being → birth → old age and death. If we take into consideration the entire relationship between the law of objects (things that are grasped on to and clung to) and the prolongation and extinction of lust, or the consideration of attachments in their savory and unsavory aspects, the problem of co-dependency becomes fairly obvious. In the same cluster of texts we find the simile of the firewood.[16] The firewood is upādāna (clinging), which is here depicted as stacked up on a cart for carrying away. As the fourth link in the causal chain, it carries the additional sense of being fuel for the fire of lust (taṇhā, burning desire). The relationship of lust and clinging (as well as the extinction of that relationship) is described in terms of firewood becoming fire, and thereby becoming a fuel to keep the fire going. The co-dependency at work behind the image is clear. The law of objects teaches that from the viewpoint of assāda, lust is prolonged, and thus leads to the accumulation of all sufferings and skandhas: lust → clinging → being → birth → old age and death; while viewed from its aspect of ādīnava, the extinction of lust leads to the extinction of the totality of sufferings and skandhas: the extinction of lust → the extinction of clinging → . . . . the extinction of old age and death.

Here we are given an important clue to the exegesis of the simpler fivefold doctrine in the Mahānidānasutta that takes its starting point from lust. Namely, if we look closely at the double perspective of the savory and the unsavory, from which the law of objects is regarded here, the chain of origination from old age and death → life → being → clinging → lust itself comes down, in the end, to the mutual grounding of clinging and lust. This gives us a succession whose totality can be expressed as follows: old age and death → life → being → clinging ⇄ lust. Lust is like trying to quench a burning thirst by drinking salt water: the more one drinks, the more one is driven mad with thirst. Clinging, then, is the kindling and fueling of lustful desire, a sort of subconscious second nature, something along the lines of Kant's understanding of fundamental evil as a "transcendental tendency to evil." Looked at from the viewpoint of clinging, lust is no more than the tip of an iceberg that has broken the surface of the sea of consciousness.

Probably the best illustration of this is the passage called "The Great Tree," which appears in the same series of sūtras.[17] There lust is likened to a great tree that spreads its roots out far and wide under the ground and grows by drinking in earth and water. If people fertilize and water the tree at the right times, it will grow into a great tree and have a long life. But if one wants the tree to wither and die, it is not enough merely to stop nourishing it, nor even to cut it down at the trunk. One must dig up its roots. But even then, if not all of the roots are removed, even the slenderest of rootlets may continue to grow and spread and bud new branches. Of course, in order not to leave so much as a single strand behind, one has to dig a great hole about the base of the tap and follow it to the outermost shoots, burning the roots out as one goes, grinding them up into powder, drying them in the sun, flushing them down the river.

The image is helpful for understanding the viewpoint of enjoyment within which lust grows and expands. In the primitive Buddhist view of human nature nāmarūpa (name-form) was also called nāmakāya (name-body) and satkāya-dṛṣṭi (the attachment to one's own body). It was seen as being in this world by sinking roots in the form of worldly passions, while the co-dependent element of vijñāna was the trunk that grew out of these earthy roots, opposed to the earthiness of the roots by the principle of clarity or knowledge. This would seem to head us in the direction of an opposition between light and darkness, but in fact both are fed by the same sap of kleśa (worldly passions) that flow through the human mode of being. The rational discrimination of consciousness and the correlative judgments of good and evil may prune the branches of appetite but they do not uproot the tree. When the violent wind of impermanence strikes terror into one, then the extinction of all sufferings and skandhas, the elemental negation of the human mode of being, becomes a real possibility. That is the real issue in the extinction of lust. Those who ignore the co-dependency of clinging ⇄ lust and think it enough to deny the burning thirst of desire reduce the problem to a simple matter of trimming branches.

As Akanuma Tomoyoshi has shown in a comparative study of Chinese and Pali texts,[18] the analogies of the city, the sheaves of reeds, the lamp wick, the firewood, the great tree, and so forth, both in the Chinese translation of the sūtras and in the original Pali texts, were probably, on the whole, originally aimed at explaining collectively the existential significance of co-dependence. In one group of texts that belongs to the scriptures he is concerned with, we find two sūtras dealing with the question of nāmarūpa and vijñāna. There we find it taught that when things subject to the law of objects are viewed in their savory aspect (assāda) both nāmarūpa and vijñāna are manifested, and the progressions nāmarūpa → six senses → . . . . old age and death, as well as vijñāna → six senses → . . . . old age and death, are explained by citing the analogy of the great tree; on the other hand, seen from their unsavory aspect (ādīnava), the extinction of nāmarūpa and vijñāna in all things is explained, including the old age and death grounded on them. These passages would seem to suggest that the texts that show the co-dependency nāmarūpa ⇄ vijñāna, as well as the sūtras just referred to, were probably all originally compiled with the same problem in mind.

As good illustrations of how the co-dependency nāmarūpa ⇄ vijñāna lurks in the background and yet plays an important role, one might cite the fourth and fifth sections of the Suttanipāta (the Atthakavagga and the Pārāyanavagga).

With regard to recent literary research from America and Europe on the Suttanipāta, we may make mention of the concluding remarks that E. M. Hare appended to his translation of the work, and which Edward Conze alludes to in his book *Thirty Years of Buddhist Studies.*[19] There Hare argues the point that almost all of the doctrines presumed to be basic to primitive Buddhism—beginning, of course, with the four noble truths, the noble eightfold path, the five skandhas, the six transcendental powers, the four dhyānas and eight levels of concentration, but including also the Buddha-Dharma-Sangha trinity, impermanence, suffering, non-ego, and other classifications of the dharma—are not to be found in the Suttanipāta. From there he goes on to point out that these sorts of fundamental doctrines were probably not established within primitive Buddhism at the time the text was composed.

Conze observes that when this discovery is combined with the seven scriptures proposed in the royal edicts of King Aśoka, we come to some extremely important conclusions. Now, leaving aside scholarly disputes over which currently extant sūtras these seven texts of King Aśoka correspond to and taking a liberal enough view to include all the possibilities, the fact that by and large there are very few places in them that deal with the fundamental doctrines of primitive Buddhism, and that they contain a good deal of material that from the vantage point of the present do not look terribly important, is hardly a new revelation.

The reasons for this have so far gone as follows. Since Aśoka chose these texts with lay Buddhist believers uppermost in his mind—and this he also took to be the missionary aim of those who left to become monks—they were not being proposed as matter for doctrinal research by specialist monks.

Conze's point was that if we add to these considerations what Hare had to say about the Suttanipāta, not only the constitution of what is known today as the primitive Buddhist canon can be placed after the time of King Aśoka (since prior to that time the sacred texts were only beginning to develop), but so can the doctrines that were transmitted orally prior to the establishment of the sacred texts. From such a point of view, Conze argued, it is possible to sustain a trustworthy and objective study of primitive Buddhism that is literally accurate and detailed.

In Japan, Nakamura Hajime is well known for the careful literary criticism he has done taking the Suttanipāta as the point of origin, and the well-nigh revolutionary conclusions he arrived at.[20] It is not a simple matter to pass judgment on Nakamura's work without going into concrete details one by one because, unlike Hare and Conze, he did not begin with a new plan of research but arrived at his conclusions through meticulous investigations from Pali and Sanskrit sūtras and from Chinese and Tibetan translations of the sūtras. Nevertheless, his conclusions may be considered close to the thinking of Hare and Conze.

As for myself, there are points at which I must part camp with Hare and Conze. In my opinion, the Suttanipāta by no means represents merely doctrine at an undeveloped stage, but rather intended to lend support to particular doctrines through the promulgation of teachings on the life and silence of the Buddha. This becomes clear if we look at the Atthakavagga and the Pārāyanavagga sections of the Suttanipāta, said to belong to the oldest strain of its teachings. These doctrines proceed from a standpoint that emphasizes the contemplative state of ākiṃcanya-āyatana (and its accompanying cessation of all mental activities, or naiva-saṃjñā-nāsaṃjñā-āyatana) as a mental attitude of mukta (deliverance, emancipation), from which it transmitted a certain interpretation of consciousness and name-form, contact, the six senses, lust, burning desire, and so forth according to a ninefold or tenfold causal chain of dependent origination rather than a twelvefold one. That is, it directed its attention to an explanation of the transition from contact to burning desire based on the vijñāna ⇄ nāmarūpa relations of the tenfold theory of dependent origination. There is another aspect to this unique commentary on the causal chain of dependent origination from the standpoint of the contemplative state of ākiṃcanya-āyatana as ultimate mukta and from the standpoint of the asceticism advanced for its achievement, an aspect not to be overlooked, because it provides us with a valuable key for reflecting on the fourfold realm of ārūpya-dhātu and niroda-samāpatti. The religious meaning and doctrinal significance of primitive Buddhism's doctrine of the four dhyānas have not been adequately recognized in Japan. Accordingly, when the problems that later arose concerning the deliverance from thought, the contemplation of ākiṃcanya-āyatana, naiva-samjñā-nāsaṃjñā-āyatana, and so forth come into question, one has the feeling that their religious psychology, their unique body-mind view, their general world view, and the like are not able to be given deeper attention for this reason. The fourth and fifth sections of the Suttanipāta show how important a clue the contemplation of ākiṃcanya-āyatana is for clarifying the relationship between the theories of depending and centering.

These fourth and fifth sections of the Suttanipāta, dealing with the surrender of speculation and dispute, which Hare has gathered together into a single section, deserve special attention. The contents of those sūtras that warn against disputes are widely scattered, but representative of them is the following from a section entitled "On Contentions":

From dear things rise contentions and disputes,
Grief with laments and envy in their train,
Pride and conceit with slander's tongue in wake:
Contentions and disputes are envy-linked,
And slander's tongues are born amid disputes.[21]

It seems to guard against and retreat from those deeds through which this type of quarrel and dispute arises as the karma of kleśa that wounds the self as well as the other. But if one reads the text closely and attentively, there is more to it than just that. In a unique way the sūtra is pursuing the relationship of lust, clinging, contact, name and form, and consciousness (avidity) in the doctrine of dependent origination, and arrives at the practice of overcoming name-form and consciousness in absolute denial by means of tetralemmic discrimination, or in the insight into the non-discriminating equality of the realm of ākiṃcanya-āyatana.[22] With regard to the matter of whether there can be a level of contemplation beyond this, we can only note that the sūtra does not define this dhyāna as ultimate but rather seems to retain the attitude of classifying it as a moot and unclear issue.

In this sūtra and others like it, the matter under dispute has to do with academic (metaphysical) opinions focusing primarily on questions of metaphysical theory that at the time were shaky and open to doubt because their main points had come to be formulated in terms of antinomies, and of whose actual contents we know from other canons of primitive Buddhism and the celebrated research that has been done on them. (For example, we have the questions of Māluṅkyāputta mentioned in the early pages of chapter 1, and to which we return in the next chapter.) Allusions are made to the previous example left by the Buddha, but in the case of the Suttanipāta the critique is directed less against actual details of content of the antinomies than against the individuals who clung to such opinions. To cling to one's own opinion and insist on it, we are told, is the work of an underlying desire, and this sort of clinging results in anger and deceit and skepticism and other corruptions. The stupidity that sees all other standpoints as in error and one's own view as correct, argumentation carried on with the aim of winning applause, and so forth are seen as the form proper to metaphysical judgments. They are seen as grounded on a perversion of the desire for possessions into a preoccupation with nāmarūpa that ends up clinging to the ego. Once one has passed beyond these disputes, there is no longer any reason to be preoccupied with whether one's own stance is "superior" to that of another, or "inferior," or "equal."

But if we look carefully at what is involved in the sort of standpoint discussed in the sūtra, one that does not allow itself to be swayed this way and that by problems of superiority, equality, and inferiority, we see that not only is one not pestered by metaphysical questions; but that one aims positively at a critical attitude focused on accusing the attitude behind metaphysical judgments of giving expression to burning desire with all the resentment and haughtiness and insolence and double-talk that go with it. This way of dismissing questions about the world, the existence of spirits, and so forth without entering into the details of the metaphysical problems that concerned the world or religious thought at the time is common to these texts. It points to a critical attitude that, leaving aside the question of how profound it was in its actual workings, may be said to be more radical than even the famous critical attitude of the Buddha towards metaphysical questions in refusing to answer the questions of Māluṅkyāputta (see chapter 1). The common object of criticism in these sūtras is the agitation produced in the subjective attitude of one who traffics in these sorts of problems, independently of actual concrete details. The full force of their insistence fell on a repudiation of covetousness towards nāmarūpa and a letting go of one's hold on everything in the world.

If this standpoint is stressed, the tendency appears to maintain as great a silence as possible with regard to the four noble truths, the eightfold noble path, and other doctrinal matters, if not to ignore them altogether. (This runs against the grain of contemporary scholarship, but I shall leave it to another occasion to describe how these doctrinal explanations are stressed in Buddhism from its earliest beginnings.) The reason is that those who took such a standpoint were possessed of a particular experience through the centering of samādhi, which gave them a confidence and firm footing that could not be shaken. What sort of experience was this?

In describing the death of the Buddha, the main body of the Nirvāṇa Sūtra portrays a peculiar wedding of the theory of the four dhyānas and the eight samāpatti (stages of concentration) that lead to perfect nirvāṇa. It may be that this theory of contemplation was authorized with the experience of the Buddha as its ultimate reference point and assumed its place in the world of Buddhism at the time that the prose sections of this sūtra were being completed. The enlightenment of the Buddha depended on the theory of the four dhyānas, which I take to be centered on compassion and to consist in the realization of indifference (upekkhā), thus forming a single whole with the four immeasurables (catvāry apramāṇāni). But if it is combined with the catvāry apramaṇāni one would also expect it to be combined with contemplation of the four arūpya (formless states).

Those of the disciples of the Buddha who took a position of encouraging the quiet of solitary interiority, which was the ideal of the Suttanipāta, must have preferred the latter to the former, however, and found it to reverberate more persuasively with their own point of view. In its beginnings, the contemplation of the four arūpya was a form of kasiṇa meditation consisting in denying objects by abstracting them in contemplation, as we saw in chapter 2. That is, a concretized reflection on the subjective and the objective goes through a process of elimination in which at a certain level the object suddenly loses its actuality, the self ceases to be the self, and infinite space and time shed the weight of reality and manifest themselves in softly shining rays of light. In this way the idea of a macrocosm-microcosm relationship functioned within contemplation even as far as the basic elements of earth, fire, water, and air were concerned, so that, for example, internal fire came to be fused experientially into the fire of the external world. It is like drawing a curtain down before one with a hole at eye level through which a fire on the other side is visible. As one gazes intently at the fire, one first has the sense of a device overlaid on an object, but gradually the objectness of the object gets lost, until finally the world as a whole can be felt as something that reveals itself as filled up with the brightness of that fire. (The same thing that occurs in the "localizing" method of kasiṇa has been observed in contemporary psychology. For example, I place a disk before my eyes and parallel to my forehead. By tilting the disk little by little I would expect it to begin to appear elliptical, but in fact it continues to look as round as before. This is so because objectification entails fixation within a single setting. Whereas if this power to control the setting is not functioning, as when one looks at the same disk through a hole in a curtain, the disk will look elliptical when it is tilted.) Vijñānānantyāyatana (the contemplation of unlimited knowledge) is a stage of samādhi wherein the limitless space of the subject-object unity is filled up with the shining light of consciousness. In contrast, the contemplative state of ākiṃcanya-āyatana is a realm of the non-existing that transcends the infinite space of this bright light as a "nothing at all." This passing beyond all taste for the world of bright light is awakened to as the most radical form of the self-denial of the subject. "There the sun does not shine, the moon and the stars do not give forth their light, yet neither is there darkness." The phrase captures well the essence of the limitless space that encompasses and transcends the subject-object unity in the nothingness of ākiṃcanya-āyatana, the domain of the non-existent that has transcended both the primary form of nāmarūpa (the *Lebenswelt*) and the limitlessness of vijñāna.

There are numerous places in the fourth and fifth sections of the Suttanipāta that discuss name-form and consciousness, name and form and consciousness, name and form, name and body. Many of the concluding poetic verses also argue for centering on ākiṃcanya-āyatana, or some similar form of samādhi, as the supreme standpoint. In two related but separated passages we read, "Where there is no nāmarūpa there is no vijñāna," and "Where there is no vijñāna there is no nāmarūpa." We cannot here go into the poems one by one to explain them in detail, but it is clear that the standpoint of the contemplation of ākiṃcanya-āyatana is the key to understanding the co-dependency of nāmarūpa ⇄ vijñāna in both its forward and backward progressions. Since the standpoint of the Suttanipāta is that of the contemplation of ākiṃcanya-āyatana—and this also holds true for the sections it has in common with the Dhammapada—it is unavoidable that at certain points it will fall wide of the fundamental doctrine of the Buddha. To take an example close to home, if I had to guess the doctrine of Shinran only from Yuien's *Tannishō,* I should never expect Shinran to have composed something like the *Kyōgyōshinshō* (see chapter 3). Without Yuien and others like him, there is no doubt that Shinran's teachings would not have spread so far and wide. But at the same time, if there had only been Yuien and others like him, they would never have been able to come up with the true teaching of Shinran, no matter how many of them there had been.

Finally we may establish the fact that the notions of nāmarūpa and vijñāna that we find in the co-dependent relationship nāmarūpa ⇄ vijñāna belong within the intellectual and religious history of India, where from ancient times they have been laden with the highest significance, where they possess a long linguistic history, and where their lifeline runs through the very time of primitive Buddhism itself.

The first manifestation of Puruṣa (the primordial human) was Vāc (the word) and also Virāj (the dawn's light, the great red sea of eastern clouds). Already here a relationship of co-dependency comes about inasmuch as Virāj is born from Puruṣa and Puruṣa from Virāj. The meaning of this initial manifestation is that the revelation of the Absolute is seen as a light that has not yet reached the earth—in precisely the same way that Saint John depicts the Logos as dwelling with God. Accordingly, we are presented with a situation in which the earth continues to be cloaked in darkness, with the light shining in the eastern sky as the red wellspring of life. Revelation continues to abide at one with the Absolute even as it comes forth here as the Vāc (word), light, and life.

In the second manifestation, nāmarūpa in its mode of being as (1) word is shown to be also (2) an androgynous human or, alternatively, an epicene cow or primordial beast. This primordial human is then manifested further as (3) a cosmic tree, which is its correlative. Incidentally, the myths that Plato cites also speak of an androgynous being (*Symposium*) and a cosmic tree hanging upside down from the sky towards the earth (*Timaeus*).

In the next and third manifestation we see the primordial human and the beast approach the near side, where the waiting magicians (mountain hermits or gods) grab hold of them and cut them up for sacrifice. The myth of this "dissection of the giant" is tied into the opening up of the cosmos, the arrival of light from the far side to the near side. In passing through this stage the cosmos (the first manifestation of nāmarūpa), which was formerly at one with the Absolute, is divided into heaven and earth, and every existing thing is split into nāma (form) and rūpa (matter). In this way the world is formed of individual things composed of nāma and rūpa. Here we have the situation where the light reaches the phenomenal world and the world, which has been penetrated by this light, is dissected by discriminating knowledge. The phenomenal world gets bathed in bright light, but this has a double significance: it means that the world is made manifest and is split into two tiers. On the one hand, the world becomes transparent through the power of discriminating knowledge; on the other, its identity with an elemental ground is thereby hidden from view. In his interpretation of this elucidation of the phenomenal world, the Vedantic philosopher Śaṅkara envisions it as the one casting a transparent veil over the phenomenal world: the closure of truth is at the same time the disclosure of truth.

In the fourth place, the world is seen not only to come about as a result of the split of nāma and rūpa but also to be sustained by nāmarūpa. Both heaven and earth are upheld by a cosmic pillar (the cosmic tree mentioned earlier). Even the movement of the sun leans on this pillar for support. It is both the cosmic pillar that towers up from the bowels of the earth to the pinnacle of the sun, and the cosmic tree that breaks its way down into the earth with its lower roots and pierces up into the heavens with its upper branches. Nāmarūpa brings this divided reality to a unity without forfeiting its dividedness.

In the phenomenal world day alternates with night. When night falls the schism is healed and all is once again restored to a primordial oneness. The effect of this shift from day to night is only temporary, but still it is a time when all distinctions return to a primary unity. When night comes, consciousness (vijñāna) seeks refuge in the cosmic tree, like small birds folding in their wings to nest for the night. The birds perched on the lower branches fly up to the higher branches in the treetops, until at last they soar off into that primordial oneness that transcends the great tree—namely, all its manifestations as nāmarūpa.

As we mentioned briefly in passing earlier, Bultmann has observed the influence of the Gnostic idea of the primordial human in Saint John's account of the incarnation of the original Logos, arguing that in the time before Christ there existed a Gnostic sect in the regions about Palestine in whose traditions we find this theory of a primordial man upheld.[23] There are numerous literary problems that crop up in trying to substantiate this, but from a religious point of view it seems to be a highly plausible assumption.

What I have been attempting here is to classify according to types, rather than systematically to organize, what appears in the Rig Veda as a mere haphazard collection of intuitions. The problem of nāmarūpa (and vijñāna) is also preserved in the Upanishads, as we see for instance in the thought of Yājñavalkya.[24] There the attempt is made, starting from the unity of brahman and ātman, to overcome the division of the world into nāma and rūpa and bring order to it from within. The notion of awakening found there is plainly something held in common with Buddhism.[25] In primitive Buddhism the relationship between name-form and consciousness is rooted in these traditions and draws heavily from their rich storehouses.

·6·

An Existential Interpretation of Dependent Origination

The Questions of the Buddha

As we read in part three of the Aṇguttara-Nikāya ("Gradual Sayings"), the Buddha spent his youth in three palaces within his father's residential quarters built to provide the comforts appropriate to each of the three periods of winter, the rainy season, and summer. In the garden were three ponds, in each of which a different color of lotus blossom flowered. Wherever one went in the palaces, cold, heat, dust, weeds, and fog were nowhere to be found. Such was the white canopy that was spread over his life. During the rainy season the Buddha remained within the palace walls, surrounded by women who entertained him with song and dance. Food and drink were available in overflowing abundance. Verse 38 reads:

> To me, monks, thus blest with much prosperity, thus nurtured with exceeding delicacy, this thought occurred: Surely one of the uneducated manyfolk, though himself subject to [the law of] old age and decay, not having passed beyond old age and decay, when he sees another broken down with age, is troubled, ashamed, disgusted, forgetful that he himself is such a one. Now I too am subject to old age and decay, not having passed beyond old age and decay. Were I to see another broken down with old age, I might be troubled, ashamed, and disgusted. That would not be seemly in me. Thus, monks, as I considered the matter, all pride [mada] in my youth deserted me.
>
> Again, monks, I thought: One of the uneducated manyfolk, though himself subject to [the law of] disease, not having passed beyond disease, when he sees another person diseased, is troubled, ashamed, and disgusted, forgetful that he himself is such a one. Now I too am subject to disease. I have not passed beyond disease. Were I to see

> another diseased, I might be troubled, ashamed, disgusted. That would not be seemly in me. Thus, monks, as I considered the matter, all pride in my health deserted me.
>
> Again, monks, I thought: One of the uneducated manyfolk . . . when he sees another person subject to [the law of] death . . . is disgusted and ashamed, forgetful that he himself is such a one. Now I too am subject to death, I might be troubled. . . . That would not be seemly in me. Thus, monks, as I considered the matter, all pride in my life deserted me.[1]

In this sūtra we find first accounts of the sumptuous life in the three palaces just described and other stories, followed by the Buddha's reflections on old age, sickness, and death. Throughout, the number three serves as a unifying device. But a comparison with the two parallel texts in the Chinese translation leads us to suspect, in the first place, that the first section on the three palaces and the Buddha's reflections on the three sufferings originally formed a separate sūtra that was later arranged into a tripartite pattern when inserted into the Aṅguttara-Nikāya; and secondly that the reflections on the three sufferings that appear in the Pali canon were originally connected immediately with the metrical hymn that follows the text and treats the three forms of pride or arrogance (mada). This passage, verse 39, reads as follows:

> Though subject to disease and eld and death,
> The manyfolk loathes others who are thus.
> Were I to loathe the beings who are thus
> 'Twould be unseemly, living as I do.
> So living, knowing freedom from rebirth,
> I conquered pride of youth and health and life,
> For in release I saw security.
> Then to this very me came energy,
> For I had seen nirvāṇa thoroughly.
> 'Tis not for me to follow sense-desires.
> I'll not turn back. I will become the man
> Who fares on to the God-life as his goal.[2]

If we compare this hymn with the previous prose reflections on the sufferings of old age, sickness, and death, we find it to be permeated by a spirit closer to the way undertaken by the Buddha. Perhaps this sort of hymn came first and the parallel Chinese texts of verses 38 and 39 grew up as a result of differences of emphasis in prose interpretation, or as superficial and profound interpretations of the same passage. In verse 38 we see reflected the mental vitality behind the religious questions of the young Buddha. The Sukhumāla Majjhima-Nikāya links these three reflections to a story from the younger days of the Buddha when he reflected under the rose-apple tree and was transported to the realm of the first dhyāna. In any event, we will not be mistaken in supposing that these questions of the young Buddha took shape as the result of a redaction dating back to an early age, or in connection with the formation of a sūtra based on the material found in verse 38.

Oldenberg considers older than these stories the simpler prose statements:

> In the very flower of his youth, young in years and full of vigor, Gotama the ascetic left his home and went forth into homelessness. Even though his parents set themselves against it and complained with tears and moaning, Gotama the ascetic shaved his hair and beard, donned the saffron robes, and went forth from home to homelessness. . . .
>
> Life at home is stifling; it is an abode of gloominess. Freedom comes with leaving home. With these thoughts the Buddha took leave of his home.[3]

For Oldenberg this prose transmits the experience of the young Buddha's leaving home more faithfully than do the other stories. But the passages he cites do not contradict what is written in verses 38 and 39 referred to above. (The first passage appears in the Mahāpadānasutta of the Dīgha-Nikāya, where it is inserted into the decision of the Buddha to leave the world.) Moreover, both these passages refer not only to the decision of the Buddha but are much more frequently cited in the canon in connection with the decision of disciples to undertake the way of homelessness. We may consider it a good expression, at once generalized and full of feeling, of what those young men felt as they left their homes for homelessness. In the departure of the Buddha they probably saw an archetype that reflected them to themselves.

Oldenberg cannot be credited with having adequately understood the rich religious content of the tale of the Buddha's encounter with old age, sickness, and death recounted in verses 38 and 39. Earlier we indicated in outline how this story developed to stimulate speculations on dependent origination in the Mahāpadānasutta, and in the Ariyapariyesanasutta (Discourse on the Holy Quest) in the Majjhima-Nikāya.[4] Further details I should like to leave for another occasion.

According to Mrs. Rhys Davids, the historical Buddha was not born crown prince of the great King Suddhodana, as legend would have it, but was probably the eldest son of an aristocrat who was no more than one of the local leaders in a small kingdom in northern India, where, on a clear day, the peaks of the Himalayas could be seen, and where a rather democratic form of oligarchy represented the political order. She surmises that in his youth the Buddha had likely led a life of chivalry, characterized by self-control, gallantry, and discipline, rather than, as later descriptions tell us, a life of comfort and sensuality, and that portrayals of him as a youth full of intellectual curiosity were probably transmitted via foreign merchants from distant Western lands (Greece).[5]

We lack literary sources on Greek merchants, but there is a book of dreams recorded in Greek (in a sort of medical book) around the middle of the fourth century before the Christian era that shows the influence of Babylonian and Indian medicine.[6] During Plato's later years it is said that the influence of Indian medicine was to be seen in his Academy, as evidenced for instance in the theory of illness that appears in the *Timaeus*.[7] According to Filliozat, who makes the point, from ancient times up to the beginnings of the Christian era the intellectual exchange between India and Greece, particularly with regard to communication on the medical arts, was far more intimate than we would be led to expect. Jaeger pushes the date of the dream book back another century. Although much depends on one's dating, if we follow Ui in placing the life of the Buddha from around the middle of the fifth century to the fourth century (d. 372), we may suppose that in the region of northern India where the Buddha was born there was an interchange going on between the East and West at the time. This later becomes important in connection with the fact that the technical vocabulary in the Buddha's doctrine of the four holy truths was said to have originally come from medical terminology (a question that we cannot pursue any further here). If we grant that extant Buddhist literary sources, including the very oldest sections of the Pali canon, cannot be traced back to before the time of King Aśoka (273–232 B.C.), it is a matter of no small consequence if we can accept that the theories of Plato and Aristotle can shed light on the question of the four holy truths. The same may also be said with regard to the connection between the skepticism extant at the time of the Buddha and that of Pyrrho of Elis.

Accounts of the Buddha's youth that depict it as a time filled up "only with the enjoyment of women" probably took their start from the passage from the Aṅguttara-Nikāya cited at the beginning of this chapter. The tale of the three palaces and so forth were probably added there in order to provide a sharp contrast point with the three reflections that follow on old age, sickness, and death. The description of the beauty of carnal pleasures for their own sake was something pursued by authors of later biographies of the Buddha.

Old Age, Sickness, and Death

If we omit the first section on the three palaces and restrict our attention to the following part, several important elements can be noted in the reflections on old age, sickness, and death.

First of all, the onslaught of old age, sickness, and death are not seen as mere biological happenings. The young Buddha is gripped by the problems of old age, sickness, and death even as he stands healthy and strong in the full flower of youth. He becomes aware of them as his own problems. He is said to be "troubled." In another text this phrase is rendered as "deviated from himself" or "took leave of himself." The word *attiyati,* which both these terms translate, actually implies an anxiety, a self-torment, a tribulation over some matter. The common element to both translations is the ambivalent attitude that appears, on the one hand, as a *consciousness* filled with anxiety over old age, sickness, and death as one's own problems; and on the other the resultant attempt to shake free of that anxiety, of the obligation to take these problems as one's own, and thus by not making them a problem transfer them to the level of *subconsciousness.* For that reason, when one witnesses these phenomena in others and experiences shameful feelings of anxiety (attiyata harāyati) well up within, one is afflicted with a sense of abhorrence, antipathy, and disgust towards the old age, sickness, and death of another. When this happened to the young Buddha he rejected this attitude of the commonplace individual as inauthentic and "not seemly" for himself. Instead, he turned this attitude inside out, on its head, as it were. In order to bring about what modern philosophy (Heidegger and Jaspers) has referred to as a *vorlaufende Entschlossenheit,* a preliminary resolve or advance religious decision, and in order to awaken the self to its authenticity, from that moment on he determined to pursue to its end the task that old age, sickness, and death had imposed on him.

As physical realities, old age, sickness, and death are not things that can literally be made to disappear merely by denying them, not even in the enlightened state of nirvāṇa. What does happen when the questions of old age, sickness, and death are resolved is that these physical phenomena cease to hold us captive. To take up the task of old age, sickness, and death in a radical way, as a task that leads one along the path to nirvāṇa, is to experience a total conversion from one's former way of living. This is the essence of leaving home and cutting oneself off from the world. This way of living, which entails cutting oneself off from desires, giving up material possessions, and embracing a chaste life (brahma-cariya), means finding in this path to existential awakening the way of absolute truth; it means turning to it and trusting in it, becoming settled in it in a state of non-regression. This much comes out clearly in the metrical hymn of verse 39.

Secondly, old age, sickness, and death are understood as a "law" (dharma) that I myself *am.* They are the limit situations of the human which I myself, in my own solitariness, must take upon myself as my own problems. But to the extent that they are the problems of the individual, they are universally valid for all people.[8]

Old age, sickness, and death must be faced within the condition of impermanence that brings us face to face with the nothingness that is our elemental ground. The primitive Buddhist community of believers were keenly aware of impermanence. The "Flower of Life" chapter of the Dhammapada says:

> Death carries away the one who gathers the flowers of sensuous passions, even as a torrent of rushing waters overflows a sleeping village, and then runs forward on its way.
> And death, the end of all, makes an end of the one who, ever thirsty for desire, gathers the flowers of sensuous passions.[9]

In the Dhammapada, as in other scriptures of primitive Buddhism, impermanence is also likened to a burning fire.[10] Fire, which brings a burning pain to everything it touches, is a particularly fitting image because it represents the relationship between impermanence and suffering in the threefold unity of "impermanence-suffering-anātman." The impermanence of all things, a fundamental tenet of Buddhism, may thus also be expressed in the formula, "Everything burns" (sabbam ādittam). After his enlightenment, the Buddha is said once to have climbed a mountain with his disciples. At that point a fire broke out on an opposite mountain, or perhaps somewhere in the town below. The disciples were thrown into commotion when the Buddha turned to them and said, "Do you think it is only the mountain that is burning? It is not only the mountain that burns, but your eyes that see it as well. Everything is burning. As much that which is seen as that which sees—all burning together. As much that which is heard as that which hears—all burning. . . ."[11]

The Doctrine of the Six Senses

The doctrine just treated brings the problem of impermanence to the core of epistemological reflection on the relationship between our sense organs (eyes, ears, nose, tongue, body, and mind) and their objects (sight-objects, sounds, smells, tastes, touchables, and mind-objects). In order to grasp the original sense behind the way of thinking that we find in the doctrine of the ṣaḍ-āyatana, it is necessary to bring into the picture one further development of the doctrine, the so-called theory of the eighteen worlds. We may line it up as follows:

1	seeing	eyes	sight-objects
2	hearing	ears	sounds
3	smelling	nose	smells
4	tasting	tongue	tastes
5	touching	body	touchables
6	consciousness	mind	mind-objects

This presentation of the elements of sense knowledge goes beyond the simple opposition of the subjective and the objective, of consciousness and its objects, to include the organs of sense as well. Might one not say that this way of thinking is without precedent in the history of Western philosophy, with the exception of Augustine, who tries to portray the structure of knowledge in trinitarian form?

In later interpretations such as Candrakīrti's (c. 600–650) commentary on the Mādhyamika Śāstra, the problem of knowledge is likened to the way things are fashioned by tools, and epistemic connections are explained after the model of the construction of an edifice. But the intent of the doctrine of the six senses, from a standpoint of the custody of the senses (which we treated in chapter 2), is to discipline the object by regulating the perceptual organ that stands between the object and our awareness of it. Thus custody of the eyes (and this goes for the other senses in the eighteen worlds as well) consists in disciplining sight-objects through a posture of "seeing by not-seeing." In the case of the everyday individual, seeing means that the objects of perception are grasped immediately. For such a one, sensation means relating passionately to objects—whether as savory or unsavory—and hence involves an attachment. But where regulation of the senses is possible, one can perceive things as they are, without attachment, like "dew resting on a lotus blossom" or "a mustard seed pierced by the tip of a cobbler's awl."

This is the Indian way of understanding perception that stems from the experience of Yoga. Here the seeing and the seeing eye together are like the look in the eyes of the painter that have become one body with the hand painting on the canvas. This look is inserted into the composition of the painting as a third, autonomous principle between the object being painted and the consciousness of the painter who is painting. The custody of the senses, meantime, is also similar to the look in the eyes of the accomplished painter. One writer has likened this to a certain man and his wife who live in a house on a busy intersection in a large city. Virtually the whole night through there is no end to the din of passing traffic. Now, the wife has a bad heart and this means that the husband must keep constant vigil for the slightest change in her condition. Thus on the one hand he has grown to disregard completely the noises of the street so that he can sleep without disturbance, but on the other hand he has learned to remain sensitive to the slightest stirrings of his wife and wake up at their occurrence.[12]

There it is not necessary, so to speak, to guide the ear or the sounds within the domains of consciousness. It means that one makes the sense function according to command—"Let these particular sounds be announced at once"—like a master telling his maid about how to handle different visitors that show up at the door.

When primitive Buddhism assumes the standpoint of the custody of the senses (indriya-saṃvara) or the holy wisdom of right mindfulness and right thinking (satisamyag-jñāna), it takes as its aim the perfection of that special power of attention that has been refined into something distinctive, something that stands between the object and consciousness of the object. Therefore, as we have noted above in passing, even though this had already been developed previously outside of primitive Buddhism in the Yogic analysis of consciousness and its awareness of the functions of perception and representation, conceptualization, thinking, and ratiocination—for example in the older sections of the Mahābhārata, which Frauwallner argues shows a strain of Yogic thought previous to primitive Buddhism—in the teaching of primitive Buddhism itself this thought took a great stride forward, perhaps as a result of the Buddha's own contemplative experience and stimulated by the epistemology and skepticism of the age. In the pre-Buddhist Yogic theory indriya-saṃvara and satisamyag-jñāna formed a preliminary stage to samādhi, that is, from start to finish both are seen as completely one with and consistent with peace of mind.[13]

Looked at from another angle, a moral spirit (śīla) has been poured into contemplation. For in addition to the internalization of morality in conscience, and its deeper extension into the universal morality of dharma, morality is elevated to the highest peak of religiosity together with contemplation, and as its crowning glory. This is the fundamental standpoint of primitive Buddhism on satisamyag-jñāna, and the doctrine of the six senses and the eighteen worlds is the theory of reflection and praxis that elevates and sublates the commonplace facts of seeing and hearing and so forth from their human everydayness to such religious heights. It is not a question here of mere epistemological reflection. Rather, it deepens reflection to a standpoint that ponders things by lifting up, expanding, and restoring our two-dimensional reflection—which grasps the things we see only in terms of subject and object—to the third dimension of our seeing eye.

Here for the first time the everyday perspective is awakened to as something polluted by what Augustine would call concupiscence. "It is not only the mountain that burns, but your eyes that see it as well." Lurking beneath consciousness, at the bottom of the object and the consciousness that takes the object as its content, at the point that the two touch one another, there lies a fundamental evil that burns ever wider and wider. In Buddhist terms, our definition and discrimination of objects is already an "obstacle to knowing arising from regarding the illusory as real," and a polluted "will to will" at one with avidyā is at work there. Mere obstructions wrought by kleśa do not constitute avidyā. It is the obstruction of knowing that is the birthplace of avidyā. The obstruction wrought by kleśa in the form of an objectifying way of looking needs therefore to be seen as a fire smoldering beneath the ashes and capable of flaring up again at any moment.

The theory of the six senses really has to do with calling the unreflective commonplace individual back to religious reflection, like the turning of a revolving stage. A more exhaustive treatment of this question in Buddhist terms will have to await another occasion, when I plan to treat the eighth link of the twelvefold causal chain: contact (sparśa). Now, when we liken the doctrine of the six senses to a revolving stage, it is the sense of impermanence that provokes the rotation. To an epistemological way of thinking, in order for thought to focus on the object in general, it is enough for consciousness to withdraw into itself and arrive at consciousness in general. But in the case of religious awareness, the awakening of each individual person is necessary in order that the individual things that exist be made into an existing totality and then be seen as this totality that they are. It is the sense of impermanence that brings this about.

Impermanence and Sympathy

To the primitive Buddhist way of thinking, it is in the feeling of impermanence that "everything" exists as an "everything." Put in terms easy to understand, in the notion of sympathy that Japanese circumscribes with the phrase *mono no aware* (the pathos of things) the totality of existence is enveloped in a single feeling. This sympathy both gives a specific form to the impermanence that draws all of existence into one (*sym-*), and at the same time contains an awareness of my own finitude and impermanence (*pathos*). To illustrate its specific form, let us cite a poem from the medieval Japanese monk and poet Saigyō:

> Pathos in body, not mind—
> Snipes rising up from a swamp in autumn nightfall.

Imagine a swamp or a pond in autumn. The darkness of night grows thicker and thicker, when all of a sudden there is a flutter of wings as a flock of snipes fly up and away. What happens, happens only here and just this once. The whole scene lasts but a few seconds and one has no idea where the birds came from nor where they went to. It is but a line drawn for a moment across my field of vision as I stand in the semi-darkness, and then quickly vanished. Merely that and nothing more.

What is more, the whole desolation of an autumn eventide is concentrated for me in this one event. The sound of the flapping wings intensifies the wordless silence, and the peak of quiet is reached in that one point of movement. And I, too, am *moved* by the event: I become the point at which that entire feeling-laden landscape constellates. At such times, however, the opposite way of thinking is likely to occur: the idea that the feeling of sympathy is not originally the pathos *of things* but a pathos *of the subject,* a private feeling-tone that I impose on things. One must beware of making this mistake. The sympathy that I sense is a self-expression of the universe and existence as a whole. My "sense" (*Stimmung*) discloses a "disposition" (*Bestimmung*) that belongs to things as part of their original nature.

Only when we see that "Everything burns" do world and ego revert to a more basic and elemental mode of being, the mode of being of burning, which precedes the opposition of subject and object; only then do world and ego become true questions of "everything." To take up an earlier image from the Dhammapada, when the waters of a flood overwhelm a village, the entire order of the town (the totality of relationships that assigns each thing its place within the town) is being caught up in the whirlpool along with me—I and Thou, people and houses, roads and bridges, trees and forests. This, too, leads us to see that the discrimination of subject and object that sets the two in opposition to each other stems originally from a feeling of their oneness in impermanence; that the world of the subject-object opposition arises from a self-awareness twisted by the fact that the feeling of impermanence is reflected in the mirror of reason. It is as if the feeling of oneness that lies at the base of the world were stood upright like a misplaced partition.

We usually consider epistemological reflection as an adequate way of reflecting on the subject and the object. But, as we noted earlier, when we take a closer look at things we see how this reflection itself is impeded from becoming a rational experience insofar as it does not include the fundamental experience of seeing things in their impermanence. In terms of primitive Buddhism's ideas on thinking, the object is constituted in a process of thinking bound to the more concrete, immediate, and sensible form that entities assume as composite configurations of color and shape: rūpa. The conditions of rūpa become clear from the root meaning of the verb *ruppati,* "to be broken," "to suffer from a fever," "to be pestered" (by snakes, mosquitos, or the like). The noun *rūpa* always carries this original sense of a painful situation indicated by the verb. This is what is implied in the comment, "There is rūpa because there is inner affliction." Modern scholars may resist the etymological derivation, but there is a profound insight to be seen here in primitive Buddhism.

Everything flows. For the subject that clings obstinately to something and refuses to let it go—and equally so for things that are not allowed to pass even though it is in their nature to pass—its rūpa becomes a hindrance and an affliction. But it is precisely from this sort of structured relationship, namely, from the whirlpool of hindrances and afflictions, that the phenomenal form of anything is constituted objectively, as a turnabout from these conditions, as a non-temporal object that transcends the flow of impermanence and is rightly rendered by the word *rūpa.* The epistemological opposition of subject and object is simply a neutralizing of the profound discord that obtains on the dimension of attachment by introjecting it onto the face of consciousness.

In order to clarify the point, I may perhaps be forgiven for indulging in a personal memory. One evening during the war I was at Kyoto Station seeing a friend off, a Mr. K., who was on his way home and to the front. Though we had already arrived at the platform, we kept ourselves engaged in small talk. We both knew well enough that we should probably never meet again, our hearts were filled with sadness at the parting, and we each knew that the other felt the same. Neither of us wanted to make the farewell a painful one for the other. But when the train began to pull away from the station, K. opened the window and leaned out in my direction, taking a firm grip on my hands. His eyes reached out and took hold of mine. Face to face, our hands locked together, I ran along the platform in pace with the train as it picked up speed. Finally our hands broke free and he took his leave waving furiously. I stood there dumbfounded and unable to move, watching the taillights of the train fade off into the distance.

Something from that experience sank roots in me. Clinging to things that pass through our lives and take their leave is a hindrance and an affliction. Had I held on to K.'s hand forever and not let go, both K. and I would have been wounded. And yet had I simply avoided his hand from the start, and he mine, that, too, would have made us prisoners of our own refusal. When I grasp his hand, I must grasp it firmly, and when I let go, I must do so resolutely. To know the right interval of time between the grasping and the letting go, is that not the very crux of the union of affirmation and negation that guides the brush of the painter? The hand that paints and the eye that sees work together as one. The special look in the eyes of the painter is his power of sight, and through the contact that takes place among his consciousness of seeing, his power of sight, and rūpa (the object or model that is being painted onto the canvas), there is established that particular realm of the vedanā (feeling), which is the painting, the artistic beauty.

My intention in progressing from a personal memory to the example of art was to offer a prelude to the treatment of religion without going into a detailed discussion of the relationship and essential differences between artistic intuition and religious experience. But a moment's further thought on the painter's intuition should serve as a clue to further reflection on the forms in which things appear to us. What we have to see is a more concretely existential way of knowing, one closer to existence itself than the approach by way of objective objects that we will to know.

Take for example a tree standing alongside a road that I walk each day. I always look at the tree in the same way and the tree always appears to me in the same shape and form. Maybe everyone who passes it by sees it the same way that I do. But, as Bergson has noted, when a painter sets about to paint the tree it reveals an aspect of its original life that is unique to that tree and none other. Perhaps this is a manifestation of the creative reality of the tree that corresponds to creative intuition. Bergson likens the standpoint of science, by way of contrast, to a horse with blinders that draws a carriage along a road without being able to see what it passes. If we recall the way we draw stereotypes from our fund of everyday habits and conventions in order to manage the practical tasks we continually meet with—like turning knobs to open doors—we see that this is in fact a pragmatic attitude of negotiating encounters with things that science and everydayness share in common. And so it happens that even though I encounter this tree every day, I have never really encountered it even once. We assume that our everyday way of negotiating with things is realistic, and that the artistic encounter is more a matter of fantasy. But from the standpoint of religion and art, the reality of the situation is precisely the other way around.

In order to get a clearer picture of the essence of science and common sense we may turn to a vehicle of a more modern sort than the horse and carriage that Bergson uses. Imagine an automobile whose windshield is one gigantic mirror turned in the direction of the driver's seat. The things that pass by in the present of the driver are only seen reflected in the mirror as the past that has been left behind, and in reflecting the past to the present the mirror shields the driver's sight from the present into the future. This is precisely the way human reason works. The totality of these reflections projected in the mirror of reason follow the laws of perspective in making their way to my here and now as I sit in the seat of the present. The centerpoint of the here and now, from which the entire expanse of that perspective on the past opens up to me, thus shifts as the car advances forward, and at the same time the perspective gets wider and wider, the background deeper and deeper. In this way the face of the mirror takes in the new things that appear one after the other and unifies them into the totality of a world of reflected images present before the driver's seat, with the most recently arrived images serving as a focal point for the unification and synthesis of the whole. The arrival of each new image is really like a homecoming because, with the forward advance of the vehicle, the various things that approach the present of the car from the future—automobiles coming from the opposite direction, the sycamores that line the road, people, the storefronts—flip around and are taken back in again by the hemispheric windshield mirror, where they are re-presented. The things that passed by before in terms of temporal progression are those that appear farther back in terms of spatial perspective, and they continue to grow smaller and smaller as they recede into the distance of the past. In general, the size of things corresponds exactly to their importance for the seat of the present.

What lies ahead in the future for the blindfolded car is blocked and obscured from view, though one might think it possible to steer one's way into the future by having recourse to the reflected images and projecting the line that reaches from the past to the present along the road that the car has so far traveled farther ahead. The road itself stretches out ahead into the future, true enough, but the ability to project its direction from the past is limited to those cases where the road is straight and level, and where there happens to be nothing coming at one head-on from out of the future. In other words, so long as one does not collide with the reality of history, and so long as the curves and bumps in the road that mark the destinies of history are all absent, the sort of control accessible to the realms of abstract or scientific knowledge, or validated by the customs and conventions of common sense, is possible.

The real world, in the proper sense of things that come at us from the future, is obstructed from view precisely because of the mirror spread out before the driver's seat reflecting the face of things arrived from the past. Those who sit there project themselves as well onto the surface of the mirror and confirm that "the self is a self." They presume that everything is to be weighed and measured from the focal point of their own here and now. The things that get represented here—the self and objective existence—are re-presentations, the exact reverse of the present that is moving into the future. All we have is the homecoming of things from the present perfect.

Making truly present objects that have been represented as re-presentations is what people like artists and poets cudgel their brains to achieve. Artistic intuition, though it does not cease thereby to lean on intuition, seeks to obtain a fullness of meaning qualitatively different from the perceptual data of knowledge. The painter strives to achieve the actuality of intuition prior to images that have been brought home and made to appear in the mirror of the past. Once we have understood this, it is easier to appreciate the preoccupation of the existential phenomenologists with the meaning of the "primary field." Merleau-Ponty, for example, includes one of Matisse's paintings of a bathing maiden in his *L'Oeil et l'Esprit* by way of illustration. The painting is simplicity itself but brings to the present the essence of the beauty of an undefiled maiden. We see her breathing and moving, but at the same time we see the movement of the painter's brush, which has not been left out of the painting. We are brought to a halt in the actual presence of beauty, which is the supreme moment in painting a picture. In depicting the essence of the maiden, Matisse has at the same time painted for us what a painting is.

The reality of artistic intuition is not the intuition of representational knowledge. The latter, to cite an earlier example, stops with the reality of the taillights on the caboose that has passed by. But the aim of this sort of art is to break down and redirect the work of attention and will that cooperate in the construction of objective reality and their disposition into the framework of memory, and once more to let these representations loose on the primary field. Here beauty and truth and holiness live life authentically.

In the conditions of the present world we find ourselves in, it has become impossible for philosophy or theology to fulfill their salvific roles adequately—even in the case of thinkers of formidable personality and profound insight, however inspiring they might otherwise be. In such an age there is no denying the appeal that art has to the feelings as a substitute for religion, especially for those men and women of our age who enjoy a rich intellectual life.

And yet no matter how close art seems to approach the Absolute, it remains a realm that is in a sense the exact opposite of religion. The primary realm of life that artists and phenomenologists strive to approach is, from their point of view, the world of absolute truth and beauty. But when one understands the co-dependency in such a world as a co-dependency of "vijñāna and nāmarūpa," it reveals itself as something bound by a straitjacket woven of avidyā and saṃskāra. Only when co-dependence becomes a non-dependence by seeing through this state of affairs is it able to effect a leap away from its causal ground and truly enter into the realms of religion.

So far we have taken our lead from sympathy to explain what is meant by *religious impermanence.* This approach involves an interpretation that is much closer to the way things are than the Abhidharma approach, which views impermanence merely as the continual change and destruction going on in objective things in analogy to the process of movement and becoming. In primitive Buddhism, however, the forms of impermanence are explained less in terms of the obstructions to knowing that arise from taking the illusory as real, which we have described above, than in terms that place the accent on opening one's eyes to the elemental ground of the hindrances of worldly passions that accumulate at the base of consciousness. The fire of impermanence in which everything burns is also the fire of desire. The following section will attempt to treat impermanence from this angle.

Impermanence and Arrogance

In the Suttanipāta the analogy is taken up of a strong wind blowing out a fire. Obviously here the fire is meant to represent the kleśa, or worldly passions, while nirvāṇa is the state of the fire being snuffed out. There are numerous such cases where fire refers to the three fires of desire, hate, and stupidity or to the fire of worldly passions. Seen from this angle, the words *Everything burns* point to the need to rethink the opposition between subject and object from the viewpoint of attachment and desire. "Burning" is a form of impermanence, and, conversely, this form of impermanence is the flickering of the flames of desire. Within this conflagration I pursue the object of my desire and set it afire in realizing that desire; and, conversely, the object lures me in and stirs up my feelings of desire. This is also implied in the notion of "burning." Hence in the image "Everything burns" the form of impermanence and the form of desire are brought together in an extremely profound manner. The theory of twelvefold dependent origination is an attempt to get down to the root causes of this two-way relationship within the human. The links that appear at the beginning, in the middle, and at the end of the chain of dependent origination show this well (avidyā . . . lust and clinging . . . old age and death).

In the passage from the Dhammapada cited earlier, death is understood as a matter of fate that attacks one suddenly and from without. In the reflections of the Buddha on old age, sickness, and death in the Aṅgut tara-Nikāya, also referred to above, these questions are understood as universal facts of human finiteness, and at the same time they are seen as a task in that one must seek the path to overcoming them. Death is the uncertain certitude, and in order to accept that fact one must, in an act of preliminary resolve, overturn the everyday mode of being of the self from the ground up, bringing the future of death to actuality in the present and allowing its questions and problems to flow pure and transparent through the very midst of the promise of youth. In fact, by the time old age, sickness, and death arrive as physical realities it may already be too late. It is said that one winter's morning the Buddha happened to pass an old man and his wife warming themselves on the roadside with a fire made of dried cow dung and whiling away their time, whereupon he instructed his disciples that the path that leads directly to enlightenment was already closed off to such as these. As the well-known counsel of the Buddha says, "Everything is impermanent—so be diligent!"

What is more, people all too often scamper about from one escape to another in order to avoid, for the time being, becoming resolved to the task. Events that might otherwise bring the problem to light are shunted one after the other, or projected onto others in the attempt to coat oneself over with a thin varnish of authenticity. I may be rich and young now, healthy and full of the pride of life, but my original condition is one of limitation. I am no less liable to the limits of old age, sickness, and death than are others, and sooner or later there will be no escaping the fact. At any moment these things might reach out and take hold of one, perhaps in the very midst of one's quest for youth and health and the joie de vivre, perhaps during a dormant moment between passions, perhaps even at this very moment. Old age, sickness, and death are the very ground of my reality, my human being. They *are* my human being itself.

The reason that I see this in others and keep it from touching me as my own affair is that I take the posture of being somehow uniquely privileged, or that such a posture actually inspires in me the illusion of being so privileged. This is why I feel disgust, antipathy, and abhorrence when I see another who is aged or sick or dying, like a rich man looking down scornfully at a poor beggar. But all of us know well enough that no one, however it be, is possessed of such a special privilege. Where death is concerned, the rich and the poor, the old and the young, the wise and the fools, the strong and the weak, all are absolutely equal.

In the end I know that whatever I might have done to escape my fate, death waits for me at the bottom of everything. The road to death is where my very human being points me. This road to underlying death is for me at once a road of radical denial and a road of radical affirmation. Death is the negation of my self; it is my downfall. And yet, as we explained in the previous chapter, to set one's foot to this road resolutely and tread it to the end (like Hegel's *zu-Grunde-gehen,* going to the ground), is at the same time a leap up from the bottom, a transition from ground to existential reality, a transcendence from denial to affirmation. It is when I am not up to the task and trouble myself over it that I stand arrogantly in front of the old age, sickness, and death of others.

For the Buddha the word *mada* (arrogance) combines the senses of pride and inebriation. It is like one who has become intoxicated, beside oneself with the vitality of youth.

One may liken the Buddha's reflections on mada to the treatment of the anxiety before death found in the existential philosophy of Heidegger, for whom the escape from anxiety is itself a sign of anxiety; or to Kierkegaard, who sees not-despairing as itself a form of despair. Kierkegaard distinguishes between a standpoint where one tries through despair not to be oneself, and a standpoint where one tries through despair to be oneself, and then finally reduces the former to the latter. Something similar is present in the general interpretation of desire and burning thirst found in the discussion of the sixth link of the twelvefold causal chain of dependent origination, namely, lust, or taṇhā. First sensual lust is spoken of in its ordinary sense, but then a distinction is drawn between lust for being and lust for nothingness. At the root of the various worldly passions of sensual lust there is an attachment to being and survival whose motto is "there is aye life for a living man." Thus, as Aristotle also notes, a merchant will cast overboard all the goods that he went to such pain and toil to acquire if it means saving his life in a storm at sea. But when the attachment to being and survival is brought to despair, or when it seems that life has lost all meaning, the attachment to being is transformed into an attachment to nothingness. In that case human suffering swings from an attachment to being to an attachment to nothingness, and then back again to an attachment to being. Despair is a sickness of the heart that catches one up in a whirlpool that casts one about from a despair of weakness to a despair of strength and back again.

The conjecture that the roots of human suffering thus lie in the attachment that accompanies lust, and that lust consists of desire, the attachment to being, and the attachment to nothingness,[14] is based on an insight into that deep dimension referred to above where impermanence and worldly passions are interlocked with each other.

Heidegger's notion of "being toward death" offers a keen analysis from the standpoint of existential philosophy of the anxiety felt before death and the attempt to escape death in the spiritual condition of modern times. But at the same time, Martin Buber is correct in pointing to the abstractness of this analysis insofar as Heidegger's "being toward death" ignores human relationships—the I-Thou relationship in particular—and his notion of preliminary resolve restricts itself to the problem of the individual.[15] While Buber acknowledges the considerable achievement of Heidegger's existential analysis of anxiety in the face of death, he argues that what Heidegger is treating is not the problem of life and death as it is faced by real people: he studies the structure of experience by first applying a tourniquet to its veins. Buber would probably argue that the true locus of reality is to be found at the point that the I-Thou relationship is realized, and that the problem of death must also be treated from this locus.

By the same token, however, the problem of death is not clarified if we restrict ourselves to Buber's I-Thou—even if we take his *Urdistanzierung* (original distance) and *In-Beziehungtreten* (entering into relationship) as principles of human existence. Perhaps the converse needs also to be considered, as Jaspers would say, that only with the "death of one's neighbor" (the Thou)[16] does the I-Thou relationship reach its fulfillment in love. Heidegger's *Mitsein* (being-with), which he sees as the existential stage of the I-Thou, is an important notion, but from the locus of everydayness, the "one" referred to when I say "someone dies" or "someone says" has only a privative meaning and does not fulfill the positive role that the Thou does. At the same time, if there is no bond to begin with, there is ultimately no possibility of establishing a bond with an other (or awakening an other to existential reality). If one had no experience of sleep, one would have no idea of what it would be to awaken an other from sleep after awakening oneself. If the Buddha had achieved complete enlightenment all at once without the mediation of a "preliminary awakening," all the efforts that the Buddha exerted to bring about a doctrine of salvation would have no way of touching human inauthenticity. We need to keep in mind that in the young Buddha's experience of "arrogance," the problem of an enlightenment from inauthenticity to authenticity was immediately understood as the relationship of an I and a Thou (the other) and involved a connection between self-awakening and the awakening of the other.

In existential philosophy the everyday individual who makes no effort to inquire into the problem of the death of the self gets buried instead in a commonplace life where relations to others are governed by rumor and appearances. But the concrete form of arrogance does not by itself establish a connection between anxiety and the other. For Kierkegaard the relationship to a Thou involved here is restricted to the relationship to an Absolute Other (God) wherein despair—as a decision made vis-à-vis this Other—must be presumed to lie at the ground of the self, even if only unconsciously. The concreteness of the Buddha's awakening, however, consists in the fact that it takes anxiety over old age, sickness, and death as the preliminary resolve of religious existentiality, and that it comprehends the freeing from anxiety in the concreteness of the inauthentically human world of I-Thou.

The Buddha's Departure from the Four Castle Gates

The Pali canon recounts that as the young Buddha reflected on how unsuitable the response of arrogance was for him, and as he set out on the path that was to carry him beyond the self that is liable to old age, sickness, and death, perversion with all its accompanying manifestations was wiped away. In the poetry of verse 39 from the Aṅguttara-Nikāya cited earlier in the chapter, the departure of the Buddha from home seems to be presented in such a way as to lead him directly into nirvāṇa, but the wider context shows that this was only a preliminary conversion of the Buddha—namely, the point at which the religious question first came to light in him—and did not entail an immediate arrival at enlightenment. The various forms that this religious question assumed were unfolded one after another and this unfolding represents his advance along the way of the religious quest. To ask a question does not immediately imply an answer. The way the Buddha had to walk to find the answer to his question still spread out far ahead of him.

As Oldenberg rightly points out, the Mahāpadānasutta in the Dīgha-Nikāya is a further evolution of the legend of the three palaces found in the Aṅguttara-Nikāya, where the questions of the Buddha are raised. As noted earlier, in place of the young Sakyamuni, another Buddha (Vipassin) is recounted as asking the questions in the Mahāpadānasutta. Protected from the sorrows and tribulations of life, Vipassin passed his days in the pleasures and enjoyments of the five desires[17] in the three palaces. Then one day, during an outing in the country, he chanced to meet an old man on the road. Learning that he himself was liable to the law of old age and could not get around it, he laments: "Shame then verily be upon this thing called birth [jāti], since to one born old age shows itself like that!"[18] On the next occasion when he meets a sick man, and after that a corpse, the same reflection is repeated. Last of all he meets a monk who has left home, and after speaking with him comes to the decision to leave home himself.

Kanakura Enshō argues that when the Mahāpadānasutta was composed, the facts of the life of the historical Buddha himself were still within living memory of the people of the time, which made it difficult to idealize him too abruptly and exalt his story into a miracle tale of the savior of the world. Thus a former Buddha was chosen in his stead, and in this way a stereotyped image of the Buddha came to take shape and stories came to be transmitted about the conditions of his birth, his life in the three palaces, his departure from home into homelessness, and so forth.[19] In my own view, the reason that sūtras that explain the ninefold and tenfold doctrines of dependent origination and end with the co-dependency and correlatedness of nāmarūpa and vijñāna also speak of the causal kinship of former Buddhas is that fifty years after the death of the Buddha, precisely at the time that the doctrine of the ninefold and tenfold doctrines were being formed, the veneration of former Buddhas mushroomed throughout the whole of India (taking into account, of course, the time that would be required for this to occur) in response to the religious and social needs of the time. As there is not time here to enter into the specific arguments required to support that contention, I only mention it in passing.

In later narrations of the life of the Buddha (where, of course, it is Gotama the Buddha himself who is spoken of), the four events of the encounters with old age, sickness, death, and the homeless monk are depicted as departures from each of the four portals of his residence—the eastern, the western, the northern, and the southern—and have therefore come to be known collectively as the "Buddha's departure from the four castle gates." This story and the ensuing account of the Buddha's departure from home into homelessness represent the parts of the Buddha's life to which later narrators have directed their greatest efforts.

From the point of view of their meaning as religious symbols, the encounter of the young Buddha with old age, sickness, and death, and his religious resolve to renounce the world in order to seek an answer to the questions they prompted in him, are of the highest importance, and their transmission in dramatized narrations of the Buddha's life have made a deep and lasting impression on the common people. They also proved a seedbed of suggestiveness for later Buddhism, as we see for instance in the biographies of famous monks from the late Heian period into the Kamakura period (or roughly the period from the middle ninth to the early fourteenth century).

In the Buddhist lands of contemporary Southeast Asia as well—for example, in Thailand—when a young man decides to leave home and to enter a neighboring Buddhist temple to lead the life of a monk for a fixed period, the event is associated with the Buddha's departure from home into homelessness. Like Crown Prince Siddhartha, the young man mounts a canopied horse and rides out of the village while his friends and relatives bid him farewell. As a rite of initiation, it is adapted to that one particular Buddhist society, but the spiritual dynamism of the story of the Buddha is visible throughout.

One of the distinctive traits of biographical accounts of the life of the Buddha is that they lend a great deal of concreteness to the process through which religious questions came to take shape within the Buddha's own experience. In the case of Jesus or Paul or Peter, we lack sufficient information from the scriptures to know what individual problems preceded their conversions. It is, rather, through a figure like Francis of Assisi that the Christian spirit took root in the Western world among ordinary people. In Saint Francis for the first time the questions of old age, sickness, and death took hold and permeated the whole being. Through his biography we are able to trace the entire process by which these questions came to fashion a unique religious spirit out of the struggles of young Francis with the pride of youth. There we can observe concretely how the entire course of his life gradually led him to forsake his home and renounce the world, just as the Buddha had done. The image of the saint from Assisi has left an indelible mark on the Christian religious spirit that the years have not erased.

It is now thought, however, that Saint Francis may have read a modified version of the life of the Buddha in the legend of Barlaam and Josaphat that had been composed in Greek in the eighth century and transmitted westwards to Europe as a Christian tale.[20] From there the formulation of the religious question and the renunciation of the world as a solution to that question that we find in Saint Francis inspired a great number of believers to follow in his footsteps after his death. Foucher argues that if one takes into consideration the concrete conditions in which they lived, the biography if Ignatius of Loyola turns out to be still closer to the life of the Buddha than Francis of Assisi's is.[21] In many religious conversions the example of idealized religious personalities is often imitated unconsciously, and we are well aware how such typical conversions can serve as what modern religious psychologists call "archetypes" for the process of religious development. In this sense, as a religious paradigm the departure of the Buddha from the four castle gates, which is present not only in Buddhist lands but even in the Western world, can also be seen as a sort of riverbed along which the living waters of religiosity flow.

Now, as we noted above, the story of the departure from the four castle gates that appears in the Mahāpadānasutta is ascribed to Vispassin Buddha, a former Buddha who preceded Gotama the Buddha historically. Of course, one would presume that the emergence of belief in former Buddhas came *after* the time of Gotama the Buddha. However, according to the Dharma Inscriptions of King Aśoka, which may well be the oldest literary source of primitive Buddhism we have, the king is said to have made a personal pilgrimage to the stūpa (tomb) of a former Buddha, Kongama Buddha; and at important points in the scriptures of primitive Buddhism, we have argued, the teachings of the Buddha are represented as recovery of ancient moral principles, as is the case with the doctrines of dependent origination, the four noble truths, and the noble eightfold path, of which it is stressed that they recapitulate the way of ancient saints and sages. If that is so, we may possibly conclude, with Schayer and others,[22] that there existed ancient transmissions dating back to a time before the historical Buddha and since lost that from quite early on may have been linked to the tradition of four, seven, or ten former Buddhas. At all events, the idea of dependent origination flows like a great stream whose course once led it into that vast lake known as the Buddha—and out again.

·7·

Freeing and the World Beyond

The Problem of Secularization

I once had the privilege of hearing Arnold Toynbee lecture on the problem of dealing with population concentration in the cities. I had never met the famous historian, and I remember attending with the idea of getting a good look at him. As it turned out, his remarks provided me with a number of valuable and helpful insights as he addressed the impact that massive concentrations of population have on the human spirit. At the time, the issue of pollution had not achieved the widespread attention that we give it today, and Toynbee was able to focus on how patterns of urban demography are capable of distorting our idea of the human. Today our priorities have been reversed, and all the recognition accorded the pollution problem in the cities of the world has turned our eyes away from what is an even greater threat to our humanity. We are still without a clue as to how the questions Toynbee raised might be solved, and the problem keeps getting bigger all the time.

Our seismologists are sensitive to the slightest alterations in the earth's crust, and formidable amounts of energy are directed to predicting possible earthquakes and warning us of approaching calamities. But when it comes to the cracks and depressions that show up in the human spirit, it is as if everyone had decided to ignore the signs of danger until the full catastrophe should be upon us. In the same way, it may well be that our greatest complicity in the pollution problem is that we have steered the issue away from the spiritual dimension that Toynbee was speaking from in order to focus on its physical aspects.

No doubt some will dismiss Toynbee's remarks as the fanciful musings of a historian. But the impression I came away with was of having encountered a true historian, one cut of the same cloth as Albert Schweitzer, whose study of past history had enabled him greatly to expand his range of vision into the future. There was another reason for my receptivity to Toynbee's ideas that day: I had just returned from a stay in the United

States, where the problem of urban population had already reached grave proportions.

At about the same time, Harvard theology professor Harvey Cox's *Secular City* (1965) was arousing great interest both within and without theological circles. In no time it became a *cause célèbre* and the center of considerable controversy, part of which has been recorded in *The Secular City Debate* (1966). I shall have to come back to this later, but in broad outline the problem of the secular city comes down to this: The concentration of population in the big cities, particularly in the United States, has brought about a situation in which clusters of urban centers—for instance, cities along the eastern seaboard, from Boston through New Haven, New York, Philadelphia, and even as far as Washington, D.C.—show signs of fusing eventually into a continuous chain, transforming the individual cities into a single megalopolis and thus manifoldly expanding the patterns of urban culture. The question is, what becomes of religion in such circumstances? The most fundamental problem, it has been said, is that religion in such a society becomes secularized. With the secularization of culture as a whole, the underlying social structure itself becomes secularized, as a result of which religious phenomena come to take on a different meaning. For example, when the distinction and opposition between the sacred and the profane, long considered to be the most elemental of religious categories, are eroded, things once held sacred, like religious ceremonies, lose all their meaning.

In such a secularized society, religion cannot long maintain its old forms, no matter how hard it tries. The current of secularization is too strong and too rapid. As a result, the significance of church buildings, holy days, and so forth experiences an abrupt shift. In the midst of such secularization how can cities survive? How can religion and, in particular for the West, Christianity survive? That is the problem.

A few years earlier John Robinson's *Honest to God* (1963) had tackled the problem from a similar point of view. Taking the familiar expression in its literal sense of "being sincere in one's relationship with God," Robinson sought a standpoint from which contemporary men and women might be able to recover honesty with God. The work had a tremendous impact and went on to become the best-selling theological work of the century. It was followed in the same year by *The Honest to God Debate,* which contained the reactions of a number of scholars to the work.

Nowadays shifts in theological fashion take place quickly; changes occur almost overnight, like new hairstyles or the rise and fall of hemlines. But the significance of the problem that Bishop Robinson posed in that book remains. One might even compare his book to a flower blooming out of season, before its time. One flower blooms, and others quickly follow. It is not so much a question of the depth of thought as a change in the spiritual climate itself.

Among the articles collected in *The Honest to God Debate* is one by Rudolf Bultmann, who also published a separate appraisal of Robinson's idea.[1] Although written in response to Robinson's book, Bultmann's reflections are more important on the level of ideas than the work they comment on. It is worth our while, therefore, to look at how Bultmann evaluates the problem that Robinson introduced.

From the very outset Robinson addresses himself to the great change that the idea of God has undergone in the minds of modern people. Traditionally God had been thought of as dwelling "in heaven," somewhere "up there." But once the modern mind had come to see the earth as a globe spinning on its own axis and rotating on its own course in space, the distinction between "up there" and "down here" lost its absolute meaning. Thus the idea of God had also to change. His existence could no longer be situated *up* there, but *out* there, somewhere outside of the earth. The transcendence of God underwent a change of directions from the heavens above to outer space. With the change from a Ptolemaic, geocentric model to a Copernican, heliocentric one, the notion of the "beyond" or the "out there" became central, and the symbolism of a God above lost its moving power.

When we stop to think carefully about the images we have of the transcendent today, however vague they may be, and on the commonsense conceptions of the transcendent, we can hardly help acknowledging that there is something to them, even though we may feel wary of swallowing them whole. Robinson's contention, however, is that the notion of the transcendent in contemporary thinking—assuming that we can really conceive of it at all today—has so altered that it can no longer be adequately expressed in the traditional word *transcendence.* For in its metaphysical sense (at least in modern philosophy) the transcendent is regarded as something that surpasses the actual sensible world, as aligning itself with one of the poles in the opposition between the yonder shore (the intellectual, the rational) and the hither shore (the sensual, the material); but for people today, this sort of beyondness is rapidly losing its meaning.

In fact, Robinson is not alone in taking such a view. The influence of Paul Tillich is so strong in his work that he has even been criticized for being too Tillichean. At several points, his idea of God can indeed be traced back to Tillich's systematic theology. The real reason that Robinson's ideas caused such a stir lay in the fact that his outspoken and provocative statements were coming from a bishop occupying an important see in London. The more we look at his ideas, the more we find that there is not really much that is new in them. In fact, in addition to the influence of Tillich and Bultmann, Bonhoeffer's thought is also in evidence. We shall return to that later.

The religious editor of the *New York Times* met Tillich shortly before the theologian's death to sound him out on these questions, and from there went to Germany to interview the elder, but still hale, giants Barth and Bultmann; finally he crossed over to England to meet Robinson and several other religious figures. With all the skill and engaging style of a journalist, he gathered his findings into an extremely interesting book, *The New Theologian,* which may be taken as a valuable general introduction to the subject.[2] As he mentioned in his book, the problematics treated there gave rise in the United States to the idea of the "Death of God," which initiated a new trend in theology that has even made its way to Japan. This current of thought contains a great many problems that merit studying in their own right. One of these, to which we shall return later in passing, is the question of how this theology differs from European atheism or nihilism and at which points it reveals its distinctive American flavor. In *The Secular City,* Cox deliberately left the problem of atheism aside in order to approach the problem of the meaning of religion in a modern, secularized world from an entirely new angle. In later works, however, Cox appeals to the atheism of Ernst Bloch to underpin his own ideas.[3] But these and other questions we shall have to leave aside here.

This World and the World Beyond

Bultmann's appeal to "demythologizing" as a method for interpreting the Bible dates from the end of the Second World War and is by now well known. Taking the world view of the New Testament as a prime example, he shows how in the Bible the world is presented as consisting of three layers: the celestial realm, the underworld, and the human world. (Robinson takes this up in his references to a three-story or triple-decker universe.) Now, the New Testament posits such a universe on the belief that within such a structure the human world is frequently visited by suprahuman powers from the celestial realm or the underworld. Thus, to take one example, it is believed that human illness is the work of evil spirits from the netherworld. According to Bultmann, the New Testament assumes that world view as self-evident, but this does not mean that it should be assumed as part of the content of faith on which modern men and women should base their lives.[4]

A similar progression of thought is to be found in Robinson. But unlike Bultmann, Robinson is not satisfied merely with removing the mythical constructions of an outdated world view. He stresses the point that in each age the scientific-philosophical world view and the conception of God (or the transcendent) must be made to correspond to each other in a positive manner. In his commentary on Robinson, Bultmann expresses agreement on this point and from there goes on to develop, from his own standpoint and in the light of the atheism of Nietzsche and Heidegger, his view of how our modern idea of God has changed.

I am convinced that, *mutatis mutandis,* all of this applies to Shin Buddhism today as it faces the question of how to conceive of the beyondness of the "Pure Land Paradise in the West." Moreover, the question of what this Pure Land Paradise and its transcendence (expressed in the *shihō-rissō*[5]) can mean for the modern mind from the standpoint of Shin faith needs to be reexamined in a novel and contemporary manner.

Robinson frankly confesses that he himself, as a modern man, cannot take seriously the idea of a God "up there." Accordingly, he sets out to rethink what it might mean to proclaim that God is "in heaven" or that God is "transcendent." Leaning heavily on Tillich, he concludes that as a transcendent being, God, as it were, transcends in the direction of the depths of the human spirit rather than transcending in an outer direction. In so doing, he aligns himself with Tillich in seeking to see God as the "ground of being."

To Tillich's existential-ontological way of thinking, God is, on the one hand, the dark but creative "deeper layer" that lies within human self-awareness and embraces the realm of the unconscious—including what Jung calls the collective unconscious; and, on the other hand, the ground of being, the transcendent ground of all existence lying still deeper, at the bottom of human interiority. By taking up this way of thinking, Robinson tries to locate the question of transcendence at the depths of our own inwardness. When we compare Robinson's ideas to those of Tillich, we miss that sense of the profound, that insight into the dynamic structure of the deepest dimension of existence that we find in Tillich. For Tillich the problem of the ground of being—or, where humanity is concerned, the foundation of life—always implies a sort of ambiguity or mystery. He is always at pains to bring two conflicting elements into a conceptual unity: the aspect of terror that humans feel towards their own ground, causing them to shrink back in awe before it; and the aspect of recognition that this ground of being is the source of humanity, through whose acceptance our existential human reality can be made new. Robinson does not go so deeply into the question. In a sense he is much closer to Bultmann in his conception of transcendence as the depths of the human; it might even be said that his is an attempt to rationalize Tillich.

Be that as it may, it is certain that God and humanity come together in a new way when God is conceived of as the ground of the human. In this sense the traditional representation of heaven could even be interpreted as a symbolic expression of the harmony in this foundational unity of the divine and the human. But is this enough? That is a problem that Buddhism shares with Christianity, though it has to ponder it from its own distinctive point of view.

The relevance of these problematics for Buddhism leads us to ask, then: Is it permissible for Pure Land doctrine to so conceive the transcendence of the Pure Land Paradise in the West? For myself, I prefer to approach the problem in a somewhat different form. It seems to me that in relation to humanity, God, or the transcendent, is indeed "up there," a reality dwelling above, or at least implying something that makes it inevitable so to symbolize it. In my view, so long as human being is determined by bodily existence, we cannot but think of God as being "up there," even in the face of contemporary physics, that is, in spite of the fact that our view of nature has acclimatized itself to the theory of relativity and atomic physics, in spite of the fact that the Copernican revolution seems to be with us to stay.

Moreover, when it comes to the "world beyond," the "yonder shore," or, for me as a Pure Land believer of extremely conservative stamp, the Pure Land Paradise, I cannot help but attach tremendous importance to the meaning of transcendence implied in the idea of *shihō-rissō,* namely, that all things are a form of ultimate truth. That is to say, what is also transcendent to the world (its yonder shore) cannot be a transcendent reality simply in the sense that God is said to be transcendent to humanity: it cannot be envisaged exclusively from the viewpoint of the relationship between God and humanity. It has equally to be understood in terms of a relationship to the world, as a world that stands over against our world as well as a Thou that stands over against an I. For me, transcendence must always have its dimension of a "Thou," it must always be transcendent in reference to religious existentiality (an "I"); and at the same time it must preserve its dimension of a yonder shore, it must be transcendent in reference to the world.

The early Heidegger of *Being and Time* and *Vom Wesen des Grundes* viewed world-transcendence in terms of human existence going out of itself and beyond itself ex-statically into the world, and the world as opening up correspondingly in its non-designative (*unbedeutsam*) truth-totality, as becoming world, as "worlding." Thus the emergence of the historical world is enabled through the existential reality of being-in-the-world. For the early Heidegger the problem of transcendence is therefore considered solely from the standpoint of such a self-transcendence. In his later period, however, Heidegger's thought shows the marked influence of Greek art, which becomes the model of reality for him. He perceives a halo behind all works of art, like the aureoles of light behind statues of the Buddha, which he sees as the world. Such a world is, of course, a place where people can really live (*wohnen*). It is a place visited from time to time by a wink from the gods above; but at the same time, so long as people dwell on earth (that is, as beings fated to die) there is in their earthliness something that suggests a chthonic force pulling at them. For his part, Bultmann does not accept the interpretation of the world as such a *Geviert,* or fourfold harmony, of heaven and earth, divine and human. As premises for his existential theology, it is enough to consider the transcendence of human existence as being-in-the-world, together with the historicity that this entails.

Of its very nature the idea of "world transcendence" implies the idea of a world beyond this world, the viewpoint of a relationship between one world and another. The transcendent, like the yonder shore, of necessity shows itself to be a world beyond, to stand in opposition to this world. Transcendence entails a sense of "from . . . to" that involves not only a transcendence from the hither shore to the yonder shore, but no less a transcendent "ad-vent" (*Zu-kunft*) from the yonder shore to the hither shore. Transcendence thus requires the encounter of these two processes. This is the way in which a world-to-world relationship is actually realized.

In a word, the notion of transcendence contains three elements: the transcendent, human existential reality, and the world. The sense of a transcendent world cannot be omitted from the notion of transcendence. If Jaspers is correct in viewing *Transzendenz* and *Existenz* as conjugates, it must also be said that transcendence and world are conjugates. Indeed, it becomes possible to conceive of a truly concrete existential "dis-stance" (*Ent-fernung*) within this world-to-world relationship.[6] Like a single bridge connecting the two banks of a river, a bridge of transcendence links the hither shore and the yonder shore. This is encounter in its religious sense. From the standpoint of Shinran as a religious seeker, this took place through his encounter with the *yoki hito* (the "good person," or "master who brings me grace"), Hōnen. The sacred name of Amida was cast as a bridge from the yonder shore to the hither shore, in the twofold sense of an *ōsō* (going to the Pure Land) and a *gensō* (returning to the world of saṃsāra for the benefit of all living beings).

In speaking of transcendence or beyondness as a matter of relationship between worlds, I do not mean surreptitiously to inject the assumption of a single universe viewed as a spatial entity—like Robinson's "out there"—in which the two worlds relate like correlative celestial spheres. In saṃsāra the realm of animals and the realm of heavenly beings are seen from the human standpoint as events of the human realm; conversely, seen from the realm of animals, humans belong to the animal world. And yet there is an encounter that occurs among those various realms, each one of which is a totality encompassing the others. Within that encounter there occurs a movement "from . . . to" at work in world-to-world transcendence.

Let us say I meet a friend on the street. Even in such a situation we cannot understand the encounter by envisaging it as two points, A and B, set on a single straight line, the distance between them growing less and less *ad infinitum.* From where I stand, everything, my friend included, falls within my range of vision; and from his point of view, I and everything else fall within his range of vision. The scene of our greeting admits of numerous scenarios. He may be aware of me long before I notice him; or he may come into my range of vision first and notice me only after realizing that I am looking at him; or we may catch sight of each other at the same time. Moreover, as an encounter it allows of different attitudes: for example, I can avoid his gaze or I can welcome it. If my seeing were only the registering of images like the lens of a camera, and if the meeting of persons were merely like the bumping together of two objects in physical space, there could be no question of transcendence or encounter in the religious sense of the term. It is for this reason that I have come to regard the meaning of transcendence as an encounter between a world of a lower order and a world of a higher order, wherein one part of that lower world becomes the locus for the encounter of both worlds.

Perhaps the best way to summarize what I have in mind is to say that transcendence necessarily includes the idea of a world set over against this world, a yonder shore opposite to the hither shore. At the base of this conception of world transcendence, in connection with which the problem of human finitude and the finitude of the human world is taken up, lies the idea of a Paradise in the West. From my standpoint (and it may be argued that hereby I myself am demythologizing the meaning of the Pure Land in the West), this means that we have to give ample consideration to what the symbol of a Pure Land signifies, as indeed only such a symbol can signify: at once world transcendence or the transcendence of the world of finite beings, and the corresponding ad-vening movement of a transcendent world and a transcendent Other. This in turn reflects on what is meant by God or Buddha: so long as human beings are what they are and live in the world, every world transcendence must in some sense imply the sense of a Paradise in the West.

In *Being and Having,* Gabriel Marcel, it will be recalled, argued that the human body has to be considered in line with the Christian notion of the Incarnation. The idea strikes me as extremely profound and enlightening. In reference to the problematic being treated here, it might mean that the necessity for God in some sense to exist "up there" with reference to humanity stems from the very fact of our existing as corporeal beings, as being-in-the-world. That God is "above" is for me a bodily revelation. So long as the locus of the world-to-world encounter is my body—so long as humans walk the earth upright and look up into the heavens—God cannot but be revealed as fundamentally "above."[7] There is no other way for God to be revealed.

Similarly, so long as people live in the world and relate to the world as beings opened to it through the mediation of bodily existence, a transcendent that is truly transcendent to the world must be thought of as "ad-vening" from the future into the present in the form of the advent of a transcendent reality. In other words, world transcendence is something that ad-venes as it trans-cends. It becomes present in the present from the future, in the form of an arrival from the transcendent yonder shore to the hither shore of the present world. I am convinced that true transcendence is something that emerges into the present ad-vening in real transcendence *towards us.* Accordingly, I find the symbol of the Pure Land in the West exceedingly significant and possessed of a meaning too weighty to be displaced or replaced by any other symbol.

A New Form of Religious Awareness

In spite of everything we have just said, the fact remains that in a world of particularly forceful secularization like our own, where science is in the van of the effort to secularize all of us, some strategy must be devised to reach a new understanding of the meaning of traditional religious symbols.

Among scholars of Shin Buddhism over the past hundred years, Soga Ryōjin (1875–1971) may be singled out for his superior speculative powers. In April of 1961, in the course of a colloquium held on Mount Hiei to commemorate the 700th anniversary of the death of Shinran Shōnin, the founder of the Jōdo Shin sect, Soga declared that "the 'body' does not change, only its 'manifestation' does."[8]

I for one have difficulty with this formulation. To be specific, we may take an example provided by Bishop Robinson. Robinson writes that as a priest in the contemporary world, and one holding an important position in the Anglican church, he finds that he cannot really pray anymore. This extremely honest and frank admission strikes us as an authentic voice come from the depths of a human soul, and as such arouses our sympathy. It is as if a believer of Shin had confessed to being unable to invoke the name of Amida as a result of living in a modern, secularized world. The invocation of the name (*nembutsu*) should be something, however, that "does not choose between moving or standing still, sitting or lying down. It should be amenable to any time, place, or occasion." This means that its utterance does not require that one first find a place of quiet and solitude to bring one's heart to pure transparency. In contrast to the idea that specially consecrated times and places are essential for the realization of the Holy—and hence are found as prerequisites in all traditional religious rites—the spirit of the *nembutsu* in both Hōnen and Shinran consists in such a realization of the Holy taking place within the everyday actions of "moving or standing, sitting or lying down."

Nonetheless, it is after all a little awkward to recite the *nembutsu* in a streetcar, or break out with "Namu Amida Butsu" in a coffee shop at the moment the waitress is serving you your coffee. But there seems nothing odd at all about hearing an old lady say "Namu Amida Butsu" while being served green tea in a teahouse. Why should it be awkward to do the same in a coffee shop? Something seems to be out of joint somewhere.

Soga Ryōjin says that the "body," the *nembutsu* as substance, does not change; but in this technological age of ours it looks rather as if the "body" is itself undergoing change and being progressively corroded. From the standpoint of the "body," there should be no sense of contradiction in reciting "Namu Amida Butsu" in a coffee shop. Quite to the contrary, the spirit of the *nembutsu* demands just such a locale. It is still possible to maintain that the awkwardness here is due to a change in "manifestation." But when the problem presents itself in the acute form of prayer having become impossible in the midst of secularized life, we cannot help concluding that this change in "manifestation" also implies a change in "body." To borrow one of Robinson's expressions, the God of modern men and women has become "A Grandfather in heaven, a kindly Old Man who could be pushed into one corner while they got on with the business of life."[9] Surely this indicates a change in God's "body" in a prayerless world.

That the image of such a "Daddy-God" is a blasphemy was pointed out with perceptive insight by Søren Kierkegaard. Writing of the faith of his fiancée, Regine Olsen, he remarked that her God was like a doting uncle who was good for a few presents at Christmas time. It is the picture of a softhearted man, a goodly uncle living in another town whom it is nice to have around because he occasionally gives us what we want. But such a God has ceased to be an immediate reality, a serious matter having to do with our every daily activity (our "moving and standing still, sitting and lying down.") God is no longer someone with whom I enter into earnest dialogue in prayer and with whom I negotiate, but has become a remote being that only occasionally visits me, like a passing breeze. But what human beings need to set up, and to set up in the very midst of this secular age, is not such a spineless relationship with a Grandfather God, but a true relationship with a true God. How can we, how must we as humans pray to God? This is the point of Robinson's quest.

Robinson was led to this way of questioning largely through the influence of Dietrich Bonhoeffer. Because Bonhoeffer was executed in a Nazi prison at the age of thirty-nine, it is often remarked that his thinking did not have sufficient time to mature, that his statements are full of contradictions, and that a good deal of what he says is downright incomprehensible. For Robinson, however, his thought represents a profound testimony of our age, and a message that it will take many more years to understand properly. He voices particular approval of Bonhoeffer's idea of a "beyond within," a "beyond in the midst of our life." In Pure Land doctrine, this corresponds to what is called *heizei-gōjō,* the accomplishing or attaining of faith in daily life.[10] In both, the transcendent is located in the midst of actual reality, and what is not found among the things of the present is not the true transcendent. Bonhoeffer contends further that the truth of Christianity consists in people living with Jesus Christ as such a transcendent. It follows as a matter of course that he does not admit of any relationship with the transcendent that does not conform to that just described. It was for that reason that Bonhoeffer sought to go beyond all traditional interpretations (those of his teacher, Karl Barth, included) which are based on the assumption of Christianity as a church-centered religion.

For his part, Barth has also asserted that Christianity is not a "religion," but what he means by the term is the belief that one can comprehend and attain the divine or the Holy self-centeredly, through one's own power, and the actual attempt to do so. For Barth this is the case with all religions except Christianity. He sees the task of theology as the elucidation of the truth of the Gospel entrusted to the church, in the name of the church and in accord with the needs of each age. Consequently, church-centeredness becomes the primary premise for the entire theological enterprise and all its deliverances. Bonhoeffer, in contrast, maintains that Christianity from the beginning, in the primitive form it first took in the ancient world, was not a religion. From the perspective of the Hellenistic world and the notion of religion current in the Greco-Roman mind, the original doctrines of Christianity were looked on as an extremely secular and profane, if not shameless, teaching.

The very thing that non-Christians saw as a "scandalous" departure from the commonsense bounds of religion—whether from a ritualistic, moral, or philosophical point of view—was what Christians in all simplicity confessed as their God. In the present secularized world, however, try as it might Christianity cannot sustain the church. What then is to be done? It is Bonhoeffer's conviction that we need to conceive of means to communicate the new contents of Christian faith in secular language, in a wholly new form with new words, a language that might sound almost immoral to the pious ears of those contemporaries closely wedded to traditional ways of thinking.

Robinson takes over Bonhoeffer's conviction and colors it with the influence of Tillich's theology and Bultmann's theory of demythologization. We might say that his fusing of these three elements, with Bultmann's idea of the proclamation of the Gospel (*kerygma*) as a pivotal point of particular importance, represents a personal reflection on his own religious faith. The ideas of Bultmann that had such an impact on Robinson also gave rise to a new theological trend, particularly marked in Germany and the United States, that has come to be known as the post-Bultmann school and is represented by such thinkers as G. Ebeling and E. Fuchs. Ebeling deserves mention for his theological presentation of the essence of Protestant Christianity by means of a new hermeneutics that he evolved by going beyond Bultmann's methods. While the influence of his mentor, Bultmann, is strong, an outstanding piece on Bonhoeffer in his 1960 book *Wort und Glaube* shows the deep impression that this latter also had on him. In other works Ebeling sets forth his own standpoint with the utmost clarity and leaves no doubt in our minds that he considers there to be a marked difference between his approach and that of Bultmann.[11] I cannot go into these matters further here, but would only add the final comment that if one compares Bultmann with his disciples, when all is said and done the master looks to me to stand head and shoulders above the rest. All indications are that the problems he raised and the position he defended will continue to leave its mark on the theological world for some time to come.

For Bultmann, the central idea is *kerygma*. When he considers the problems of history in general, he continually focuses on the world as the locus of the salvific event, and in particular on history as existential actuality in the world. Even in his most universal speculations, he never strays a single step from the existential standpoint. For Bultmann the historical world by itself is forever relative, and the meanings we comprehend in the world remain irrevocably fragmentary and relative, so that nothing absolute can appear anywhere in the world. As a result, the history of which we are conscious (and which we explore in the study of history) is incapable as such of achieving any ultimate meaning as a whole. If anything like an all-embracing meaning is to be found in history, in his view, it is only to be found in the context of the individual as a person engaged in self-understanding. Specifically, history seems to receive its structure or plot through the person of Jesus Christ, but for the moment it is enough to stress that the person is invariably required as a pivotal point around which history crystallizes and achieves its total structure as history. Only through the mediation of particular historical existence do a total meaning and direction become apparent in history. And this sort of historical existence, as well as the world which is the "seat" of this existence, is realized only on the basis of an encounter with the *kerygma.* That is, through the mediation of the decision involved in religious existence, this encounter brings the subject to its fulfillment as a historical existence, thereby brings the world to a unity, and finally brings out the ultimate significance of history.

History and Nature

In 1961 during my stay in Marburg, I had the good fortune of meeting frequently with Bultmann. At the time he was seventy years old but continued to display the lively speculative powers that were his special gift. On one such occasion, Bultmann reached into his bookshelves and pulled down a copy of the Zen "Oxherding Pictures" in the German translation prepared by Tsujimura Kōichi of Kyoto University and Hartmut Buchner.[12] "This is a remarkable book," he told me. "What it explains is the very thing that Christianity teaches. In my view, the ox stands for the human heart and chasing the ox can only mean the quest for the true self. Pursuing the true self means forgetting the self, for the self becomes the true self only when it is forgotten. In the Oxherding Pictures that idea is depicted in an extraordinarily clever way, but the content, for all practical purposes, does not differ from Christian truth. The only difference is that history does not appear in it. I do not find the idea, so strong in Christianity, that truth is realized in history."

I replied, betraying the influence that the thought of the Japanese philosopher Nishitani Keiji has had on my own thinking, "It is true that history seems to be absent in the Oxherding Pictures, but is it not equally true that in Christian teaching, particularly in its Protestant form, nature is absent?" Bultmann asked me what I meant by "nature," and I explained that I understood existential nature, the nature that must be present when existence becomes true existence, and not the nature that falls under the physical categories of time and space, or what existential philosophers call "the vulgar notion of world." I repeated my question regarding the apparent failure of Christian doctrine to take this existential nature into account. After a moment's reflection, Bultmann answered that this was indeed the case.

Bultmann then turned the question back in my direction, inquiring how I would interpret existential nature. At that moment I recalled his own interpretation of the bodily resurrection of Jesus Christ. According to Saint Paul, resurrection is meaningless if it is not bodily resurrection, and he even goes so far as to assert that if Christ did not rise up in the flesh, his own faith would be in vain. In treating the theology of Paul in his *Theology of the New Testament,* first published in 1948, Bultmann had interpreted these passages by drawing a distinction between the Greek word *sarx,* meaning the "flesh," or body of sin, and *soma,* meaning the body of resurrection.[13] In the English translation this distinction is rendered through the words *flesh* and *body* respectively. Thus the phrase "resurrection in the flesh," which appears in ordinary parlance, really refers to resurrection in the *soma,* not resurrection in the *sarx.* According to Bultmann, *soma* is the locus where real truth makes itself manifest. With that in mind, I replied, "If you want an example of the existential meaning of nature, would not the way you yourself conceive of the corporality of the risen Christ, the *soma* as the locus of resurrection, be a good example of that existential nature?" This time Bultmann sank into thought for quite a long time and then, alluding to the notion of the *Geviert* that Heidegger had just started using about that time as a symbol for the world,[14] inquired whether my concept of nature did not resemble that notion.

Having been influenced heavily by the thought of Heidegger, I had to admit that my ideas on the subject were in fact close to Heidegger's, to which Bultmann observed that he was opposed to such a way of thinking. He explained his objections by noting that although this *Geviert* is a world in which truth is disclosed, there is no place in it for a true encounter with a Thou. At that point it struck me that his criticism of Heidegger was altogether typical of Bultmann. His remarks have stayed with me to this day. Not to be satisfied with the idea of the *Geviert,* or "world-openness," through which the later Heidegger deepened his awareness of the world, but to struggle earnestly for a more congenial understanding that would include as a necessary element the encounter with a Thou, and then to proceed from this encounter to conceive of history in its full sense—that, it seems to me, is the inevitable conclusion to which Bultmann's point of view leads.

If I may be allowed a personal comment on Bultmann's approach, I would say that his "decision of faith," which posits the world as its mediation and locus of conversion, aims at exchanging the traditional idea of a historical transmission of revelation (the Word of God) in the past for the idea of a here-and-now encounter with the Gospel *kerygma* that advenes from the future. With the world as its mediation, history can thus open up from the individual history of existential reality into world history, and the existence of being-in-the-world can become a religious existence that makes its decision in the historical world. Consequently, the full meaning of history, strictly speaking, can only be conceived in terms of the meaning of religious existence as a being in the historical world. And it is the *welten* (with its connotation of rotation) of this world that accounts for the element of encounter in our religious existence by giving the existence of Jesus Christ in the past a cyclic turn and enabling us to meet the Christ-event as something ad-vening into the present from the future. In other words, through the mediation of the world, the movement from past to present is turned around to a movement from future to present, and it is there that encounter with the Word of God becomes possible.

It is the same in the case of the name of Amida Buddha. I encounter the name of the Buddha here and now ad-vening as eternity from the Pure Land. This takes place in the form of an I-Thou encounter in the actuality of the present, with the name (as the Thou) ad-vening from the future. Conversely, at the moment of this encounter, in the religious act of uttering "Namu Amida Butsu" as a decision that brings evocation and response into one, the symbolic world (in which all Buddhas continually praise the name of Amida Buddha and guarantee the truth of that name and birth in the Pure Land through its invocation) is discovered directly underfoot of the present.

In still more concrete form, this symbolic world, which represents the background for one's encounter with the name, also signifies the opening up of the world in which the *nembutsu* is transmitted historically. Just as with Heidegger's *Geviert,* this in turn means the realization of the world of all Buddhas praising and reconfirming the name of Amida—a world in which everything mirrors everything else. And just as in Bultmann's historical world, it is in this world of ours that the encounter with the Thou, the encounter with the name, takes place. In that sense, we have here a concrete synthesis of the standpoints of Heidegger and Bultmann.

In the second chapter of the *Kyōgyōshinshō,* entitled "True Living," Shinran refers to the seventeenth vow (or prayer) as "that which is praised by all Buddhas" and as "that in which all Buddhas pronounce the Name."[15] This means that all Buddhas praise Amida Buddha and exalt his name, and that by pronouncing his name all Buddhas praise Amida. Understandably, this is generally interpreted not as referring to *our* utterance of Amida's name, but to an event belonging to the absolute world where "Namu Amida Buddha" appears with the dharma. That is, it is an event that occurs among the Buddhas in their Buddha-worlds, transcendent to the world of man. It is a matter of all Buddhas praising one another and exalting the name of Amida.

Were that the whole truth, it would be difficult to see how this praise by the Buddha has anything to do with our own religious practice ("living") of the *nembutsu.* At the beginning of the "True Living" chapter, Shinran states clearly: "The great living is to pronounce the Name of the Tathāgata of Unimpeded Light." I should like to interpret the term *great living* as religious or symbolic activity wherein the practice of all Buddhas praising the name of Amida is mirrored in our own "pronouncing the Name of the Tathāgata of Unimpeded Light." Here we are aware that our utterance of the name is praise and exaltation of the name, and that our utterance of the name is in turn mirrored in the praise of all the Buddhas. This makes it clear that "that which is praised by all Buddhas" is "that in which all Buddhas pronounce the Name."[16]

In other words, the Pure Land and this world, all Buddhas and all living beings, the cosmic chorus sounding the name throughout "the ten quarters" and the career of the historical *nembutsu* on earth combine in this symbolic action to form a locus of *Geviert.* It is at this point that my encounter with Amida takes place. With Jaspers, we may refer to symbolic action of this sort as absolute action wherein all opposition of subject and object melts away, and concrete reality appears on the standpoint of action in all its purity. It is precisely there that the encounter and mutual evocation of I and Thou are realized.

This idea of the "standpoint of action" cries out for further reflection in connection with Nishida Kitarō's view of action-intuition and Tanabe Hajime's elucidation of action from the viewpoint of practice-faith,[17] but it seems to me equally relevant to the difference of approach between Heidegger and Bultmann referred to above. In any case, the "Namu Amida Butsu" that issues forth at the point where the opposition of subject and object is overcome, in the "Great Practice" characteristic of religious action, seems to me to reveal extraordinary depths of meaning and its significance for our present day to become all the clearer when explored in the light of the contemporary problematics of theology and the philosophy of religion.

Notes

Translator's Introduction

1. 親鸞と現代 (Shinran Today) (Tokyo, 1974), p. 58.

2. In 1978–79, Kadokawa Shoten of Tokyo published the collected works of Takeuchi Yoshio in ten volumes.

3. The Takada sect of Shin Buddhism was founded by Shinbutsu (1209–58), one of the disciples of Shinran, and takes its name from the original site of its head temple in Takada, Tochigi Prefecture. In the fifteenth century the temple, Senju-ji, was moved to its current location in the town of Tsu in Mie Prefecture.

4. Takeuchi authored the entry on Nishida in the *Encyclopaedia Britannica* (1967) and has written the commentary for vol. 9 of Tanabe's collected works (田邊元全集 [Tokyo, 1963]), pp. 493–508.

5. The turning point for Tanabe came with the publication of his book *Philosophy as Metanoetics* (see below, chapter 7, n. 17).

6. Nishitani's major work has been published recently in English in the translation of Jan Van Bragt, *Religion and Nothingness* (Berkeley: University of California Press, 1982).

7. The article on Watsuji in the 1967 edition of the *Encyclopaedia Britannica,* as well as the survey article on "Modern Japanese Philosophy," were both authored by Takeuchi.

8. 教行信証の哲学 (Tokyo: Kōbundō, 1941).

9. For additional information and bibliography relating to the Kyoto School, see Jan Van Bragt's "Translator's Introduction" to *Religion and Nothingness.*

10. The text of this talk appeared in my English translation in *The Eastern Buddhist* 15, no. 2 (1982): 10–27.

11. This theme, which is only alluded to in passing in the present book (p. 56), is taken up in chapter 3 of *Shinran Today,* especially pp. 76–79.

1 The Silence of the Buddha

1. See E. J. Thomas, *The History of Buddhist Thought* (London, 1953), p. 125.

2. *The Middle-Length Sayings,* trans. I. B. Horner (London: Pali Text Society, 1954), pp. 97ff. The wording has been slightly altered here.

3. If this were the case, the result would be agnosticism, which would support

the view of those who stress the poverty of philosophical thought in primitive Buddhism when compared with Indian philosophical religions of the time. See, for example, A. B. Keith, *Buddhist Philosophy in India and China* (Oxford, 1923).

4. *The Book of the Kindred Sayings* (Saṃyutta-Nikāya), part 5 (Mahā-Vahha), trans. F. L. Woodward (London: Pali Text Society, 1979), p. 370.

5. Cf. C. A. F. Rhys Davids, *Buddhist Psychology* (London, 1914).

6. Cf. for example, H. v. Glasenapp, *Die fünf grossen Religionen,* vol. 1 (Düsseldorf, 1952).

7. Thomas, *History of Buddhist Thought,* chap. 10.

8. According to this theory, our existence may be likened to a kaleidoscope into which pieces of colored glass (mainly of five sorts) have been inserted. At every turn, the pattern is jumbled into a new construction, while the pieces remain the same. So long as we keep our eye glued to the kaleidoscope, we have no way of seeing how the world (the object) or the ego (the subject) are constructed in reality. Due to the structure of avidyā, our eye remains fixed to the eyepiece and identifies with the patterns it sees there.

9. See her *Buddhist Psychology.*

10. *Die Buddhistische Versenkung* (Munich, 1922), p. 40.

11. Ibid., p. 41.

12. *The Dhammapada: The Path of Perfection,* trans. Juan Mascaró (New York: Penguin Books, 1973), pp. 49–50.

13. See my "Hegel and Buddhism," *Il Pensiero,* VII:1–2; and "The Philosophy of Nishida," *The Buddha Eye,* ed. Frederick Franck (New York: Crossroad, 1982), pp. 179–202.

14. Cf., for example, 1 and 2 Corinthians, and especially Philippians 3:12–14.

15. See her *Gotama the Man* (London, 1929), *Wayfarer's Word,* vols. 2 and 3 (London, 1942), and *Sakya* (London, 1931).

16. H. Beckh, *Buddha und seine Lehre* (Stuttgart, 1958), p. 58.

2 The Stages of Contemplation

1. The Sāmaññaphalasutta (The Fruits of the Life of a Recluse) belongs to the Dīgha-Nikāya, chap. II. ET: *Dialogues of the Buddha,* part 1, trans. T. W. and C. A. F. Rhys Davids (London: Pali Text Society, 1977), vol. 2, pp. 69–95.

2. See Ui Hakuju, 印度哲学研究 (Studies in Indian Philosophy), (Tokyo, 1925), vol. 3, chap. 3; and Kanakura Enshō, 印度古代精神史 (The Intellectual History of Ancient India), (Tokyo, 1938), chaps. 8–10. Both of these works treat of the six heretics referred to here.

3. To take Ajita Kesakambalī as an example, he is one of the ascetics who dressed in a hair shirt, similar to the European monks and mystics of the Middle Ages, or to the naked ascetics (the "gymnosophists") who wrapped their own hair about themselves as a robe. His philosophy, however, showed a tendency to sensualism and materialistic mechanism. See J. Sinnha, *History of Indian Philosophy* (Calcutta, 1956), vol. 1, chap. 7; and A. L. Basham, *History and Doctrine of the Ājīvikas* (London, 1951), chap. 2.

4. Étienne Lamotte places the site of his encounter with the Buddha elsewhere, namely, in the city of Vesāli, but in my view this stems from later legends. See his *Histoire du bouddhisme indien* (Louvain, 1958), p. 21.

5. In addition to the works of Ui and Kanakura referred to above (n. 2 above), one may also refer to Basham's *History and Doctrine of the Ājīvikas,* pp. 10ff.; E. Frauwallner, *Geschichte der indischen Philosophie,* vol. 1 (Salzburg, 1953); and J. Gonda, *Religionen Indiens,* vol. 1 (Stuttgart, 1960), pp. 283ff.

6. Frauwallner, *Geschichte,* pp. 185ff.

7. Of course what is contained in the Sāmaññaphalasutta does not reflect contemplation in the age of the Buddha as such. The "general rules for spiritual practice" should rather be thought of in terms of a fundamental spirit that characterized the age of the Buddha. The distinctive element in Frauwallner's explanation lies in the parallel he draws between the four noble truths and the twelvefold doctrine of dependent origination.

8. See his *Die buddhistische Versenkung* (Munich, 1922), and *Das Gebet* (Munich, 1923).

9. Sāmaññaphalasutta, par. 102 (see n. 1 above), p. 95.

10. The Pali words (sīla, jhāna, paññā) have been replaced here with their Sanskrit equivalents to avoid confusion.

11. Heiler, *Das Gebet,* p. 268; idem, *Versenkung,* pp. 10f.

12. *The Dhammapada,* trans. Juan Mascaró (New York: Penguin Books, 1973), vv. 146, 47, 48, 128, 212, 215, 46, 414.

13. Heiler, *Versenkung,* pp. 19f.

14. See my "Existentialism and Buddhism: The Dialogue between Oriental and Occidental Thought," in *Religion and Culture: Essays in Honor of Paul Tillich,* ed. W. Leibrecht (New York, 1959), pp. 291–365.

15. Heiler, *Versenkung,* p. 19.

16. The Mahāsatipaṭṭhānasutta (The Setting-up of Mindfulness), from which this quotation is taken, appears in part II, 293, of the Dīgha-Nikāya. ET: *Dialogues of the Buddha,* part 2, p. 330.

17. The *Milinda Questions* (London, 1930). See also the Samyutta-Nikāya, v. 10 (ET: *The Book of the Kindred Sayings,* part 1, trans. C. A. F. Rhys Davids [London: Pali Text Society, 1979], pp. 169–70), and the Milindapañha, secs. 27–28 (ET: *Milinda's Questions,* vol. 1, trans. I. B. Horner [London: Pali Text Society, 1969], pp. 36–38).

18. M. Heidegger, *Sein und Zeit* (Halle, 1935), pp. 262ff.; idem, *Vom Wesen des Grundes* (Frankfurt, 1955), p. 42. Regarding the thought of the later Heidegger, see my "Existentialism and Buddhism," pp. 294–304. Particularly important is his later turn to an elucidation of the notion of *Lichtung* (opening, clearing) in *Zur Sache des Denkens* (Tübingen, 1969), pp. 72f. This may rightly be compared to Nishida's "locus of nothingness," which is treated in my essay, "The Philosophy of Nishida," *The Buddha Eye,* ed. Frederick Franck (New York: Crossroad, 1982), pp. 179–202.

19. Heiler, *Versenkung,* pp. 19–20.

20. The same theme that the Buddha treats in his sermon on the mountain (see chapter 6, "The Doctrine of the Six Senses") is expressed in terms of the present tension between the pleasant and the pitiful in the unreality of the modern city.

21. See Nishitani Keiji, *Religion and Nothingness,* trans. Jan Van Bragt (Berkeley: University of California Press, 1982), chap. 2, sec. 1.

22. It is worth remarking here that this will to escape or release differs somewhat from the philosophical resolve of "being towards death." For Heidegger nothingness is unveiled in anxiety; it is in anxiety that beings as a whole are rendered null and void. But in this "slipping away" that has beings as a whole submerge into nothingness, human beings are transformed in their *Da-sein* and question the totality of existents as such. It is true that in this philosophical question beings are brought into question as a whole, but the connection between being and "sense and meaning" is not yet clear. Only through the negation of life and the world in a religious decision does anxiety in the face of nothingness, or rather doubt swept up into the whirlpool of nothingness, become a central question. Thus it is not Heidegger's question, "Why is there being rather than nothingness" that corresponds to this religious situation, but rather the saying of the Buddha: "In truth this world is caught up in toil. One is born, grows old, and dies, leaving this existence to be born again. There is no way out of this suffering to be found. How is one then to be released from this suffering, old age, and death?" Even the theory of the five skandhas, which analyzes beings as a whole in terms of five groups of existential elements—and which I see as occurring in the experience of contemplation—is religious before it is philosophical insofar as exitence in the world is played out in the arena of human *Dasein.*

On the other hand, in this abyss of *nichtigenden Nichts,* the negative is likewise transformed into the positive. Heidegger's pregnant phrase, "Nothingness itself nothings," thus receives a genuine affirmative sense, namely, that the ego is able to determine itself. It is an absolute *Nichts* that embraces the ego (*ichts*—cp. J. Böhme) in its pure activity. This is precisely what Buddhism means by non-ego (anātman). In this way nullification, accompanied by a negative judgment, the insight that keeps the pitiful before its eyes in the pleasing side of impermanence, gets turned around into a pure release or *de*becoming, that is into the escape from the unsavory. The threefold insight into the five skandhas—the savory, the unsavory, and the escape—therefore constitute the dialectic of religious decision, while in the philosophical question the back-and-forth movement of "slipping away" from being as a whole and "being submerged" into it is a realization of the same dialectic that first becomes possible with the transcending of being as being in metaphysics. (See Heidegger, *Was ist Metaphysik?* [Frankfurt, 1949], pp. 35–39).

23. Sāmaññaphalasutta, v. 43 (see n. 1 above), p. 79.

24. H. Beckh, *Buddha und seine Lehre* (Stuttgart, 1958), pp. 153ff.

25. Bṛhadāraṇyaka Upanishad, I, 5, 14.

26. On the notion of "open" and "closed" morality, see H. Bergson, *Les deux sources de la morale et de la religion* (Paris 1935); for further remarks on the difference between tribal religions and world religions, one may refer to the works of Albert Schweitzer, in particular his *Die Weltanschauung der indischen Denker: Mystik und Ethik* (Munich, 1965).

27. Frauwallner distinguishes one part of the Mahābhārata that in his view goes back to a time prior to Buddhism from classical Yoga, which is inseparable from the Sāṃkhya system of philosophy (*Geschichte,* pp. 97ff.), and I follow him

here. I have taken as a starting point for the contemplation of primitive Buddhism what should logically precede it in the history of thought.

Concerning the relationship between the five commandments, Yoga, and Jainism, see Beckh, *Buddha,* pp. 158ff.; H. Jacobi, introduction to vol. 22 of *The Sacred Books of the East;* J. W. Hauer, *Der Yoga als Heilsweg* (Stuttgart, 1958), pp. 165ff.; Kanakura, *Intellectual History,* pp. 268, 408ff.; Heiler, *Versenkung,* pp. 3ff.

28. In primitive Buddhist texts there is no distinction between contemplation of the four immeasurables (catvāry apramāṇāni) and contemplation of the four Brahma states (catvāry brahma-vihāra), but the latter is tied into belief in rebirth in a heavenly kingdom after death, and I have therefore provisionally distinguished it from true compassionate contemplation, which I take as the hallmark of the spirit of primitive Buddhism, and placed it with early Yogic doctrine. The same distinction can be made with regard to later Abhidharmic analyses (See D. Schlingloff, *Ein Buddhistisches Yogalehrbuch* [Berlin, 1964], p. 115). In like manner, the doctrine of the four dhyānas, as will be stated later in the text, belong among the sixty-two heresies as an "expropriation of true nirvāṇa into visible existence" (diṭṭha-dhamma-nibbāna-vāda). Still, it correctly presents as the content of true self-centering right doctrine, and indeed expresses the religious life of primitive Buddhism.

29. *Dhammapada,* v. 284.

30. Sāmaññaphalasutta, v. 64 (see n. 1 above), pp. 79–80.

31. M. Eliade, *Techniques du Yoga* (Paris, 1948), pp. 15f.; on Yogic terminology, see Kanakura, *Intellectual History,* pp. 125, 128.

32. *Dhammapada,* v. 183.

33. *Dhammapada,* vv. 165, 160.

34. Heiler, *Versenkung,* pp. 26f.

35. Cf. M. Eliade, *Yoga: Immorality and Freedom* (New York, 1958), pp. 193ff.

36. C. G. Jung, "The Psychology of Eastern Meditation," *Collected Works* vol. 11 (London: Routledge and Kegan Paul, 1959), pp. 558–75.

37. I shall return to this again later, in chapter 6.

38. Sāmaññaphalasutta, v. 65 (see n. 1 above), p. 80.

39. Frauwallner, *Geschichte,* p. 171.

40. From the Thera-gāthā (Psalms of the Brethren), vv. 522, 523. ET: *Psalms of the Early Buddhists,* vol. 2, trans. C. A. F. Rhys Davids (London: Pali Text Society, 1980), pp. 246–47.

41. S. Radhakrishnan, *The Dhammapada* (London, 1950), p. 7.

42. From the Ariyapariyesanasutta (Discourse on the Holy Quest), v. 167, included in the Majjhima-Nikāya. ET: *The Middle Length Sayings,* vol. 2, trans. I. B. Horner (London: Pali Text Society, 1976), pp. 210–11.

43. From the Sāmaññaphalasutta, vv. 75, 77, 79, 81 (see n. 1 above), pp. 84–86.

44. Sāmaññaphalasutta, v. 76 (see n. 1 above), pp. 84–85.

45. Suttanipāta (A Collection of Discourses), vv. 970, 972. ET: *Woven Cadences of Early Buddhists,* trans. E. M. Hare (Oxford University Press, 1964), p. 141.

46. *The Visuddhimagga of Buddhaghosa,* vol. 1, trans. Nyāṇamoli (Colombo, 1964), pp. 142.

47. Hauer, *Yoga,* pp. 171ff.

48. Otherwise, of course, this is realized only in the second stage of contemplation.

49. Sāmaññaphalasutta, v. 78 (see n. 1 above), p. 85. The phrase that reads *devo ca kālena kālaṁ sammā dhāraṁ anupaveccheyya* can only mean "there are rainshowers." Otto Franke (*Dīgha-Nikaya* [Göttingen, 1913]) and J. Bloch (*Canon Bouddhique Pali,* vol. 1) read *devo vā naṃ kalena,* which means that not so much as a rainshower falls.

50. Sāmaññaphalasutta, v. 80 (see n. 1 above), p. 86.

51. Sāmaññaphalasutta, v. 82 (see n. 1 above), p. 86.

52. Cf. T. W. Rhys Davids and William Stede, *Pali-English Dictionary* (London: Pali Text Society, 1921–25).

53. "Talks of Instruction," XIV, in R. B. Blakney, *Meister Eckhart: A Modern Translation* (New York, 1941), p. 13.

54. From the Tevijjasutta (Union with God), vv. 43–79, Dīgha-Nikāya (see note 1 above), pp. 317f.

55. Suttanipāta, vv. 143–52 (see n. 45 above), pp. 23–25.

56. See Heiler, *Versenkung,* p. 25: "Limitless compassion for all living things is the strongest and surest guarantee of upright moral conduct and requires no casuistry. Whoever is full of such compassion is sure to cause no wound or injury or harm to anything, but to exhibit patience and forgiveness and help so far as possible, and all the actions of such a one will bear the stamp of uprightness and love of humanity. . . . I know no more beautiful prayer than that with which the ancient Indian play ends (as the English of an earlier time used to address their kings): "May all living things be free of pain."

57. Meister Eckhart, *Schriften* (Düsseldorf and Cologne, 1959), p. 37.

58. Eckhart, *Schriften,* pp. 47f.

59. Schweitzer, *Die Weltanschauung,* pp. 87ff.

60. The same question that Schweitzer puts appears already in the Mahāyāna text, the Vimalakīrtinirdésa. In reply, a satisfactory explanation of the notion of "great love" (mahāmaitrī) is offered, a notion that is related to the contemplation of the four immeasurables. See E. Lamotte, *L'Enseignement de Vimalakīrti* (Louvain, 1962), pp. 263–69.

3 Centering and the World Beyond

1. *Kyōgyōshinshō* (教行信証), VI, 3. ET: *The Teaching, Practice, Faith, and Enlightenment,* Ryukoku Translation Series, vol. 5 (Kyoto, 1966), p. 165.

2. 正像末和讃 (Shōzōmatsu-wasan, The Praise of the Grace of Amida Buddha in the Last Things), n. 53.

3. *Kyōgyōshinshō,* VI, 39 (see n. 1 above), p. 194.

4. *Tannishō* (歎異抄), I. ET: *Notes Lamenting Differences,* Ryukoku Translation Series, vol. 2 (Kyoto, 1962), pp. 15–16.

5. *Tannishō,* III, (see n. 4 above), pp. 22f.

6. Hōnen Shōnin (1133–1212) was Shinran's teacher and founder of the Japanese Pure Land sect.

7. Zendō (613–81), the Japanization of the Chinese name Shan-tao, was the

fifth of the Seven Patriarchs of Shin Buddhism, and was one of the most prominent teachers during the T'ang Dynasty.

8. *Tannishō,* II (see n. 4 above), pp. 20f.

9. *Jōdo-wasan* (浄土和讃), n. 31. ET: *The Hymns on the Pure Land,* Ryukoku Translation Series, vol. 4 (Kyoto, 1965), p. 59.

10. The passage appears in v. 10 and has been somewhat abbreviated here. The complete text of the sūtra appears in vol. 49/2 of the *Sacred Books of the East* (Oxford University Press, 1894), pp. 89–102.

11. "When a mother ape falls into danger, her young immediately cling fast to her, and when she makes a leap to safety, they are saved, by the act of the mother it is true, but in such a way that the young *cooperates* a little, because it clings to the mother *by its own act.* It is therefore a synergist. But when danger threatens a cat with her young, the mother cat takes the young in her mouth. The young one does nothing for its salvation. It remains merely passive. All cooperation is excluded" (R. Otto, *India's Religion of Grace and Christianity Compared and Contrasted,* trans. F. H. Foster [London: SCM Press, 1930], p. 56).

12. Shōtoku Taishi (574–622) was a Japanese prince and devoted advocate of Buddhism, and is commonly credited with having secured the introduction of Buddhism into Japan.

13. See M. Kōsaka and K. Nishitani, 日本的なるもの－その系譜と構造 (The Genealogy and Structure of Things Japanese), *Jiyū,* December 1959, pp. 110–31, January 1960, pp. 104–22.

4 The Problem of Dependent Origination

1. From the Mahānidānasutta (The Great Discourse on Causation), v. 1. This text appears in the Dīgha-Nikāya, XV, 1. ET: *Dialogues of the Buddha,* part 2, trans. T. W. and C. A. F. Rhys Davids (London: Pali Text Society, 1977), pp. 50f.

2. Cf. W. Geiger, trans., "Saṃyutta-Nikāya: Die in Gruppen geordnete Sammlung aus dem Pāli-Kanon der Buddhisten," *Zeitschrift für Buddhismus und verwandte Gebiete* IV (1922):37, 129f.

3. Cf. his 仏教思想研究 (Studies in Buddhist Thought), (Tokyo, 1943); and 仏教汎論 (An Outline of Buddhism), 2 vol. (Tokyo 1947–48).

4. See the Mahāyāna-samparigraha Sāstra, translated into Chinese by Paramārtha (499–569), a priest of West India who came to China at the invitation of Emperor Wu of the Liang Dynasty.

5. A. Schweitzer, *Die Weltanschauung der indischen Denker: Mystik und Ethik* (Munich, 1965).

6. H. Beckh, *Buddha und seine Lehre* (Stuttgart, 1958).

7. The point is stressed in P. Tillich, *Biblical Religion and the Search for Ultimate Reality* (Chicago: University of Chicago Press, 1956); and R. Bultmann, *History and Eschatology* (Edinburgh: University Press, 1957).

8. 原始仏教の実践哲学 (Tokyo, 1974).

9. J. Chevalier, *Pascal* (Paris, 1922), pp. 177–78.

10. T. Watsuji, 仏教哲学の最初の展開 (The Early Development of Buddhist Philosophy), *Collected Works,* vol. 5, (Tokyo, 1977), pp. 113–15.

11. Watsuji, *Collected Works,* 5:310ff.

12. E. Husserl, *Die Krisis der europäischen Wissenschaften und die transzendentale Phänomenologie,* ed. Walter Biemel (Nijhoff: The Hague, 1954).

13. *Zur Sache des Denkens* (Tübingen, 1969).

14. Cited in H. G. Gadamer, *Philosophical Hermeneutics,* trans. David E. Linge (Berkeley: University of California Press, 1976, p. 157.

15. *Essays in Metaphysics: Identity and Difference,* trans. K. F. Leidecker (New York, 1960).

16. *Zur Sache des Denkens,* pp. 67ff.

17. Cf. A. B. Keith, *The Religion and Philosophy of the Veda and Upanishads* (Cambridge: Harvard University Press, 1925).

5 Dependent Origination and Co-dependency

1. From the Saṃyutta-Nikāya, XII, 2, 20. ET: *The Book of the Kindred Sayings,* part 2, trans. T. W. Rhys Davids (London: Pali Text Society, 1982), p. 21.

2. Saṃyutta-Nikāya, XII, 1, 1 (see n. 1 above), pp. 1–2.

3. Saṃyutta-Nikāya, XII, 7, 65 (see n. 1 above), pp. 72–75.

4. Mahāpadānasutta (Buddhas, Bodhisats, and Arahants), chap. XIV of the Dīgha-Nikāya. ET: *Dialogues of the Buddha,* part 2, trans. T. W. and C. A. F. Rhys Davids (London: Pali Text Society, 1977), pp. 1–41.

5. Saṃyutta-Nikāya, vv. 4–9 (see n. 1 above), p. 5.

6. Mahāpadānasutta, v. 32 (see n. 4 above), pp. 25f.

7. See my essay, 縁起説に於ける相依性 (Co-dependency in the Theory of Dependent Origination), published in a special collection of essays commemorating the fiftieth anniversary of Kyoto University's Department of Literature, 1956.

8. Probably war or pestilence or some other disaster befell the city and destroyed it. Examples of this are to be found as late as the twelfth century.

9. "The City" (see n. 3 above), pp. 74f.

10. Saṃyutta-Nikāya, XII, 7, 67 (see n. 1 above), pp. 79–81.

11. *Phenomenal form* here refers to a relationship of inseparable correlatedness between the one and the many such that the many come about in virtue of the one, and vice versa. *Mutual interpenetration* extends this to the correlatedness of the activity of each individual element to the activity of the whole. The former principle is often likened to the correlatedness of the water of the sea with its waves; the latter, to rays of light penetrating one another without hindrance.

12. See *Açvaghosha's Discourse on the Awakening of Faith in the Mahāyāna,* trans. D. T. Suzuki (Chicago: O.C.P., 1900).

13. Mahādināsutta, chap. 15 of the Dīgha-Nikāya (see n. 4 above), pp. 50–70.

14. Cf. vol. 4 of *The Book of the Discipline,* trans. I. B. Horner, (London: Pali Text Society, 1982), p. 6.

15. Saṃyutta-Nikāya, XII, 6, 53 (see n. 1 above), pp. 60f.

16. Saṃyutta-Nikāya, XII, 6, 52 (see n. 1 above), pp. 59f.

17. Saṃyutta-Nikāya, XII, 6, 55 (see n. 1 above), pp. 61f.

18. T. Akanuma, 漢巴四部四阿含互照録 (Nagoya, 1929), pp. 193–94.

19. E. Conze, *Thirty Years of Buddhist Studies* (Oxford: Bruno Cassirer, 1967), p. 7; E. M. Hare, *Woven Cadences of Early Buddhists* (Oxford University Press, 1947), pp. 212–17.

20. Nakamura's principal work on primitive Buddhism is to be found in his collected works (中村元選集), published by Shunjūsha of Tokyo, vols. 11–14 (1969–71).

21. Suttanipāta, v. 863. ET: Hare, *Woven Cadences*, p. 127.

22. This is the tetralemmic differentiation into (1) existing, (2) non-existing, (3) both existing and non-existing, and (4) neither existing nor non-existing.

23. Rudolf Bultmann, *Das Evangelium Johannes* (Göttingen, 1962), pp. 12f.

24. Maryla Falk, *Nāmarūpa and Dharmarūpa* (Calcutta: University of Calcutta, 1943). S. Radhakrishnan, *The Principal Upanishads* (London: Allen and Unwin, 1953), pp. 162ff.

25. Bṛhad-āraṇyaka Upanishad I, 4, 7. Cf. Radhakrishnan, *Principal Upanishads,* p. 168.

6 An Existential Interpretation of Dependent Origination

1. *The Book of the Gradual Sayings,* vol. 1, trans. F. L. Woodward (London: Pali Text Society, 1979), pp. 128–29.

2. *Gradual Sayings,* p. 130.

3. H. Oldenberg, *Buddha: sein Leben, seine Lehre, seine Gemeinde* (Munich, 1961), pp. 105–6.

4. *The Collection of the Middle Length Sayings,* vol. 1, trans. I. B. Horner (London: Pali Text Society, 1976), pp. 203–19.

5. *Gotama the Man* (London, 1929).

6. W. Jaeger, *Paideia: The Ideals of Greek Culture,* vol. 3 (Oxford, 1939), pp. 39–40.

7. J. Filliozat, *The Classical Doctrine of Indian Medicine: Its Origins and Its Greek Parallels* (Delhi, 1964), pp. 229ff.

8. I have been criticized for qualifying the Buddha's reflections on the "fate" of old age, sickness, and death as the "law" of old age, sickness, and death. On the one hand, I am of course obliged to follow the lead of specialists who know more about the Pali language than I. But on the other, in the case of the passage cited here it is clearly a question of the law (dharma) of these realities that we are being given to consider. W. Geiger argues that in such cases as this the use of *dharma* carries the sense of "reverting to such-and-such a law," which he understands as a law of nature. He renders the first part of the poem of verse 39 as "Since they are liable to sickness, old age, and death, [since they are] as they are determined to be, Therefore do commonplace individuals harbor antipathy [towards one another]" (*Pali Dhamma vornehmlich in der kanonischen Literatur* [Munich, 1921], p. 147). Whether one says "are fated" or "are subject to a necessary law," so long as one grants that it is a matter of fate, for instance, that I happen to be color blind or that Plato had a broad forehead or that Socrates had a snub nose, there is nothing any of us can do about it, whether we realize it or not. In those cases, we are not dealing with matters of essential determination. Thus in the case of old age, sickness, and death, they are physical facts that not even the

Buddha could transcend after his enlightenment, as we noted earlier in the text. Here the things that cannot be surpassed through enlightenment are taken into mind and reflected on intently as the original finitude to which the self is fated. In order for one to comprehend those matters of fate as one's own problem and come to a decision with regard to them, the need arises to resolve to renounce everydayness with one's whole heart and soul. It is precisely at this point that we are dealing with a task that holds true for all people. The "dharma" that is connected to those questions is, in other words, an existential category. It was this existential category, seen as dharma, that the young Buddha awakened to in his reflections. As we noted in chapter 4, the "dharma" of Abhidharmic thought belongs to another dimension.

9. *The Dhammapada,* vv. 47–48, trans. Juan Mascaró (New York: Penguin Books, 1973), p. 42.

10. *Dhammapada,* v. 146 (see n. 9), p. 56.

11. This story has been explained in the Vinaya (I, 34) as an admonition by the Buddha to certain of his disciples who had previously been devoted to fire-worship on Mount Gayā. In a parallel passage (IV, 19–20), no mention is made in the Buddha's sermon of causality (which is a kind of sermon pattern or stage setting). See also the parallel text in VI, 71. If the Buddha can be said to have insinuated any criticism in his words, it would have been in the form of light-hearted teasing. In similar jeering fashion the Buddha remarked of those practicing ablutions that if the hearts were something that could be purified through bathing, one would be no better than a waterfowl. The parallel is instructive. (See Udāna, v. 6. ET: *The Minor Anthologies of the Pali Canon,* part 2, trans. F. L. Woodward [Oxford University Press, 1948], pp. 7–8; *The Book of the Discipline,* vol. 4, trans. I. B. Horner [London: Pali Text Society, 1982], pp. 45–47.) The editor of the incomplete tales of the Buddha in the Vinaya probably took that transmission as a model for developing in an interesting manner the Buddha's sermon on burning. For that reason the spirit of this sūtra is altogether absent (in a religious or philosophical sense) from traditional interpretations, which have overlooked its point. The text has yet to be understood in the light of the possibility that it was really trying to make clear the doctrine of the six senses and the relationship between vijñāna and nāmarūpa.

12. Ernest Wood, *Yoga* (London: Cassell, 1962).

13. E. Frauwallner, *Geschichte der indischen Philosophie,* vol. 1 (Salzburg, 1953), pp. 170ff., 189f.

14. After the three worlds (the world of the senses, the world of form, and the formless world of pure spirit) were established, the threefold desire of sensual lust, lust for being, and lust for nothingness were set up to correspond to them. But texts that describe it in the terms mentioned in this chapter are scattered throughout the scriptures and probably represent its original meaning.

15. Martin Buber, *Between Man and Man* (New York: Macmillan, 1969), pp. 163ff.

16. K. Jaspers, *Philosophie,* vol. 2 (Göttingen, 1956), pp. 221f.

17. The five desires for property, sexual love, eat and drink, fame, and sleep.

18. Mahāpadānasutta, Dīgha-Nikāya, XIV, 22. ET: *Dialogues of the Buddha,* part 2, trans. T. W. and C. A. F. Rhys Davids (London: Pali Text Society, 1977), p. 19.

19. E. Kanakura, 印度古代精神史 (The Intellectual History of Ancient India), (Tokyo, 1938), pp. 296ff.

20. H. Thode, *Franz von Assisi und die Anfänge der Kunst der Renaissance in Italien* (Vienna, 1934).

21. A. Foucher, *La vie du Bouddha d'après les textes et les monuments de l'Inde* (Paris: Bibliothèque Historique, 1949), p. 112.

22. Stanislaus Schayer, "Pre-Canonical Buddhism," *Archiv Orientální* 7 (1935): 122–32, especially pp. 124–25; "New Contributions to the Problem of Pre-hīnayānistic Buddhism," *Polish Bulletin of Oriental Studies* 1 (1937): 8f.; *Vorarbeiten zur Geschichte der mahāyānistischen Erlösungslehren* (Munich, 1921).

7 Freeing and the World Beyond

1. R. Bultmann, "Der Gottesgedanke und der moderne Mensch," *Glauben und Verstehen,* vol. 4 (Tübingen: Mohr, 1965), pp. 113–27.

2. Ved Mehta, *The New Theologian* (New York: Harper & Row, 1965).

3. See E. Bloch, *Das Prinzip Hoffnung* (Frankfurt, 1959).

4. Bultmann's method of demythologizing aims at (1) eradicating this kind of mythical view of world and life, which has lost its relevance for the present age, and thereby removing from the scriptural content those elements that constitute an unwarranted obstacle to the acceptance of the faith for modern men and women; (2) reinterpreting the myth by means of existential philosophy in those cases where the myth expresses something that religious existence experienced on a transcendent level; and (3) bringing into fuller relief through these steps the full form of the "scandal" distinctive to Christianity. The last point in particular is seen by Bultmann as the central task of his biblical exegesis.

5. *Shihō-rissō* 指方立相 refers in Shin Buddhism to the location of the Pure Land Paradise in the West; literally, the indication of direction and determination of form.

6. Heidegger interprets existential distance as an overcoming of separation (*Ent-fernung*). The Japanese philosopher Kūki Shūzō (1888–1943) has followed him here.

7. The Japanese words for "god" 神 and "above" 上 are both pronounced the same: *kami.* This does not, however, imply etymological derivation.

8. Soga uses the categories *tai* 体 (body, *quidditas*) and *gi* 義 (manifestation, *modus*).

9. John A. T. Robinson, *Honest to God* (London, 1963), p. 41.

10. *Heizei-gōjō* 平生業成 is the idea that the authenticity of the believer's faith is not first attested to at the hour of death, by entering the Pure Land with feelings of gratitude and an untroubled heart, but that true faith must realize and prove itself each day, in the midst of everyday life.

11. Cf. for instance *Das Wesen des christlichen Glaubens* (Munich, 1965).

12. This booklet tells the story—in ten pictures, to which explanatory poems by master Kuo-an and others are appended—of an oxherder looking for a stray ox until he finds it and brings it home. In the form of a parable it depicts the process of the quest for the true mind of the self. Towards the end, the ox becomes completely docile, and we see the oxherder returning home sitting on the back of the cow and playing the flute, without even bothering anymore with

the tether. From that point on, all concern for the ox is forgotten. The German translation alluded to here is *Der Ochs und sein Hirte,* trans. Kōichi Tsujimura and Hartmut Buchner (Pfullingen, 1958).

13. *Theology of the New Testament,* vol. 1, trans. by K. Grobel (London, 1952).

14. The notion of the *Geviert* was alluded to earlier in this chapter. In brief, it means that sky and earth, gods and mortals are bound together into a unity, with all four mirroring one another. This is what is symbolized by the quadrate, the square, or the fourfoldness.

15. 教行信証 *Kyōgyōshinshō,* trans. D. T. Suzuki, in *The Collection of Passages Expounding the True Teaching, Living, Faith, and Realizing of the Pure Land* (Kyoto, 1973), p. 14. The translation of this work cited earlier (chapter 3, note 1) is less suited to show the exegetical problem being treated here.

16. The exact wording of the beginning of chapter 2 of the *Kyōgyōshinshō* (p. 15 [see n. 15 above]) reads:

> As I reverently reflect on the outgoing *ekō* [Merit-transference] I find therein the great living and the great faith.

The adjective *great* has been added to *living* (practice) and *faith* with the intent of exalting them. Merit-transference has two directions: the outgoing phase (*ōsō* 往相) is the direction from us to the Buddha; the coming phase (*gensō* 還相) is the direction from the Buddha to all living beings insofar as it is correlative to *ōsō.* Merit-transference is the working of Amida Buddha's Compassion in the form of the name: the working of an absolute love wherein the substantiality and totality of the Buddha are bestowed as such on the hither shore. In this working there is an outgoing phase and a coming phase. Living (practice) and faith are both discussed from the viewpoint of the outgoing phase.

The text reads further:

> The great living is to pronounce the Name of the Nyorai [Tathāgata] of Unimpeded Light. In this living are embraced all good things and all the roots of merit. They are instantly perfected [as soon as the Name is pronounced; that is, the ultimate desire of man is promptly fulfilled therein]. The Name is the treasure-ocean of the merits accruing from the absolute reality of Suchness. [The Name is the absolute truth as Suchness; it is the ocean of merit wherein this truth is realized as it is, in a unique way, impossible to duplicate]. Therefore, it is called the great living.
>
> So it is that this great living issues out of the Prayer [or Vow] of Absolute Compassion, for which reason the Prayer is known as that which is praised by all Buddhas, or that in which all Buddhas pronounce the Name, or as that which is heartily applauded by all Buddhas.

The "True Living Chapter" in fact explains the text of the seventeenth vow as a prayer that the name shall be uttered in praise by all Buddhas. Shinran then cites the Sukhāvatī-vyūha-sūtra (The Larger Sūtra of Eternal Life):

> If, upon my attaining Buddhahood, all the innumerable Buddhas in the ten quarters were not approvingly to pronounce my Name, may I not attain the Supreme Enlightenment.

17. Nishida's notion of "action-intuition" is developed in 働くものから見るものへ(From Acting to Seeing), a work published in 1927, a translation of which is presently being completed by David Dilworth and Valdo Viglielmo. Tanabe's notion of "practice-faith" is best understood from his 1946 book 懺悔道としての哲学(Philosophy as Metanoetics). Unfortunately, Tanabe's writings have not appeared in English translation, though plans are currently under way to publish this work in a translation I prepared in collaboration with Valdo Viglielmo, beginning back in 1966.

Glossary of Sanskrit and Pali Terms

While the Sanskrit and Pali words that appear in this glossary (as well as their Japanese or Chinese equivalents) often admit of a number of possible meanings depending on their historical and literary context, the explanations given below are restricted to the way they have been used in the present work. The entries have been composed principally with the aid of Nakamura Hajime's three-volume Cyclopaedia of Buddhist Terms (佛教用語大辞典 [Tokyo, 1970]).

ādīnava S, P. [患 gen] The unsavory aspect of taṇhā or the five skandhas, in contrast with assāda.
ahiṃsā S, P. [不害 fugai] The injunction against killing or harming any living thing.
ākiṃcanya-āyatana S. [無所有処 mushou-sho] The realm of the non-existent attained contemplatively in samādhi.
ālaya-vijñāna S. [阿梨耶識 ariyashiki] The "store consciousness" in which all of life's experiences are potentially contained in advance and actually stored after their occurrence. In providing a basis for continuity and psychic heredity, this idea has often been accused of smuggling back in the permanent self that Buddhism is at pains to reject.
anantaram S. [即 soku] A copulative indicating the inseparability of two terms, like the front and back sides of each other. It says that A, such as it is, is one with B, and vice versa; or that A is A because it is likewise not-A (B), and vice versa.
anātman S. [無我 muga] Non-ego, the absence of ātman.
anitya S. [無常 mujō] Impermanence. The state of flux, changeability, and transiency that characterizes all things.
anuloma P. [順 jun] The forward progression of the causal chain of dependent origination, which proceeds from effects to causes in constituting the world of avidyā; the opposite of paṭilomam.
arūpa S. [非色 hishiki] The absence of form, or rūpa; ārūpya-dhātu.
ārūpya-dhātu S. [無色界 mushikikai] The immaterial world or realm without material beings, composed only of the four mental skandhas of vedanā, saṃjñā, saṃskāra, and vijñāna.

āśraya-parāvṛtti S. [転依 ten'e] The overturning of the ground of our wayward existence; the inversion of kleśa and attainment of nirvāṇa.

assāda P. [味 mi] The "savory" aspect of taṇhā or the five skandhas, to be contrasted with ādīnava.

ātman S. [我 ga] Ego, personality, I.

avidyā S. [無明 mumyō] The absence of vidyā; the darkness of ignorance, the fundamental unknowing at the root of our existence.

avyākrta S. [無記 muki] The silence of the Buddha's refusal to answer metaphysical questions.

bhāva S, P. [有 u] Being, the opposite of nothingness or emptiness.

bodhi S, P. [菩提 bodai] Enlightenment, the conquest of avidyā through the awakening to perfect wisdom.

bodhisattva S. [菩薩 bosatsu] One who undertakes the path to enlightenment; one who strives to attain the wisdom of the Buddha; a future Buddha.

brahma-cariya P. [梵行 bongyō] The practice of complete celibacy.

brahma-vihāra S, P. [梵住 bonjū] The achievement of karuṇā towards all living things. The holy state of catvāry apramāṇāni.

catvāry apramāṇāni S. [四無量心 shi muryōshin] The awakening to infinity of a mind that has cast away all its fetters in upekkhā. Traditionally it has been interpreted to embrace the four immeasurables of infinite benevolence (mettā), infinite compassionate mercy (karuṇā), infinite compassionate rejoicing (muditā), and infinite indifference (upekkhā).

cetasika S. [心 shin] A general term for mental states or activities of mind; heart or mind understood as the principle underlying our human existence.

dharma S. [法 hō] The ultimate constituent of existence; the law that governs all things; the essence or nature of a thing, and hence by association the things themselves; the ultimate truth taught by the Buddha.

dharma-dhātu S. [法界 hokkai] The dharma realm, which can be taken either as a general name for "things" or as the underlying spiritual reality regarded as the absolute ground of all that is.

dhyāna S. [禅定 zenjō] Contemplation, samādhi, understood as a process of spiritual advancement involving stages. When writtenı 禅 [zen], it is taken to mean the actual stages of contemplation themselves, although there is no change in the Sanskrit term.

diṭṭha-dhamma-nibbāna-vāda P. [現在涅槃論 genzai nehanron] This-worldly theories of nirvāṇa, hence considered heretical.

idappaccayatā P. [縁性 enshō] The kinship or bond of one thing with another that brings that thing into being.

indriyesu guttadvāro S. [感官の防護 kankan no bōgo] The custody of the senses. Also: *indriya-saṃvara*.

jarā-maraṇa S. [老死 rōshi] Old age and death.

jāti S. [生 shō] Birth, origination.

jīva P. [命 myō] Life, the vital principle, vital powers.

kalpa S. [劫 kō] An extremely long period of time. Though sometimes used for the age of the world itself, it is usually thought of as the time of eternity or infinite time, or as a unit of such time, which can then be further distinguished as small, medium, or large.

karma S. [業 gō] Human deeds and the residue they leave behind them as effects.

kasiṇa P. [処 sho] A word that functions grammatically as a locative, generally to indicate the point at which an organ of perception and its object come together, and hence can be variously qualified to yield different disciplined forms of knowing (such as the contemplation of ākiṃcanya-āyatana or ārūpya-dhātu).

kleśa S. [煩悩 bonnō] Morally defiling worldly passions.

kṣaṇikavāda S. [刹那論 setsunaron] Doctrine concerning momentary lapses of time, sometimes referred to as 1/65th of the time it takes to snap one's fingers, or the shortest unit of time as opposed to the kalpa, which is the longest.

mano nāma vijñāna S. [意名識 imyōshiki] Among the Vijñānavādin, the idea that consciousness produces illusions by creating its own objects by virtue of its own latent powers.

mukta S. [解脱 gedatsu] Deliverance, liberation, release from the bonds of illusion and the tribulations of this world.

nāma S, P. [名 myō] Name; mental activity as distinguished from the form (rūpa) of things.

nāma-kāya S, P. [名身 myōshin] The totality of mind and body in general, equivalent to nāma-rūpa.

nāma-rūpa S, P. [名色 myōshiki] In the Upanishads, the collective noun for the phenomenal world as a whole, including both name and form. Taken over as such into ancient Buddhism, it came to designate the two aspects of individual entities—the mental or spiritual (nāma) and the physical (rūpa)—and as such found its way into the twelvefold theory of dependent origination.

nidāna S. [尼陀那 nidana] The name given to each of the links or bonds or primary causes that make up the chain of dependent origination.

nirodha S, P. [滅 metsu] Extinction, passing away; the opposite of samudaya.

nirodha-samāpatti S. [滅尽定 metsujinjō] Samādhi in which all mental activities have ceased; a state of mental harmony (samāpatti) achieved with the extinction (nirodha) of the various activities of consciousness.

nirvāṇa S. [涅槃 nehan] The final state of release following enlightenment, in which even the skandhas that constitute empirical existence have ceased. Literally, the snuffing out of the flame (of illusion or desire).

nissaraṇa P. [出離 shutsuri] Escape, release from the world of saṃsāra.

pañca-nivaraṇāni S. [五蓋 gogai] Five sorts of kleśa that cloud the mind and heart. The five hindrances of avarice, anger, drowsiness, frivolity and moodiness, and doubt.

paraspara-apekṣā S. [相依相関関係 sōesōkan kankei] Co-dependent correlatedness.

paṭilomam P. [逆 gyaku] The return or reverse progression of the causal chain of dependent origination, which eliminates effects by eliminating causes and thus leads back to nirvāṇa; the opposite of anuloma.

paṭicca-samuppāda P. [縁起 engi] Dependent origination.

pātimokkha P. [戒本 kaihon] Code of precepts for monks and nuns governing their life-style.

pīti P. [喜 ki] Joy, gladness, delight.

prajñā S. [般若 hannya; 慧 e] Knowledge of the truth attained in enlightenment; the perfect comprehension of the totality of all existence; consummate wisdom.

praṇidhāna S. [願 gan] Resolve, will; sacred vow.

rūpa S. [色 shiki] Form. The concrete materiality of things as distinguished from mental activity (nāma).

ṣaḍ-abhijñāḥ S. [六通 rokutsū] The six superhuman powers possessed by the Buddha and bodhisattvas through the four dhyānas: the power to appear at will anywhere and to move unhindered through space; of unlimited vision of all things, great and small, near and far; of unlimited hearing; to intuit the minds of all beings; to know all forms of previous existence of oneself and others; and the power of insight into ending the stream of saṃsāra.

ṣaḍ-āyatana S. [六入 rokunyū] The six regions through which mental activity takes place, namely, the mind and the five organs of perception; the six senses.

samādhi S, P. [定 jō] To settle, fix, compose oneself in meditation. Strictly speaking, we should distinguish between samādhi in general (a class name for the various forms of meditation) and dhyāna (the specific form of contemplation that involves the progress through stages). As a meditative form of centering of the mind, it should further be distinguished from kasiṇa meditation.

samāpatti S. [等至 tōji] A state of rest in which body and mind have reached equilibrium. The arrival at consummate dhyāna through a series of stages.

saṃgha S. [僧伽 sōgya] Together with Buddha and dharma, one of the tri-ratna, or Buddhist trinity, indicating a community of Buddhist believers, in particular those banded together for monastic practice. In China and Japan the term later came to be applied to individuals who renounce the world to lead an ascetic life (in which case it is reduced to the single character 僧).

saṃjñā S. [想 sō] One of the five skandhas; the mental activity in which the material shape and perceptible traits of an object are known.

saṃsāra S, P. [輪廻 rinne] The turning of the wheel of birth and death; transmigration.

saṃskāra S. [行 gyō] Volitional impulses; the latent capacity to give shape to existence through the exercise of will power. As a mental activity, it is distinguished from vedanā and saṃjñā, together with which it is included as one of the five skandhas.

samudaya S, P. [集 jū] To gather, collect, accumulate; the uprising of the mass of things, as opposed to their passing away (nirodha).

sati-samyag-jñāna S. [正智正念 shōchi shōnen] Vigilance and right mindfulness.

satkāya-dṛṣṭi S. [有身見 ushinken] A clinging to the body as one's own possession, brought about by the egoistic unification of the five skandhas.

śīla S. [戒 kai] Commandments; the keeping of the commandments; rules for a moral life to be upheld by converts to Buddhism and their corresponding commitment to avoid evil deeds.

skandha S. [蘊 un] The aggregates or constitutive elements of all existence, including our own existence. They are five in number: rūpa (form), vedanā (feelings), saṃjñā (perceptions), saṃskāra (volitional impulses), and vijñāna (consciousness).

sparśa S. [触 soku] Contact; the sense of touch.

stūpa S. [塔 tō] A tumulus or burial mound for the bones or remains of the dead; also used to contain other sacred relics.

sukha S. [悦楽 etsuraku] Happiness.

śūnyatā S. [空 kū] Emptiness, absolute nothingness. From the time of primitive Buddhism, and particularly in prajñā Buddhism, the fundamental conception of ultimate reality.

svabhāva S. [自性 jishō] The self-nature or self-existence of anything, in terms of which that thing continues to be what it is and to subsist in itself.

taṇhā S, P. [渇愛 katsuai] The attachment to illusion likened to a throat parched and burning with thirst. The flames of lust or desire.

Tathāgata S, P. [如来 nyorai] One of the epithets of the Buddha of obscure grammatical origins, taken by later commentators to contain the double sense of the "thus gone" and the "thus come", that is, one who has gone the way of enlightenment and come from the world of truth, as the previous Buddhas have come or gone.

tisro-vidhāḥ S. [三明 sanmyō] The three insights; the last three of the ṣaḍ-abhijñāḥ.

tṛṣṇā S. [愛 ai] Lust; the blind attachment to and longing for the world of illusion.

upādāna S, P. [取 shu] Clinging, the ninth link in the twelvefold doctrine of dependent origination.

upekkhā P. [捨 sha] One of the catvāry apramāṇāni, that of the perfect indifference attained through complete equanimity and detachment from all bodily illness or spiritual anxiety as well as bodily pleasure or spiritual joy.

vedanā S, P. [受 ju] Feelings of all sorts, pleasant, unpleasant, or otherwise; one of the five skandhas.

vicāra S, P. [伺 shi] Detailed investigation and mental deliberation; ongoing reflection; the opposite of vitakka.

vidyā S. [明 myō] Knowing; the light of knowledge, as opposed to avidyā.

vijñāna S. [識 shiki] A general name for consciousness and the activities of mind. The so-called Yogācāra Buddhist school that professes a theory (vāda) affirming the reality of vijñāna and denying the reality of the objective world is also known as the Vijñānavāda.

vijñānānantyāyatana S. [識無辺処 shikimuhenjo] A contemplative state in which knowledge becomes unbounded and limitless.

vitakka P. [尋 jin] General consideration or investigation as a mental activity; as a form of contemplative thought, it differs from vicāra, the pursuit of clarity and distinctness in consciousness, by aiming rather at the discovery of more general principles.

yama S. [制戒 seikai] The five śīla given in the Yoga Sūtra as the first of eight stages leading to samādhi: the injunctions against taking life, lying, stealing, unchastity, and intoxicants.

Index